Kristen
God bless you

Life After Lucy

Keith Thibodeaux (signature)

The True Story of
Keith Thibodeaux —
"I Love Lucy's"
Little Ricky

Psalm 32

Life After Lucy

The True Story of Keith Thibodeaux — "I Love Lucy's" Little Ricky

by
Keith Thibodeaux
with
Audrey T. Hingley

New Leaf Press

First Printing: May 1994
Second Printing: July 1994

Library of Congress Catalog Number: 93-87255
ISBN: 0-89221-256-X

The television program series "I Love Lucy"™ is copyrighted by, and used with the permission of, CBS, Inc.

"I Love Lucy"™ is a trademark of CBS, Inc.

Front cover photo by Robert Vose.

Back cover photo of Thibodeaux family: Thomas Howard Photography, Clinton, MS.

Dedication

*I dedicate this book to
my wife, Kathy, and daughter Tara,
the people I love most in this world!*

Special Thanks to

My Lord and Saviour, Jesus Christ; Audrey Hingley, my good friend, who worked very hard to help me tell my story; my parents, Mary Ann Thibodeaux and Lionel J. Thibodeaux, for being my parents and loving me; Mary Denton and Bo Denton, my in-laws, for their support and help through the years; Honey Denton, for being the sweetest grandmother around; David and the Giants, who have been such a big part of my life; Mark Ridgeway, my good friend all these years; Billy Baker, for showing me what it means to be a servant; all the dancers and staff of Ballet Magnificat, for their encouragement and love; Lucie Arnaz Luckinbill and Desi Arnaz Jr., for their continuing friendship, and thanks to their mom and dad, the late Lucille Ball and Desi Arnaz; and New Leaf Press, for providing the forum in which I can share my story.

— Keith Thibodeaux

Special Thanks to

Keith Thibodeaux, who felt we were a good team to tell his life story — thanks for your faith in me! — my husband, Brian, for his unfailing encouragement and love and for being so understanding about the many hours needed to make this book a reality; my son Robert, God's gift to our family, who also suggested the book's title; my father, Clyde Tyler, for being the world's best dad; my dear Aunt Rose Blake, a godsend in my life; for the encouragement and prayers from friends and my church family at New Creation Church; to four special friends — April Blue, Linda Mikell, Stephanie Ashby, and Maisie Bell — for your prayers and encouragement; and everyone at New Leaf Press who believed in this book.

. . .

This book would not have been possible without people who consented to share with me their memories of Keith and their lives together. I appreciate all of you, and your memories, very, very much!

. . .

Lucie Arnaz Luckinbill, Desi Arnaz Jr., Kieth Dodge, Madelyn Pugh Davis, Jim Clark and the Andy Griffith Rerun Watchers Club, Mary Ann Thibodeaux, Lionel J. Thibodeaux, Brad DeHart, Dan Sauer, Gary Lamson, David Huff, Rayborn Huff, Clayborn Huff, Kathy Thibodeaux, and Tara Thibodeaux.

. . .

I dedicate my work on this book to the memory of my beloved mother Pauline Martin Tyler (1915-1991), who always loved me, supported me, and encouraged me. Mom, you believed in this book and here it is . . . . I love you and look forward to seeing you in heaven!

— Audrey T. Hingley

Contents

Keith Thibodeaux at age 5 becomes Little Ricky Ricardo.
Let the journey begin.

1

The World's Tiniest Drummer

"You look great, Keith," my dad commented, stepping back for the final inspection of my appearance. Dressed by Dad in black short pants, a white shirt, and a striped jacket, I looked younger than my five years. My small size and new short pants completed the "kid" look.

Carefully slicking my brown hair back, Dad took one last look at me as I turned all the way around. Then nodding his approval and smiling as he took my hand in his, he urged, "Come on, it's time to go."

It was a typically sunny Los Angeles day in 1956, full of bright sunshine, blue skies, and promises. In spite of the beautiful weather, I felt a knot forming in my stomach. As we walked outside and got into Dad's car, my apprehension about this latest audition welled up within me. Even though I didn't fully understand what all the fuss was about, I knew instinctively that today was very important to my dad.

Whenever I had an audition, or had to appear in a public performance, Dad would say, "Now, Keith, I want you to do good today." Those words — *"Keith, I want you to do good"* — always echoed in the back of my mind.

I could sense Dad's nervousness and anxiety as he drove me silently to Desilu Studios' Motion Picture Center in Hollywood where "I Love Lucy" was filmed. I had never even seen the popular sitcom on television, but Dad talked about it all the time. It was one of his favorite shows.

I didn't realize that over 200 youngsters had already auditioned in New York and Hollywood for the role of Little Ricky Ricardo, the new TV son of the series' stars, Lucille Ball and Desi Arnaz. All I knew was that my audition for the Little Ricky role was very important to my dad. I sensed somehow that my "doing good" today could be the key, not just for my career, but for his own dreams of making it big in show business.

I looked at Dad. He was concentrating on maneuvering the car between other cars in the lanes of traffic. With his hands gripping the steering wheel tightly, he appeared intent, his eyes looking straight ahead.

Short, with dark curly brown hair, Lionel Thibodeaux was not particularly handsome. In fact, most people thought my mother, a petite, soft-spoken woman — not quite five feet tall — had the looks in the family, with her dark brown hair and brown eyes.

Dad's outgoing personality and captivating charm, however, drew people to him, and he always had a lot of friends. A warm, emotional person, Dad was a hugger.

My father was born in Baton Rouge, Louisiana, on March 5, 1927, to Lionel Joseph Thibodeaux Sr. and Eunice Thibodeaux. His dad was from Parks, Louisiana, near Breaux Bridge, about 10 miles from Lafayette.

My grandfather, whom I called "Papop," was an engineer who worked for the state highway department, and was always being transferred around the state. Papop was about six feet tall, and he always wore a hat that seemed to make him even taller! He traveled a lot because of his job, so my dad's childhood was spent constantly being uprooted, going to different schools, and having to make new friends all the time. Maybe the constant moves had something to do with helping my dad become the person he is today. Instead of withdrawing, like some kids do when they move all the time, he was outgoing, friendly, and loved meeting people. He still does. His family was staunchly Roman Catholic.

My mom, too, was a loving person, but she seemed to have difficulty showing emotion and expressing love. I remember her hugs as a child, and I knew she loved me, but expressing emotion seemed to be difficult for her. I think a lot of it had to do with her mother dying at a young age, and her dad abandoning the family.

My mother, Mary Ann Chitty, was born on July 21, 1930, in Breaux Bridge to Birdie and Leo Chitty. Her father was an engineer, too. Her mother died at age 41, when Mom was only 17 years old. After my grandmother died, Grandfather Chitty couldn't cope with her death, and he just sort of took off, leaving his eight children to be raised by my Aunt Gladys. He was a Baptist, but when he married Birdie, who was Catholic, he agreed to have all the children raised as Catholics. So both sides of my family had a strong Catholic religious tradition.

When Mom and Dad met in Breaux Bridge, Louisiana, Dad had just gotten out of the service and was still at loose ends, trying to find his niche in life. When they married on February 5, 1949, Dad was 21 and Mom, at 19, was a recent high school graduate. I was born the following year in Lafayette. My parents' first home was the house where Mom was born on Main Street in Breaux Bridge. They later moved to Kirby Street in Lake Charles, Louisiana, and finally to Bunkie.

With Dad's Cajun upbringing, he made it clear that the man was the head of the house — no ifs, ands, or buts about it. A strict disciplinarian whose word was law, Dad backed up his authority with his belt whenever I got out of line. Still, I never doubted his love for me.

Dad's nickname, even back in those days, was "Hollywood." Fascinated by movies and the entertainment industry, Dad wore zoot suits and liked to dress in a flashy style. At one point, he played drums with a group that performed the big-band style of music for proms, graduations, and weddings.

During those early years of married life, Dad had a lot of different jobs, most of them in sales, which suited his people-oriented personality. When I was born, he was working as an insurance salesman.

As other cars sped past us on the Hollywood Freeway, I looked out the window at the swaying palm trees and tried not to think about what I would face today at Desilu Studios. Although I had been performing as a professional drummer since I was three years old, I still got nervous around strangers. To keep my mind off the audition, I tried to remember how it had all started.

My earliest memories involve listening to music and keeping time by beating on pots and pans with sticks, knives, and forks. I also liked to strike up a beat on the garbage cans outside; I pretended they were drums.

With the sounds of Benny Goodman, Count Basie and His Orchestra, and Duke Ellington music constantly filling our home back in Louisiana, I quickly developed a sense of rhythm. With the radio always tuned to big-band sounds, the beat and the rhythm of the pulsating orchestra music caught my ear.

One evening after Dad came home from work at the United Gas Company in Bunkie, a neighbor phoned, wanting to talk to him.

"I notice that your son goes out every day and beats on the garbage cans," she began.

Dad, thinking she was upset about the racket I was making, immediately apologized to her. "Oh, I'm so sorry! I'll certainly talk to him and have him stop." Dad told me her response surprised him.

"Oh no, Mr. Thibodeaux, it sounds to us as if he is making some rhythm — so we don't really mind! He seems to enjoy it. I just thought I'd tell you about it."

At dinner that night, I absent-mindedly started tapping on my plate with my knife and fork.

"Keith, will you please stop that?" Mom said wearily, passing a bowl of mashed potatoes across the table to Dad.

"Wait a minute, Mary Ann," Dad said.

He put a final scoop of mashed potatoes on his plate, handed the bowl back to Mom, and looked at me thoughtfully. "It sounds as if he's making rhythm. Maybe we ought to get him a drum."

A few days later, Dad came home with a toy drum tucked under his arm for me. I was thrilled with the present!

Now I could listen to music on the radio and keep time with it on my little toy drum. Besides loving big-band sounds, I especially enjoyed marching band music and going to parades.

One time Grandma Thibodeaux, whom I called "Mamom," took me to a music concert in Lafayette, where I sat spellbound for more than two hours, mesmerized by the sights and sounds of all the different bands and orchestras on the program lineup that evening.

I played that toy drum until I beat it up and then announced to my parents, "I want a real drum."

Dad, who always had a way of getting things done, went to a friend, the local music teacher, and mentioned my natural talent and interest in playing the drums. The man offered to give Dad a snare drum. That was my first real drum! I was only two years old.

My parents probably thought I was going through a childhood phase and would grow out of my fascination with drumming, but I kept wanting to play. I seemed to have a natural ability to control the drum sticks and imitate any beat that I heard.

Always the promoter, Dad, who was a district zone chairman for the Lions Club, told someone about my unusual talent. The next thing I knew, I was playing for a group of adults at the Lions Club. Using just my snare drum, I kept time with the music of a record player set up in the corner of the room.

That was the beginning of my public performances.

Soon I was asking Dad for more and knew exactly what I needed. "I want a bass drum to go along with my snare drum, and a tom-tom, and a floor tom-tom, and cymbals," I begged.

Dad later told me that at first he wasn't sure if I was really good at drumming. He kept telling himself, *After all, this is my kid. Maybe I'm not being objective about his ability.*

The more people raved, however, the more Dad started to believe in my natural talent.

Requests for me to come and play drums for different events increased, and Dad finally agreed to purchase a complete drum set for me. Part of the attraction was the novelty of seeing such a tiny little guy like me sitting behind a professional drum set and pounding away, with my head barely showing from where I sat behind my drum kit.

As word about my drumming ability spread, other Lions Clubs began calling Dad, asking if I could come and play for their meetings and events. Soon I was playing at amateur shows, on radio programs, at promotional events, and for all sorts of different functions and talent shows.

One friend remembers seeing me playing drums outdoors on the back of a flatbed truck at a car dealership in Lafayette.

By age three, I had been invited to attend the National Drummers Convention in Jackson, Mississippi. One of the country's top drummers, who had heard me play in Lafayette, asked Dad to bring me to Jackson.

I still have a yellowed newspaper clipping that Mom kept from our local paper in Bunkie, with the headline, "Bunkie Discovers 'Honest-Injun' Prodigy: 3-Year-Old Drummer." The story reported,

> Not only can Keith handle the drums, but he seems to have an in-born love for performance. Keith watches the audience with intelligent brown eyes that mirror the satisfaction of the moment. Occasionally, he self-consciously cocks his head to one side, as though momentarily overcome with stage fright, but he never misses a beat. When he completes a piece, he waits expectantly for the applause, and appears to enjoy every second of it.
>
> Offstage, he's a normal three-year-old, romping with small neighbors at games of Indians and cowboys. But put him behind those drums, and that's something else again!

It is true that I loved playing the drums, but I was also scared whenever I had to play in front of people. Sometimes it wouldn't affect me, but at other times I got really nervous. Despite my problems with anxiety and fear, I started to dream about being a professional drummer when I grew up.

Another local newspaper report noted,

> Bunkie's infant prodigy, Keith Thibodeaux, is receiving so many honors he doesn't know what to do about it — except keep beating the drums. Yesterday his dad was driving around Bunkie with the set of drums in the family car. Keith was sick with a little cold, and his parents wanted him to stay in bed — so the only thing to do was hide the drums.

Keith is sporting a new gold key, given him as a honorary citizen of Abbeville. The little fellow received his key, along with state superintendent of education Shelby Jackson and Ted Weems.

His folks received word last week that he won a New Orleans' amateur show, and the prizes are on the way. Yesterday a Lafayette radio announcer called to say that the folks are still telephoning about the little lad's appearance there Sunday night.

Amid the local hoopla about me, Dad's brother heard that Horace Heidt was coming to Lafayette on a talent search for his musical variety television show on CBS-TV. Called "The Horace Heidt Show," the program featured undiscovered professional talent.

Dad had never heard of Heidt until my Uncle Terrell explained that the well-known band leader conducted radio talent shows and cross-country tours. Heidt had also headed a popular radio program called "Pot O' Gold," which was the first radio show to extend prizes beyond the studio audience to listeners across America.

A native of Alameda, California, Heidt began his Youth Opportunity Program in 1948, as the first touring company to visit cities across America in search of undiscovered talent, helping ambitious young people to stardom. Art Carney, who later played opposite Jackie Gleason in the popular "The Honeymooners" TV show, and Gordon McRae, who became a well-known actor, were among Heidt's discoveries.

When the touring company came to Lafayette, Uncle Terrell, who had always been very supportive of me and my drumming, went to Horace Heidt's people and told them, "I have a three-year-old nephew who is a great drummer."

At the time, Heidt had another child drummer traveling with the show, Allen Brenaman, who was about eight years old. Known at the time as among the world's best young drummers, Allen was one of Heidt's "show stoppers."

Somehow Uncle Terrell managed to arrange an audition for me with Heidt's people anyway, and they decided to put me on the show. Heidt didn't know his talent scouts had added another child drummer to the performance bill in Lafayette.

The big night arrived. When I, a little bitty three-year-old, performed with Horace Heidt's orchestra, the hometown crowd went wild, cheering and applauding. They loved my drumming.

"What do you think? Does my son have any future as a drummer?" Dad asked Heidt after my show.

Despite the crowd's response, Heidt's answer was terse: "No, I don't believe he does."

Disappointed, Dad went back to his job with the gas company; I went home to play cowboys and Indians; and that was that.

Two weeks later, Horace Heidt telephoned Dad.

"Mr. Thew-be-dough, I would like to have your son come with us on tour," Heidt said, mispronouncing our last name, which phonetically sounds like Tibah-dough.

My astonished father listened as Heidt explained that there had been such a response to my performance that he had a change of heart.

"I'll pay him $300 a week," Heidt offered. That was a lot of money in 1954.

When Dad pointed out that he'd have to quit his job, since obviously I couldn't go out on the road by myself, Heidt replied in an exasperated tone, "Oh all right, I'll make it $500 for both of you, and that's it! Will you come?"

At age three I had risen from drumming on trash can tops to touring with a big-name professional orchestra. Dad and I traveled from coast to coast and in Canada, with the show televised in different cities. This was a big step for a toddler not long out of diapers.

My first appearance with "The Horace Heidt Swift Premium Hour Show" came on March 26, 1954, in Durham, North Carolina. The next week, we did a show in Washington, DC, and the week after that we played New York City. We flew to each show, and soon one performance date blurred into the next. One minute I'd be in a plane, and the next I'd be in front of a bunch of people in a darkened auditorium.

Between shows, I spent a lot of time by myself in hotels wondering what my best little buddy back in Louisiana was doing.

I'd think about how we would play cowboys and Indians together in his sandbox. Some days we'd get our mothers' brooms and pretend they were horses, "riding" the brooms around the yard and whooping it up with heart-felt Indian war cries.

Now I had no one my age to take part in my childhood fantasies.

Heidt billed me as "pound for pound, the greatest drummer around" or as "the world's tiniest drummer."

Some nights I'd be ready to play, but other nights I just didn't want to perform and Dad would have to urge me to go out on the stage.

One night in South Dakota, I simply refused to go on, and Dad had to tell Horace Heidt.

"Heidt almost had a heart attack, because we couldn't persuade you to go on," Dad told me later.

I guess my bursts of rebellion didn't happen very often, or I'm sure my tour with Heidt's company would have been short-lived!

Dad and Mom viewed my new-found celebrity status differently. Mom later told me she wasn't concerned about my "going professional." Apparently, she didn't think it would ever go any farther than the Heidt tour.

She thought, *Well, he'll just do this, and then it will be over.*

By this time, my sister Katie had arrived, and Mom was pregnant with my brother Dwight. She had her hands full at home and just accepted the fact that my dad would be on the road, taking care of me.

Dad, on the other hand, saw this first tour as just the beginning of my career. In fact, once he realized that I had potential, Dad pushed me, doing all the talking, all the managing. He always had been captivated by Hollywood, and going with Heidt probably seemed like the big time to him. In a way, it was.

Eventually Dad worked his way up to a position as one of Heidt's talent scouts for the touring show.

Bits and pieces from that time in my life stand out in my mind.

In Maine, I remember going to a restaurant and staring wide-eyed at a tank full of lobsters. In Chicago, I recall talking to Mom on the phone as I looked out the hotel window and gazed at a large lake filled with sailboats.

The big cities were much different — and seemed very far away — from tiny Bunkie, where probably only 2,000 to 3,000 people lived at the time. With the help of my dad, I would write "I miss you, Mommy" letters. Whenever I got homesick, I tried to picture Mom standing in the kitchen of our older, one-story frame house that stood next to a lake.

My mom's kitchen table resembled a dinette booth, so whenever Dad and I ate out — which was almost every day — I was reminded of home. In my childlike way, I would invariably repeat, "Look, Dad, a booth like the one we have in our kitchen."

That remark would lead me to other thoughts of home.

"Remember the time it rained so hard that the backyard flooded?" I liked to ask Dad, who probably grew tired of my same old stories. "There were snakes everywhere!"

I still cringe today at the thought of all those water moccasins slithering in heaps all over the grass.

Joining in with my reminiscing, Dad would say, "I'll never forgot the day your mama jumped up on a chair and screamed when a tiny mouse ran across the kitchen floor!" Then we'd both laugh as loud as possible, and I'd feel better for a while.

It was exciting to be in a different city almost every other day, but it was also scary. One night I woke up in our hotel room completely alone. My dad had slipped out for a minute. It was dark, and I was all alone. I huddled under the covers, shivering.

My fear brought to mind another fearful night. When I was two years old, a terrible thunderstorm rumbled through Bunkie. With the lightning flashing across the sky and loud thunderclaps, the storm had raged until I saw what appeared to be the outline of a skeleton on my bedroom wall.

Running to Mom and Dad's room, I had begged to sleep with them, but they told me to go back to my own room. I went back to my bed, pouting and mad at them because I was so scared.

There, alone in the hotel room, I tried to be brave, telling myself, "Dad will be back soon. I know he will."

To bolster my courage, I reminded myself of the day when I was two years old and had swallowed a bubblegum ball. I stopped breathing and was choking and turning blue. Dad rushed me to the hospital, and the doctors dislodged the ball before it was too late.

Dad has always been there when I needed him, I told myself.

Still, I couldn't shake the feelings of insecurity that often crept into my young mind and later would torment my life.

My time with the Heidt show ended in 1955, in California. The taste of the big time was in Dad's blood now, and he thought there would be more opportunities in the entertainment business in California.

Although Mom wasn't thrilled with moving her family across the country, she went along with Dad's wishes, leaving behind her sisters and other family.

In the beginning, we stayed at Horace Heidt's ranch in Sherman Oaks in the San Fernando valley north of Los Angeles, just a few miles from Hollywood. My dad found a job with a Firestone tire company, and we settled in at Heidt's ranch, which one visitor described as resembling "a combined circus winter quarters, resort hotel, and museum."

Heidt had built a comfortable home, surrounded by citrus trees, on a large tract of land in the valley. Extra bedrooms had been added to the house for guests, and Heidt had a small bungalow on the property that he used as an office. The ranch also included garages that housed the show's road cars and trucks, a rehearsal hall, tennis courts, a golf putting green, and a swimming pool.

Near the rear of the main house, a row of connected bungalows, resembling a motel, had been built as living quarters for Heidt's touring troupe. We lived in one of the bungalows. Since there were no kitchens in the individual cottages, everyone ate together in the main dining room. With all its buildings and amenities, the ranch looked like a resort hotel.

Mom, a true Southerner, didn't like California at first and said, "I feel as if we're living in a motel. It just doesn't seem homey to me." That was understandable, but Dad was head of the house and she didn't question him.

My first friend in California was Bobby Pachorek, a kid who came from a family of 13 children. He lived in a neighborhood near the Heidt ranch, and we met in a nearby field one day. Later, our mothers developed a friendship and have remained friends to this day.

I spent a lot of time at Bobby's house where we played baseball and just did regular fun, kid things together. Playing with Bobby was a welcome change from the grueling road tours and stage performances.

Little did I realize that my life as a performer was far from over. In fact, it was just about to begin.

One day Dad heard through a friend of his, Fred Dodge, that Lucille Ball and Desi Arnaz were conducting a talent search to find a little boy to play their TV son on "I Love Lucy."

Dodge, a feisty guy and nonstop talker, was the typical Hollywood agent type. Through Dodge, Dad arranged my audition for "I Love Lucy."

In later interviews, Desi said he saw me on Heidt's show, called my father, and set up an interview. Dad doesn't remember it that way.

I looked up as the car slowed. We were nearing Motion Picture Center.

"This is it, Keith," Dad said, as we turned into the entrance drive. He smiled, and patted my hand.

Even though I had no real idea of the significance of this day, I sighed. I knew I had to "do good" today. For Dad.

2

A Drummer, Not an Actor

As Dad and I were ushered into the studio that day, I noticed Lucille Ball first. She had the brightest, reddest hair I'd ever seen. Wearing white slacks that emphasized her slim figure, she seemed very tall to me.

Lucy focused her wide, big, blue eyes on me as Dad and I walked over to where she was standing. After we were introduced, she smiled and gave me a hug. "Has he studied acting?" she asked Dad, all the while looking down at me and inspecting my appearance very carefully. I remember thinking how pretty she was.

"No," Dad answered truthfully.

"Well, what *does* he do?" she said with just a hint of impatience in her voice.

"He's a drummer," Dad replied.

"You mean he plays drums? A set of drums?" Lucy asked. She glanced at me again, with a look on her face that told me she thought the idea of me playing the drums was ludicrous.

"Yes, and he can also play a conga drum," Dad told her politely.

At that point, Desi Arnaz arrived, dressed in a loose white shirt and baggy trousers.

"Who ees thees?" he said in his heavily-accented Cuban voice, looking at me with a warm smile.

Someone noticed that a set of drums was in place on the sound stage for "The Danny Thomas Show," which was next to the "I Love Lucy" set.

Dad took my hand, and we all walked over to the drums so I could play for Lucy and Desi.

Dad leaned down and squeezed my hand.

"Okay, Keith, this is it," he whispered. "Go ahead and play. I want you to do good today!"

I walked over obediently, sat down behind the drum kit, and began to play.

I don't remember everything that happened or much that was said that day, but when I started playing the drums, Lucy and Desi began to act excited.

Then Desi came over and asked, "Mind if I play, too?"

I got up and let Desi have the stool. When he finished he said, "Okay, now it's your turn."

First I'd play the drums awhile; then Desi would take over and play. Then I would play again, then Desi would play. We kept taking turns. It was fun.

Sheldon Leonard, who produced "The Danny Thomas Show," was on the set that day, and came over to watch us. He started talking in a lively voice to Dad, amazed that a five year old could play the drums like a pro.

While Desi and I were taking turns on the drums, I heard Lucy say excitedly, "This is the kid! This is him! This is Little Ricky!"

Everyone was talking about how I actually looked as if I could be Desi's son. That look, combined with my drumming ability, apparently cinched the deal in Lucy and Desi's minds.

I don't remember anything about the rest of the day, but I soon became aware of the significance of being chosen to portray Little Ricky Ricardo.

Since the search for a child for the Little Ricky role had sparked a nationwide talent search, my selection did not go unnoticed by the press. In writing about me, one journalist speculated, "His future seems bright indeed," adding that Lucy and Desi had "pulled a coup" in signing me to the show. He dubbed me "a bright little package."

Desi told an interviewer, "He's a remarkably talented youngster, and there will be plenty for him to do besides 'Lucy' — if the show doesn't last that long."

Of course, I didn't understand just how much of an entertainment phenomenon "I Love Lucy" had become. Since the show's debut on October 15, 1951 — ironically replacing the one-season "Horace Heidt Show"— it had become a blockbuster hit. Within six months of the first airing, "I Love Lucy" became the first program to be seen in 10 million American homes, an amazing statistic when you consider that by 1952, there were still only 15 million TV sets in the entire United States!

Telephone companies reported reductions in calls during the show's half-hour duration on Monday nights from 9:00 to 9:30 p.m. In fact, some stores actually closed early because customers were home watching their favorite TV show. Magazine articles relentlessly examined the "whys" behind the program's success.

Although the comedy didn't seem like anything special when it first went on the air, viewers identified with Ricky and Lucy. Many of the scripts revolved around real issues in marriage: Lucy trying to stick to a household budget; Ricky and Fred complaining to Lucy and Ethel that housewives did nothing except stay home all day; or Lucy's desire to put more romance into her marriage.

Such everyday themes were translated into slapstick comedy as the Lucy character was always getting involved in some crazy scheme, usually enlisting Ethel as her partner in plotting. Added to the slapstick approach to marriage was the image of a star-struck Lucy, forever trying to worm her way into her husband's nightclub act to fulfill her own dreams of show biz glory.

The show was funny, classic comedy at its best, even when some of the plots stretched imaginations to the limit. As one writer of the day pointed out, "The viewer is somehow persuaded that any wife might buy $700 worth of meat for a deep freezer, or glue a beard to her face in a campaign against her husband's mustache."

"I Love Lucy" also made show business history with its technical and production innovations. It was the first TV show to use three cameras simultaneously, imitating motion picture production. It was also the first television series filmed live before a studio audience and aired nationwide. The decision to film the show made it possible to have prints instead of then-common kinescopes, which were films taken off the television screen.

In making the decision to do "I Love Lucy" on film, Desi Arnaz invented the rerun. As a result, filmed episodes would be available for endless rebroadcasting, changing all of television. The appeal of reusable, filmed programs eventually caused television production to shift from New York, where it began with the great live shows of the early days of television, to Hollywood. It also made Lucy and Desi millionaires.

Lucy gave birth to her real-life son, Desi Arnaz IV on January 19, 1953. Coincidentally, that same day her TV son, Little Ricky Ricardo, was "born" on the show. More Americans watched the Little Ricky birth episode on TV than watched the 1953 inauguration of the country's thirty-fourth president, Dwight D. Eisenhower! The viewing audience for that one episode was estimated at 44 million people.

After the TV birth of Little Ricky in 1953, six-month-old twins Richard Lee and Ronald Lee Simmons had been brought in to alternate playing the baby Little Ricky. By the summer of 1953, a search was underway for another set of twins since child labor laws governing the use of the Simmons twins, who were not yet a year old, were so restrictive.

Joseph David Mayer and Michael Lee Mayer, 14-month-old twins signed to replace the Simmons duo, stayed with the show until I was selected in 1956. The Mayer twins were not old enough to play a kindergarten-age Little Ricky role, and their mother had decided to retire them from show business.

Now it was my turn.

For Dad, having his son as a star on such a popular TV show was like a dream come true. I'm sure he had visions of stardom for me resulting from my national television exposure and a bright future for him made possible by show business connections he would inevitably make. So on my behalf, Dad signed a seven-year contract with Desilu Productions Inc. on March 13, 1956, as "I Love Lucy" prepared to go into production for its sixth season on CBS-TV.

According to the contract's terms, my salary would begin at

$300 per week, with a guaranteed minimum of 40 weeks annually, and an escalation to $1,000 per week by the end of the contract period. At the time, Vivian Vance and William Frawley, who played Ethel and Fred Mertz, were being paid $2,000 each per episode.

The contract stated that I would furnish my "exclusive services" to Desilu Productions, spelled out to include television, radio, movies, phonograph records, merchandising, commercial tie-ups, and stage or personal appearances.

I would be paid minimum rerun fees as prescribed by the Screen Actors Guild (SAG) TV Supplement, and should any television film I appeared in ever be theatrically released, I'd be paid the minimum fee for that as well.

For TV commercials requiring my services, Desilu would also pay minimum fees as described in the Codified Screen Actors Guild TV Film Commercial Agreement. Desilu also had the right to loan me out to "any other person, firm, or corporation," and my contract could be assigned to any other person, firm, or corporation.

Along with all this exclusivity, the contract stipulated that my services would be furnished for Desilu in "all other fields of entertainment, over any media now known, or that may become known or invented in the future." Desilu really covered all their bases; basically, they pretty much owned me.

For example, I never received any income for a "Little Ricky" clothing line produced by Chips and Twiggs, a respected clothing manufacturer based in Philadelphia, even though I was sent on a summer promotional tour in 1958 in support of the line. The suits had the "Little Ricky" label inside.

I made department store appearances back east and used a thumb-print stamp to stamp my autograph because so many people came out to my public appearances to meet me. Hundreds of fans lined up to oooh and ahh over "Little Ricky."

Dad says a company executive in Philadelphia gave him a bottle of scotch, and I got some free clothes, but that was about it. I have no idea how much money that clothing line generated for Desilu Productions.

Although the contract was a good deal, it probably was not a

Desilu Productions Inc.

846 NORTH CAHUENGA BOULEVARD • HOLLYWOOD 38 • CALIFORNIA

HOLLYWOOD 9-5981

March 13, 1956

Mr. Lionel Thibodeaux
c/o Miss Edith Jackson
6801 Hollywood Boulevard
Hollywood 28, California

Dear Mr. Thibodeaux:

It is hereby understood that you agree in behalf of your son, KEITH THIBODEAUX, a minor, that he will furnish his exclusive services for Desilu Productions Inc. or its assigns on radio, television, motion pictures, phonograph records, merchandising, commercial tieups, stage or personal appearances, as well as all other fields of entertainment, over any media now known or that may become known or invented in the future. Desilu may assign him to perform services in any of the above-described media at its sole discretion in accordance with the terms and conditions listed below:

1. TERM: Seven (7) years, to commence with the week of March 19, 1956, each year consisting of fifty-two (52) consecutive weeks.

2. EXCLUSIVITY: Services during the term hereof shall be exclusive to Desilu and he will not render services for any other person, firm or corporation or for his own account without Desilu's prior written consent. He will not allow his name, voice, likeness or endorsement to be used by any other person, firm or corporation without Desilu's prior written consent.

3. TERMINATION: Desilu may terminate his services as of the end of any contract year on notice to be given at least thirty (30) days prior to the conclusion of any contract year.

4. COMPENSATION: For the performance of his services during the term hereof, Desilu will pay him the following compensation for a minimum of forty (40) out of fifty-two (52) weeks each year during which we may require his services. (It is understood that he will be paid for forty (40) weeks each year whether we require his services or not):

        1st year — Three hundred dollars ($300.00) per week.
        2nd year — Three hundred fifty dollars ($350.00) per week.
        3rd year — Four hundred dollars ($400.00) per week.
        4th year — Five hundred dollars ($500.00) per week.
        5th year — Six hundred fifty dollars ($650.00) per week.
        6th year — Eight hundred dollars ($800.00) per week.
        7th year — One thousand dollars ($1,000.00) per week.

We may deduct, withhold, or put in trust any monies required to be deducted, withheld, or put in trust under the law or by reason of any court order.

    5.   TELEVISION RESIDUALS:

        A. For each television film in which he appears Desilu will pay him the minimum rerun fees as described in the SAG-TV Supplement.

        B. For the theatrical release of any television film in which he appears, Desilu will pay him the minimum fee for the theatrical release of any such television film.

    6.   TELEVISION COMMERCIALS: For each commercial in which his services are required, Desilu will pay him the minimum fees as required for said television commercials as described in the Codified SAG-TV Film Commercial Agreement. Desilu shall have the right to loan out his services to any other person, firm or corporation in Desilu's sole discretion.

    7.   OTHER SERVICES: If Desilu or its assigns requires him to render services for any other person, firm or corporation and compensation in addition to the amount set forth herein is required pursuant to any applicable collective bargaining agreement in effect and having jurisdiction over any of his services hereunder, Desilu will be required to pay any additional amounts needed to bring the compensation he receives up to the minimum compensation required by any such applicable collective bargaining agreement. Desilu shall be entitled to receive the gross amount paid by any other person, firm or corporation for his services.

    8.   LABOR UNIONS: Nothing herein shall be in violation of any collective bargaining agreement or labor agreement applicable to any services rendered by him pursuant to this agreement.

    9.   INCAPACITY: Minimum of three (3) weeks before any termination.

    10. ASSIGNMENT: Desilu may assign Artist or Artist's contract to any other person, firm or corporation.

    11. LOAN OUT PROVISIONS: As generally provided in term agreements as used in the major Motion Picture Studio Agreements.

                    Very truly yours

                    DESILU PRODUCTIONS INC.

                    By _____

ACCEPTED AND AGREED:

_____
Lionel Thibodeaux

_____
Edith Jackson

-2-

great deal. Dad later came to believe he could have asked for more and gotten it, but he relied heavily on my agent, Edith Jackson, whom he had met through Fred Dodge. It was Jackson who negotiated my contract deal with Desilu Productions.

Edith Jackson, an older woman who wore her hair in a little bun at the nape of her neck, looked to me like an 1800s-era schoolmarm. She had been an agent for only five years, and Dad perceived her as a frustrated actress who was thrilled by the idea of working in the entertainment business. Although she represented other actors, I was her biggest client.

Even as a kid, I remember that she struck me as being kind of slow, and I'm sure, as a negotiator, she was no match for either Lucy or Desi. But to Dad — a salesman from Louisiana infatuated with Hollywood — Desilu's contract seemed not only fair, but like a dream come true.

Television was so new, and few people in those days, especially someone with limited show business experience like my father, could foresee the income implications for things like merchandising or promotional tie-ins. It was not the way contracts are today, where stars routinely stamp their name on a pair of jeans and negotiate a handsome return in exchange.

Dad's dreams for my future were likely heightened by all the news reports about my addition as an "I Love Lucy" cast member. Prior to the beginning of the sixth season of the show — when I was first to appear — Lucy told a reporter there would be a shift of emphasis on the show to the Little Ricky character. Little Ricky's age would be pushed up from a baby to five years old to accommodate more interesting script situations for Lucy, Ricky, Fred, and Ethel.

It was Desi who came up with my name change, suggesting the name "Richard Keith" for professional purposes, which was often shortened to "Ricky Keith." Desi told Dad that the name Thibodeaux was too hard and too long to remember, and people couldn't pronounce it.

Dad took for granted that my new stage name would be added to the list of credits on the original filmed "I Love Lucy" episodes. When that didn't materialize, he expected Edith Jackson to take over the matter. When nothing happened, Dad complained to her about it.

"Why isn't Keith's name included in the credits for the show?" Dad had questioned Edith.

"Don't worry," she replied nonchalantly. "I'll check into it."

When nothing happened, Dad complained to her again.

"I'm doing my best, Lionel," Edith answered weakly.

Dad eventually quit raising the credits issue, and nothing more was ever done about it.

Later, Dad came to believe that credit was not given to me because Lucy planned to bring Desi Jr. into the show, perhaps in a later series utilizing the Lucy character. (Lucy did eventually bring Desi Jr. and her daughter Lucie to a later TV series, "Here's Lucy," as her television children; the series ran from 1968 to 1974.)

With my name not listed in the "I Love Lucy" credits, the public would not likely be aware of the difference. Though this was speculation on Dad's part, it's interesting that most observers have noted that in the public's mind, Little Ricky and the real-life son of Lucy and Desi were one and the same once I assumed the role on "I Love Lucy."

As Desi Jr. and I grew older, people thought he was Little Ricky, and in turn, mistook me for Desi Jr. Whatever the reason, my name was never listed in the original program credits.

After signing with Desilu, our family finally moved from the Heidt ranch to an attractive rented, one-story house with three bedrooms at 4213 Wilkinson Street in Studio City. The stucco, Spanish-style house was about a 20-minute drive from Motion Picture Center.

Annette Funicello, who gained fame as one of Walt Disney's Mouseketeers, lived a block away. Ironically, her first husband, Jack Gilardi, later became my agent for a brief time period.

When we moved into our new house, Mom was pregnant with my sister Leslie, who was born at the end of 1956. That made four of us, including myself, my five-year-old sister Katie, and my three-year-old brother Dwight. Eventually, the Thibodeaux family would expand to six children, with the addition of my sister Debra in 1958, and my brother Brian in 1962.

As a full-time mother at home, Mom had her hands full, and

she only came once or twice to "I Love Lucy" filmings. It was difficult for her to spend time at the studio because she would have to find someone to watch the other kids. Unlike Dad, who loved the aura of show business, Mom was too busy caring for her family to be impressed by Hollywood. Lucy, Desi, and all the glamour surrounding them didn't faze her. "They're just people," she would say with a shrug.

California's child labor laws stipulated that at least one parent had to be with a child on the set, so Dad quit his job with the tire company to chauffeur me to the studio and help me practice my lines. He had saved a little money and was able to deduct a portion of my salary to help with family expenses.

Until the "Jackie Coogan law," earnings of minor children belonged exclusively to a child's father, but in 1938, due largely to the controversy over the earnings of the well-known child actor Jackie Coogan, California's civil code was changed. The statutes governing child labor allowed parents of a minor child to deduct "reasonable sums" for the "support, care, maintenance, education, and training of the minor," as long as up to one-half of net earnings after taxes and other expenses were set aside in a trust fund, or some other savings plan, for later use.

About a year after I signed with "I Love Lucy," Dad started working at Desilu in the public relations department, under department head Ken Morgan, who was married to Lucy's cousin, Cleo.

Lucy was loyal to family and her close friends, and many of them worked for Desilu. Everyone joked about Lucy practicing nepotism — a big word for a little kid, but I eventually learned it meant favoritism by placing relatives and friends in high positions.

Dad started out working in the photography department and did some office work for public relations events. Eventually he helped set up press conferences and arranged still photography shoots.

As Dad's career became more and more tied to Desilu, and as our family continued to grow, pleasing Desi and Lucy became even more important. Dad became close to the famous couple, even joining Desi in some of his later much-publicized carousing.

Dad says that one reason he didn't make more of an issue

about the credits situation is that Desi repeatedly assured him that he would always see to it that I was "taken care of." And, with Lucy and Desi as his bosses, Dad didn't want to rock the boat.

When he finally left Desilu Productions in the 1960s, Dad left as assistant to a Desilu vice-president, George Murphy, who later became a U.S. Senator.

Going to work at Motion Picture Center at 846 North Cahuenga Boulevard was a real adventure for a child. The huge complex, built on a seven-acre lot, had nine sound stages. Four of the sound stages had been converted into theater-style filming sites for Desilu shows filmed before a live audience. The "I Love Lucy" sound stage on Stage 9 had bleacher seating for an audience of 300 people.

I remember going through the back lot, opening a big door, and finding myself suddenly standing on the sound stage. Stages for Lucy and Desi's New York apartment and the Connecticut home where the Ricardos would move during the sixth season of the show were set up there, as well as seating for the studio audiences present at each week's filming. With dozens of different nooks and crannies to explore, it was as if I had my own fantasy playground.

In Hollywood, the size and opulence of an actor's dressing room reflected the status and importance of the role played in any show. My first dressing room was a drab partitioned-off cubicle and in no way compared to the plush suites that Lucy, Desi, and the other actors on our show enjoyed. That changed, however, on my sixth birthday in December 1956.

Lucy came on the set that day carrying a big birthday cake and smiling at me. "Happy Birthday, Keith!" she said gaily. Always looking for a reason for a celebration, Lucy often had a cake brought in whenever someone connected with the show had a birthday.

Instead of gathering around the cake, the entire cast and crew were standing nearby smiling as if they all shared a secret.

"We have a surprise for you, Keith," Lucy announced. "Come over here for a minute." Obediently, I walked over and stood beside Lucy while she tied a blindfold around my head.

"Come on, Keith. Go with me," she said, taking my hand and leading the way.

Finally, we stopped, and I heard the sound of a door opening. After a few more steps, Lucy untied the blindfold.

"Happy birthday, Keith!" Lucy shouted. "Here's your new dressing room!"

Amazed, I stared at the burst of blue color all around me. With blue walls, a blue overstuffed sofa, and plush sky-blue carpeting, my new dressing room had all the amenities.

A pint-sized director's chair with my name emblazoned on its canvas back sat in the middle of the room.

"Thanks, Lucy," I said excitedly as I walked around looking at all the pictures lining the walls and the school desk where I could do my schoolwork during filming breaks.

"How do you like it, pardner?" Desi asked.

Shyly, I replied, "I really like it."

"Here you are, Keith," Lucy said, handing me a set of keys. "The keys to your very own dressing room!"

I didn't know what to say. Having my own keys impressed me more than anything else.

I continued to look around the room, noticing the big star on the door with my name on it, and I suddenly felt very special.

As we walked back to the sound stage to eat birthday cake, the entire crew smiled at me and shouted, "Happy Birthday!" as I passed by.

In honor of my birthday, John, one of the stage hands, performed a magic trick for me, which he often did during breaks on the set.

Having such an elaborate dressing room meant, in my mind, that I had "arrived" on the show. Often during filming breaks, I'd go to my dressing room and color in my coloring books.

On a typical day, Dad and I would be on the set at 8 a.m. As soon as I arrived, I would check in with my teacher from the State Board of Education, Miss Barton.

A buxom, somewhat matronly, white-haired lady, Catherine Barton was soft-spoken and always kind to me. She served as my private tutor and had previously worked with the child star of TV's

"Rin Tin Tin." Later, she tutored Ron Howard, who played Opie on "The Andy Griffith Show." Miss Barton was extremely protective of me and functioned as a combination schoolteacher and babysitter. I came to love and respect her.

Miss Barton didn't put up with any nonsense from Desi.

More than once she confronted him about not complying with the State Board of Education requirements.

"Mr. Arnaz," she would say in her schoolteacher's voice, "I hope you don't expect Keith to remain overtime for additional filming today."

"Listen, Catherine, dear," Desi would respond in an overly restrained voice that only hinted at the anger he must have felt. "We have a deadline to meet, and we need Keith for this shot!"

"I can't permit that, Mr. Arnaz," Miss Barton would say, looking the famous actor square in the eye. "It's not my rule. It's the Board of Education's rule."

At that point one of the producers would pipe up and say, "You're up against a stone wall with the Board of Education, Desi. They could really make this hard for Keith — and for us — if you don't let the kid go for the day."

Desi would stand silently for a moment, chewing on one of the thin Cuban cigars he always smoked. Then he would glare at Miss Barton, the fire in his eyes indicating he was trying to hold back and keep his Latin temper from exploding.

"Okay! Let him go!" Desi would shout, finally giving in to the inevitable. "It's a wrap for Keith today!"

Stomping away, he would mutter under his breath, "I don't know how we can get any work done around here with all her (expletive) meddling!"

In spite of Desi's outbursts, Miss Barton usually won these battles of the will.

A little schoolroom had been set up in one of the vacant dressing rooms where Miss Barton and I worked on my school subjects. To break up the daily routine, Miss Barton and I would play games or take long walks around the lot. I especially liked visiting the studio commissary for a cold drink whenever we finished our work early.

On the days I had to shoot the show, I would check in with

Miss Barton and then be sent to makeup. At first I thought being made up was very strange, but I grew to like it, finding the process relaxing. They put very dark makeup on me because the filming was done in black and white and also to give me that Latin look — to appear as much as possible like Desi's son. My brown hair, which was slicked back and sprayed, appeared black on television.

At the first of the week, I would sit with Desi, Lucy, and the rest of the cast, as well as the director and writers, while we went over the script for that week's show.

My first day on the set, I responded to Lucy by saying, "Yes, Miss Ball."

"Listen, if we are going to be spending a lot of time on this show together, we'll have to call each other by our first names. It's Lucy, Desi, Vivian, and Bill. We're all on a first-name basis here," Lucy insisted.

We would rehearse around a table where we were sitting. I listened attentively and felt privileged and special because I was the only kid there. I knew I was part of a big show.

Script changes were made at that time, and sometimes Dad would suggest alterations in my lines since I had trouble pronouncing some words.

The second day, we moved from the table to the set where we went over the script again.

On the third day, with the lighting crew's work done, and the various crews and cameras assembled onstage, we'd do blocking. That involved the placement of chalk marks and masking tape on the floor to indicate the positions the cameras would take for various shots. All the actors, including myself, would be told where to stand onstage. This was particularly important since "I Love Lucy" was shot like a stage play.

The fourth day was dress rehearsal.

Finally, the show was filmed live in front of a studio audience.

When I began, we filmed the show on Friday nights. Later on, filming was switched to Thursday nights, so Lucy, Desi, and the kids could leave Friday for long weekends in Palm Springs.

I filmed my first episode of "I Love Lucy," titled "Lucy and Bob Hope," in June 1956. The show aired in October, and my role was minimal. I appeared in a brief baseball sequence, complete with an elaborate mockup of Yankee Stadium's grandstands on the sound stage.

Dad says that Hope mentioned to Lucy that I was "very talented," and expressed interest in having me on one of his shows, but nothing ever came of it.

I remember he was very kind to me, but I don't remember much more about Bob Hope or that particular show since my appearance was so brief. The episode was the first one of the new season, introducing me to viewers as the now-older Little Ricky.

In the two episodes following my opening appearance on the "Lucy and Bob Hope" episode, my character was featured a little more prominently. "Little Ricky Learns to Play the Drums" and "Little Ricky Gets Stage Fright" were both filmed in June for October air dates.

In "Little Ricky Learns to Play the Drums," I had to beat on a drum in a monotone fashion. Actually, this was sort of odd for me — a professional drummer — to pretend to pound very unprofessionally and noisily! The premise of the show, however, was hysterical.

The nonstop, monotonous rhythm makes Lucy and Ricky function to the unending beat. When Lucy squeezes oranges for Ricky's juice, she does it to the drumbeat; when she scrapes burned toast, it's in time to the beat.

Fred and Ethel come to Lucy and Desi's apartment to complain about the constant pounding that is driving them crazy.

After Little Ricky stops the drum beating for a moment, Fred says, "What a relief! I thought he'd never quit!"

An argument between the Ricardos and the Mertz's ensues, with Fred threatening to evict the Ricardos.

In the middle of the argument, apartment neighbor Mrs. Trumball appears. Suddenly, everyone is frantic to discover that Little Ricky has disappeared. By the show's end, they find me curled up on the Mertzs' sofa, fast asleep.

My favorite and most enjoyable "I Love Lucy" episodes were the ones where I could play the drums. Music had to take a back seat to acting at this point in my life, but whenever possible I'd grab my sticks and spin through one of my drum routines.

Although I was a right-handed drummer and set up my drum kit as a right-handed drummer would, my grip for my sticks was left-handed. My style made me look sort of odd when I played.

I remember one time the famous drummer, Buddy Rich, saw me play.

Dad asked him, "Do you think Keith should try to change his style to play the drums with a traditional right-handed grip?"

Buddy Rich studied my technique for a while. "His cymbal work is very fast," he remarked to my Dad. "If he's that good, just leave him alone!"

The fact that I was a drummer and not an actor sometimes worked against me. I hated memorizing lines, and it was hard for me to deliver them. My focus wasn't very good back then, but I tried to do my best.

The assistant director, Jay Sandrich — today, a well-known television director — would stand behind the scenes. When the red light came on, he would always be there to prompt me so I wouldn't miss my cue.

Madelyn Pugh (now Madelyn Davis), one of the show's writers, recalls: "We were very pleased with Keith's addition to the show because it gave us so many more story lines, especially with him being a drummer! In the beginning, we were very careful not to give him too many lines because he was so little. We knew he was a drummer, not an actor."

At times I would simply freeze during rehearsals.

"It was as if he was almost in shock," Madelyn remembers.

I simply could not say my lines.

Lucy would be telling me one thing, Desi another, the director another, and Dad another. I felt caught in the middle between everybody.

According to Madelyn, during one incident, Desi came over, took me on his lap and gave me a hug, speaking softly to me.

Desi had a sweet and compassionate side to him that, in spite of his temper, made me feel comfortable around him. I felt an affinity with Desi; he had a Latin name, and I had a French name. He played the drums, and I played the drums. We had more in common, and he seemed more down-to-earth than Lucy.

I had another problem, however, that no amount of comforting or coaxing could solve — I stuttered.

Sometimes, when the show got to a certain point, I would stutter and forget my lines. Unlike drumming, which was as natural to me as breathing, acting was hard. I had to work at it.

Dad coached me to say my lines a certain way; and if I didn't say them as he instructed, he would get upset with me. I also had a lisp, and sometimes I wouldn't say my lines distinctly enough and would have to repeat them. I didn't understand what all the fuss was about.

On the first show with Bob Hope, instead of saying "Joe DeMaggio," I called him "Joe Maggio." Then Desi came in, and he too called the famous ball player "Joe Maggio." The writers had decided to write it that way on purpose so it would sound as if we had similar speech patterns.

In my mind, I thought my speech difficulties just added to the show. After all, Desi's Spanish-tinged mispronunciations of English words were a comedy plus on the show, and I was supposed to be his son, wasn't I?

Dad would stand on the sidelines during filming, and I'd look to him for direction. If you watch any "I Love Lucy" reruns where Little Ricky appears, you'll notice I often seem to be staring off in the distance. Actually, I was looking at Dad, searching for his approval and direction in how I was saying my lines.

During the tapings of the show, the writers and other VIPs watched from a little platform behind the last row of seats in the studio's bleacher section. My dad often sat with Madelyn Pugh and the other writers.

"Once I took my son, Michael, who was about four years old, to a show with me," Madelyn recalls. "Someone gave him a piece of Lifesaver candy, and it got stuck in his throat. Before I knew it, he was choking. Michael was my first child, and I was so terrified I didn't know what to do. Keith's dad grabbed him, took him downstairs away from the platform turned him upside down, and shook him until he spit out the candy. He saved Michael's life, and I have never forgotten it."

Although I don't remember the incident myself, it didn't surprise me to learn how my father responded. Dad had once rushed me to the hospital when I choked as a child. I guess he was well-able to handle such emergencies after his experience with me.

I vividly remember filming my second segment for the show, "Little Ricky Gets Stage Fright." In this episode, Little Ricky, prior to his first music recital, is gripped by a terrible case of stage fright. Actor Howard McNear was featured in the role of Little Ricky's music teacher. Howard and I later worked together on "The Andy Griffith Show," where McNear portrayed Floyd, the barber.

To combat Little Ricky's stage fright, Lucy suggests that he play at Club Babalu — the former Tropicana Club, which Ricky Ricardo had bought an interest in and renamed. Finally, Ricky persuades his son to play at the club.

On the night of the performance, the ukulele player gets sick, and Little Ricky refuses to play without his strumming buddy. Lucy comes to the rescue, dressed in a striped blazer, and joins Ricky Jr. and his Dixieland Band in performing an upbeat number, "Five-Foot-Two, Eyes of Blue."

More than any other episode, "Little Ricky Gets Stage Fright" has always stood out in my mind. It wasn't until recently that I learned why I could recall this episode so vividly — as if it had happened only yesterday.

For that particular episode, I had a lot to memorize, and this was one of the shows where I forgot my lines.

I remember Desi yelling excitedly, "We're losing time!"

That statement wasn't unusual. Because of my age and the child labor laws, time was of the utmost importance when I was filming the show. If I made a mistake, I couldn't always do it over if my time was up because I had to leave the set.

Desi's yelling really scared me.

I sort of shriveled up inside. Normally I was a very quiet child on the set, but I got to the point that day where I could barely speak.

Finally, Lucy went to my father about the problem with my lines. "Tibbie, what do you think we should do about the situation?" she asked.

My father, Lionel J. Thibodeaux, was called L.J. by my mother, but Lucy always called my dad Tibbie.

"I don't know, but something's got to be done. He's just too tense," Dad replied.

Someone suggested that they send me to a speech therapist. That helped during the daily rehearsals, but when the time came to actually film the episode live before the studio audience, I was still having some problems. I was stuttering a lot, which I lapsed into whenever I was upset.

Desi told my father, "Oh my God, we've got to do this show! We'll have to call the doctor."

It wasn't until recently that I learned how the adults in my life chose to deal with my stuttering problem.

My mother was the first person to bring up the subject with me.

"What did that man do to you in the dressing room?" Mom questioned me one day not long ago.

"What man?" I asked.

"You used to talk about a man with a round pocket watch that he swung back and forth, and you would have to watch it," Mom explained.

At that point, something clicked in my mind, and I began to remember such incidents.

I then went to Dad and asked him about the man in the dressing room.

"A therapist was brought to the set," my dad recalled, "and he took you to a dressing room to talk with you."

"Yes, I remember that," I said. I knew I had regular speech therapy sessions for a period of time.

"What about the day, during the actual filming of the show, when I just froze?" I asked, recalling vague memories of this doctor being with me in my dressing room. "I remember he would play games with me using a round disc going back and forth in front of me."

"I don't know for sure if you were hypnotized that night or not," my father answered. "But I know you were hypnotized more than once."

"That must be why the memories of filming that particular episode are still so fresh in my mind," I thought aloud. "I never realized the guy was a hypnotist! I thought he was a playmate who would help me get through my lines and stop my stuttering."

My dad didn't say anything else.

"How could they do that to me?" I asked. "Modern medicine may accept hypnosis as one of their tools, but to me, it has its roots in occultic practice."

Dad could tell I was very upset, but he just looked at me.

Of course, I know that Lucy and Desi did not realize there was any danger in hypnosis. To them it was simply therapy, a way to get me to stop stuttering.

With Horace Heidt on his television show.
Viewer response was instrumental in Heidt hiring me.

3

Who Am I?

My relationship with Lucy and Desi was really strange. On the one hand, they were like parents to me. On the other hand, they were my bosses — as well as Dad's.

Every morning, Desi would stride onto the "I Love Lucy" set, give me a hug, and in a booming voice ask, "How's it going, pardner? Are you ready to play the drums today?"

Desi was a great guy who knew how to make people feel loved and accepted. Lucy, on the other hand, had a more complex personality, and I often found myself in awe of her.

On the set, Lucy usually dressed casually in slacks, sweater, and flat shoes, and ran around with curlers in her hair. It seemed she always had a cigarette in her hand. On show nights, when she came out of her dressing room with her hair done and all made up and ready for the filming, a new Lucy appeared. Even as a child, I was aware of how pretty she was, and she could make me feel shy by just looking at me. Lucy was always a "star" to me.

Sometimes when Vivian Vance, who played Ethel Mertz, came on the set in a particularly pretty dress, or if she looked especially thin, Lucy would say, "Look, I'm the star, you're working for me. Find another outfit."

Vivian was an attractive woman and a year younger than Lucy, but she was always made to look like "frumpy Ethel" on the show. She played the wife of Bill Frawley, who portrayed Fred Mertz, and he was 25 years her senior. Vivian and Bill never got along and were always at each other's throats.

I don't think Vivian and Lucy cared that much for each other at that time, either. There appeared to be some friction between them. Later in life, however, they became quite close.

Vivian was a professional in every sense of the word. She was nothing like the homey Ethel character that she played. Although Vivian could be a very warm person, she was usually distant with me. When she wasn't doing her lines, she would retreat to her dressing room.

I had no way of knowing it at the time, but I later learned that Vivian spent a considerable part of her "I Love Lucy" years in psychoanalysis. She evidently had a lot of problems, and her husband at the time, an actor named Phil Ober, supposedly was the cause of most of them.

Because of his voice, Bill Frawley always seemed sort of gruff to me, much like the Fred character he portrayed. He was a big-hearted man who just came to work and did his job. Like Fred, his bark was probably much worse than his bite.

I noticed that Bill always acted like a gentleman around the ladies and was courteous when they were present.

Although I was always very aware that they were actors — professionals doing their job, in many ways, Bill and Vivian were like an aunt and uncle to me. I could talk to Bill more easily than I could to Vivian.

Every morning, Bill and I met at the doughnut table on the set. "How's it going today, Keith?" he would say every day. "How's the world treating you?" I felt like an equal when Bill talked to me like that — not like a kid. In fact, he always treated me like a peer and didn't talk down to me.

I called everyone by their first name, and even though I was just a kid among all these adults, I thought I had to act like an adult. Despite my insecurities, I felt I was an actor, too, and it was an honor to do a show like "I Love Lucy."

We were all in it together, and there was a kind of camaraderie between us as actors. In many ways, it was like any other work-place: We had a job to do and tried to perform to the best of our ability.

At the height of "I Love Lucy's" popularity, fan mail came in at the staggering rate of 10,000 letters a month. I started to get fan mail, too, and lots of it. I still have several of the notes.

One, addressed to "Master Richard," reads,

> I love to watch you perform on "I Love Lucy." You must really love it also. Getting to play those drums and being surrounded by such wonderful people! Could you please, if possible, send me a photograph of yourself? Thank you.

Another note, addressed to "Richard Keith," said,

> I watch the "I Love Lucy" show all the time and enjoy it very much. It is one of my favorite programs. I like it because it is funny. I would like a picture of you.

The episode, "Deep-Sea Fishing," which we filmed in September for a November air date, was especially intriguing to me. The show was one of several we did with a Florida setting.

In this episode, Lucy and Ethel make a bet with Ricky and Fred on who can catch the biggest fish. To ensure their victory, Lucy and Ethel go out and buy a hundred-pound tuna and plan to hide it in the Ricardos' hotel bathtub. Ricky and Fred come up with the same idea and also buy a hundred-pound tuna. A hilarious routine involving each couple trying to hide their fish from the other ensues, until they eventually discover each other's plan.

With things out in the open, the Ricardos, Little Ricky, and Fred and Ethel go out for a day of real deep-sea fishing. At first, Little Ricky is the only one who catches anything. Then Lucy gets a nibble, followed by Ricky getting a bite.

When Ricky's fishing pole goes overboard, he dives in after it, only to be reeled in by Lucy. When a squirming fish is discovered in Ricky's jacket, Lucy claims she has won the bet because she "caught" Ricky, and hence, the fish.

To do the deep-sea fishing scene, the crew had to dig a hole in the set and fill it with water and bring in an actual yacht. Although the entire scene took place there on the set, for some reason, it was very believable to me. I knew we were inside Motion Picture Center, but, as far as I was concerned, we were out on the open seas!

Each "I Love Lucy" show was done like a three-act stage play, which was studied, rehearsed, and then performed in sequence, live, in front of a studio audience. At the height of its success, Desilu Productions employed over 2,000 people to work on its various shows, with nearly 100 people employed for each "I Love Lucy" episode.

Major expansion was going on the year I joined the show, with Desilu projecting more than 200 hours of television shows to be in production for the upcoming season. When Desilu needed more money for expansion, Lucy and Desi struck a deal to sell 179 "I Love Lucy" programs, which would be the total at the end of the 1956-57 season, for $4,500,000, as well as its percentage ownership of another Desilu produced TV show, "December Bride," for $500,000.

Desi and Lucy received an extra million dollars to be exclusive CBS-TV performers for 10 years. Looking back, getting the rights to "I Love Lucy" was an incredible deal for CBS, although at the time it seemed like an excellent price, and the money enabled Desilu to keep growing.

Because we were shooting a live show, the pressure on the set was tremendous. I sensed that a lot of peoples' jobs were on the line every week. If a crew member wasn't doing his job right, Desi did not hesitate to let them know it. Employees who were not productive on the set got their walking papers!

Even at my young age, I was aware of the high costs of the lights, the production people, and all the things that went into producing a television show with the kind of professionalism Desilu Productions expected and required. I knew that the incomes of all the people involved depended on the show's success. From my child's viewpoint, if I had been asked to describe the mood of the set in one word, my reply would have been short and to the point: tense.

After only a short time on the set, I began to feel great pressure to please Lucy and Desi. And pleasing Lucy was a difficult task because she was a perfectionist. Lucy had a big heart, but she also could be cold as ice. To me, doing "I Love Lucy" was never a fun-and-games time. It was never relaxed. There was always an undercurrent of tension and pressure in the air.

Although Lucy and Desi both demanded perfection, their demands manifested themselves in different ways.

Desi once told a reporter, "Only quality attracts the public, so we deal in quality." It was probably this emphasis on quality that led to his expectations of perfection.

During the sixth season — the season I joined the show — Desi also assumed the role of producer, adding even more to his Desilu responsibilities. In spite of his natural genius, the pressures on him must have been enormous.

Desi had a quick, hot temper and was easily excitable, often exploding on the set. But generally, he was easy-going and laid-back in temperament, despite his flare-ups.

There was another side to Desi, too — a warm, compassionate side that didn't hesitate to help those in need. When Desi learned that the daughter of one of the grounds keepers at Desilu Studios needed an operation and the family didn't have the money to pay for the surgery, he told the man, "Go to my office. There's a check waiting for you."

"God bless you, Mr. Arnaz," the gardener said with tears in his eyes as he pumped Desi's hand.

While Desi had a tenderness about him, Lucy seemed more rigid. On the show, Lucy was a zany, wacky wife, and Ricky put up with her; in real life, she wasn't zany, and she would confront Desi. They had a passionate relationship, and both of them were very emotional people.

When arguments on the set arose, I tried to stay out of the way of the adults as much as possible. When I heard people curse, I didn't like it and inherently sensed it was wrong. Most of the time, the adults on the set tried not to use foul language when I was around, so if they did, I knew they were really mad!

On the set, when Desi would start yelling, even though he wasn't yelling at me, I would get upset. I was a sensitive child, and that probably made it worse.

During rehearsals, Lucy, Desi, Vivian, and Bill would sometimes argue heatedly over lines. One would say to the other, "You're not going to read that line like that, are you?" Sometimes Lucy would chew out Vivian and Bill, and I'd think, *Uh-oh, me next!*

Many times I sat at the table during rehearsals with my head down and my stomach churning. Lucy would kiss me or hug me as a gesture of reassurance during such episodes, but her hugs didn't lessen the stress and anxiety I was beginning to experience constantly.

In the fall of 1956, during hiatus time from the show, I began attending parochial school at St. Victor's Catholic Church on Sunset Strip in West Hollywood. Miss Barton continued as my tutor during the months that episodes were being filmed.

On the first day of school, I was really scared. Not only was this a completely new experience for me, but for the first time in my life I would be around kids all day. At first, the idea sounded great, but I soon found that being in a classroom full of other children only made me more introverted. This probably resulted not only from my basic shyness but from the fact that, since the age of three, I had traveled and worked with adults.

The kids at school had heard I was Little Ricky, but they didn't treat me like a TV star or a celebrity. In fact, the other kids picked on me because I was the shortest and smallest child in the class. Whenever it came time to choose sides for a game, I was always the last one picked because I was so small.

Attending St. Victor's served to emphasize the tremendous dichotomies in my life. One day I'd be in school, trying desperately to fit in and be accepted by the other kids; the next day, I'd be back on the "Lucy" set in an entirely different world.

Years later I read a magazine interview in which actor Dean Stockwell, lately of "Quantum Leap" TV fame, reminisced about his child stardom days. Stockwell said, "The life of a child star is so fraught with responsibilities that it frustrates normal interests and associations with other children. It's a miserable way to bring up a child."

I wasn't miserable as a child, but I'd have to agree that acting does affect normal associations with other kids. At a time when most kids are carefree — their biggest worry is getting a good grade on a school quiz or making the Little League team — my life was becoming increasingly complicated. Not only did I have the normal school issues to deal with, but I had to satisfy all the adults in my life and on the show.

And I was barely six years old.

Despite all the pressures, I got a feeling of exhilaration from being onstage, out in front of all the lights and cameras. The whole world seemed to be watching me.

Sometimes I'd forget my lines, and since the show was filmed live, they'd have to stop the filming and have me do my part over again. Fortunately that didn't happen very often.

I guess my favorite episode of "I Love Lucy" would have to be "Lucy and Superman," filmed in the fall of 1956. Like most kids my age, I loved the "Superman" TV show with George Reeves as Superman.

The plot for this episode revolved around Lucy planning a party for Little Ricky's fifth birthday at the same time that Lucy's friend, Caroline Appleby, played by Doris Singleton, was planning a birthday party for her own "Little Stevie," played by Steven Kay.

The mothers argue over the same date for their child's parties, and both refuse to budge. So Lucy and Caroline Appleby try to outdo the other with their child's birthday bash.

Caroline hires a clown and a magician. Lucy realizes that Superman is in town and begs Ricky to ask the TV star to attend Little Ricky's party. Without waiting for confirmation, Lucy brags to Caroline that Superman will be at Little Ricky's party. Unable to top the maneuver of getting Superman, a defeated Appleby agrees to change Little Stevie's party to a different day.

When Lucy finds out that Ricky can't produce Superman after all, she enlists Ethel in a scheme whereby Lucy will disguise herself as Superman. Lucy climbs outside to a ledge and just as she is about to make her entrance, the real Superman shows up. Little Ricky and his friends are thrilled, and so is Lucy — until she discovers she has been locked out on the ledge. A rain storm begins, and Superman has to come to the rescue of a soaked Lucy.

One of the funniest lines in the show was when Superman tells Ricky Ricardo, "You mean to say you've been married to her for 15 years? And they call me Superman!"

When George Reeves came on the set, I felt he *really* was Superman, even though I knew he was an actor.

When he shook my hand, I thought, *Wow, he really is super!*

He picked me up in his arms and said, "Keith, how'd you like to go fly with me?"

I just looked at him, spellbound. He was a hero to me, and for a moment, I was caught up in the myth that television creates, even though I knew in reality he was just an actor. I couldn't help but entertain the thought that he was Superman — even as I watched him climb a ladder so he could come in "flying" through the window.

Although I liked being in front of the lights and cameras, I never liked the Little Ricky character and wished he could be more of a regular kid. I thought Little Ricky was sort of namby-pamby, and I wanted to be Tom Sawyer.

When Dad coached me with my lines, he had me say them in a cutesy, "little man" way. Other than when Desi directed the show, Lucy and Desi left my dad to deal with me. I never said anything to Dad about it, but I felt like a puppet, with him standing in the wings, coaching me.

Since I was a kid myself, I thought I knew more how a real boy should act. I remember thinking that the television son, Richie, on "The Dick Van Dyke Show" seemed more natural because he had some smart-aleck lines.

If I said my lines the way I thought they should be said, Dad would reprimand me with, "Oh no, Keith, that's not the right way to do it!"

It wasn't that I felt unloved by Dad, but I did start feeling as if my job was more important to him than my feelings; I felt I had to do what pleased him. Dad wanted me to be something he envisioned for me. He didn't see me as a person in my own right.

On the drive home on Friday nights after we filmed the show, I'd ask, "How was it tonight, Dad?"

If he said, "Keith, it was great, you were great," I felt fantastic.

But if he said, "I was disappointed in you tonight, Keith. You could have done better," I felt as if I had done something really wrong.

Dad kept presents in the trunk of his car, things like little toy soldiers or a doctor's kit, and would give them to me after the show's taping. If he thought I had done a particularly good job that night, I'd get the present along with lots of praise. If he was disappointed, I'd still get the present, but he seemed to give it grudgingly.

I remember one night on the way home, after my Dad said I had done particularly well, I asked him, "Dad, why did God pick me to be Little Ricky?"

Dad looked surprised at my question.

"He put you there for a purpose — to make people happy."

"But Dad, God could have chosen anybody!"

Dad reached over to the passenger seat and smoothed my hair. He was smiling at me. "I don't know, Keith. I guess God's just got a reason, a purpose, for you to be Little Ricky."

I vividly recall my first meeting with the Arnaz children, Lucie and Desi Jr. It took place at Lucy and Desi's mansion at 1000 North Roxbury Drive in Beverly Hills.

Lucy and Desi's house wasn't a mansion in the opulent, overdone, Hollywood sense of the word. But the very large, white, two-story Williamsburg-style house was a mansion as far as I was concerned since it was nothing like the modest home where I lived with my family in Studio City.

Located just north of Sunset Boulevard, several streets over from the now-famous Rodeo Drive shopping district, the Arnaz home included a guest house out back, a swimming pool with a pool house and cabanas, and a garage.

I later learned that Lucy and Desi bought the house in 1955 for $85,500 after deciding to move closer to town from their ranch in Northridge. In today's real estate market, the house would be valued in the millions of dollars. Jack Benny lived next door, and Jimmy Stewart lived four doors down.

Beverly Hills is actually a separate city with a separate government, its own police force, and its own school system. It is not Los Angeles and never has been. A mere five and a half square miles today, it's a wealthy oasis with odd boundary lines. Money has always been the prime requirement needed to live there. Although long associated with movie and TV stars, doctors, lawyers, and wealthy business people also call Beverly Hills home.

In those days, Beverly Hills was a more close-knit neighborhood than it is now.

I remember being driven to Lucy and Desi's house, and taken to the foyer, where Lucy greeted me. As soon as I walked in, I noticed the big, winding, grand staircase leading up to the second floor. I stood silently in the foyer as Lucy called to the kids upstairs.

"Lucie! Desi! Come meet Keith!"

They both came walking down the stairs, pausing halfway to look at me quizzically, as if to say, "Who's this kid?"

In a few minutes, however, we were all playing happily together. Lucy was very strict about who her children could play with, and she must have felt safe about our friendship since she had personally recruited me as a playmate for Lucie and Desi. I played with both of them, and eventually was taken into the Arnaz family, becoming almost like another child of Lucy and Desi.

I'd often stay overnight at the Arnaz's Beverly Hills home and became familiar with all the people who worked there.

The house was fully staffed with nurses for the children, cooking and cleaning help, a chauffeur, and a gardener. A security guard would arrive at dusk, walking around the property with a big flashlight until dawn.

Willie Mae Barker, the maid, had been with Lucy and Desi for years and helped raise the kids. Sometimes it seemed they had more mothering from Willie Mae than from Lucy. When Desi Jr. would feel lonely or sad, I'd sometimes see him snuggle up to Willie Mae.

She was allowed to discipline us, too. Once she took a switch to Desi Jr. and me because we got in the swimming pool — boy, that stung, even with my swimming trunks on!

Lucy's mother, DeDe, also helped out a lot when Lucy had to be away.

The Arnaz's chauffeur, Frank, used to take us everywhere. He always told wonderful stories!

Hazel Pierce, who was Lucy's stand-in on the show and a close friend, lived in the guest house. Stand-ins do just what the name implies: they "stand in" for the stars during rehearsals or during long periods when lighting and other technical problems are being worked out. She and her husband, Wesley, were a dance team, and had been friends with Lucy since she first came to Hollywood.

Hazel was older than Lucy, and when Wesley died, Lucy sort of took her in. You can see her in many "I Love Lucy" shows, usually in the background as the blonde and skinny extra.

Hazel was a very nervous person, and ditsy in a kind of Gracie Allen/Stan Laurel kind of way. Instead of "What?" she would say, "Hello?"

Lucie recalls that Hazel would be walking down the hall, carrying a big stack of papers, and Lucy would scream, "Hazel! Get over here!" really loud, causing Hazel to throw the papers in the air in surprise.

Lucie says the kids teased her like this, too, because, although they loved her, Hazel was sort of a natural target.

Jack Benny lived next door to the Arnaz house, and in the summers, with the windows open, we could hear the famous performer playing the violin up in his room. The sometimes melancholy sounds drifted on the cool summer breezes.

We liked to peek over the wall between the two houses and look into his swimming pool, which had a huge octopus with long tentacles painted on the bottom!

Since I was three years older, Desi Jr. looked up to me and tried to imitate me during those early years. He didn't come to the "I Love Lucy" set very often, so most of our time together was spent playing at the various Arnaz homes. I spent many weekends with Desi, Lucy, and the kids either at the Beverly Hills mansion, the house in Palm Springs, or at Desi's ranch in Corona.

During the filming of the show in the winter when the family would go to Palm Springs, I'd come along, too, as a playmate for Desi Jr. They had a house on a golf course there. I spent summer weeks with them at the beach house.

Desi Jr. and I often took long walks on the beach at Del Mar, and our favorite place was a secluded beach called the Cove. When the tide came in, we could see crabs and all kinds of sea animals scurrying along the shoreline.

One day on our way to the Cove, we saw a man surf fishing on the beach. "Want to meet Jimmy Durante?" Desi Jr. asked me.

"Sure!" I said, looking around. "Where is he?"

"Right over there," he answered, pointing in the direction of the old man who was fishing.

We walked over to him, and Desi Jr. asked, "How's fishing today?"

"Well, what do you know," the old man answered. "Haven't seen much of you lately, Desi. Who's this young fellow?"

"This is Keith, the boy who plays Little Ricky on the "I Love Lucy" show," Desi Jr. told him as I stared at the actor's famous big nose.

Durante flashed a smile and gripped my hand tightly. "Hi, Chickie!" he said, with a glimmer of fun in his eye.

From that time on, I was "Chickie" to Jimmy although I have no idea why! It may have been his way of making some sort of humorous combination out of my two names — Keith and Ricky — who knows?

Later, we often visited him and his wife Marge at their home in Del Mar.

Having Desi Jr. as a friend meant that I got included in many of his family's special activities. Desi took Desi Jr. and me to a football game at the stadium and even bought us Los Angeles Rams uniforms. In many ways, Desi Arnaz was like a surrogate father to me. He taught me, along with his own kids, to swim, fish, and ride horses.

One night when I was staying with them, Desi announced, "Tomorrow we are going to the races."

I got really excited. The racetrack was right across the road from the beach in Del Mar so the trainers would sometimes exercise their horses by riding them into the surf. I had often watched the large animals run and splash in the water — their every muscle in motion.

The next day, as we prepared to leave for the racetrack, Desi said, "Here's $60 for each of you to use betting on the races. You pick your horse, and one of the adults will place the bet for you."

Desi had his own private box at the track and had invited Jimmy and Marge Durante to join us that day.

"Okay, Chickie and Desi," Jimmy said after studying the racing form, "this is the horse you want to bet on."

Before long, I developed my own style of betting and would

choose the long shots because they paid more money if I won. Plus, I liked rooting for the underdog. Some days when we would return from a day at the track, our winnings would be good. My largest winning came to $160.

When the race started, each of us cheered for his own particular horse. By the end of each race, one of us would still be cheering while the others sat dejected because their horses lost. Our depression was temporary, however, because right away we'd be looking forward to the next race.

Desi Arnaz, however, took losing very seriously. As long as he was winning, he was all smiles. Losing was another matter, and he often got very upset — and everybody knew it. Desi wanted to be a winner in everything, and he didn't accept defeat easily.

Ineptness was another trait he refused to tolerate — in anybody, including himself. When we were out fishing on his boat and someone lost a fish we had on the line, it was like the end of the world.

Although Desi was involved in more activities with the kids and me, Lucy was always giving me presents. One time she gave me two drum sets for my birthday! One set was for me to have at home, and one was for stage use. Both were the exact same Gretsch drum sets.

Lucy also bought Desi Jr. an identical drum set, so there would be no feelings on his part that I was getting any special treatment from his parents.

I still have my set, which has been restored, and I still play them. That particular year makes the set a collector's item, not counting the fact that Lucy gave them to me!

Lucy and Desi knew how much I loved playing cowboys and Indians, so they bought me an authentic Indian teepee, complete with a wooden floor. It was so big, I don't know how they even got it to our house!

In some ways I knew them better than my own family because of all the time I spent with them.

In later years, Lucie once told me, "At times I wondered if you had a family, Keith! You spent so much time with us that I thought maybe you just liked being with us more than being with your own family."

The few times that Desi Jr. did visit the "I Love Lucy" set, it must have been hard for him. During the shows, Lucy would sometimes have me in her arms, kissing me. On television, I was pictured as the son, not Desi Jr.

Although Desi Jr. and I became close friends, there was always an undercurrent of rivalry between us, a sort of unspoken competition. I was older, and usually did better in sports than he did. When we played games together, I usually beat him. When I won, it would frustrate him.

But the rivalry between us was a healthy, brotherly-type rivalry. Desi Jr. looked up to me because I was older; I was like a big brother to him. We developed a close, loving relationship that continues to this day.

"Everyone thought you were really Lucy and Desi's son," Desi Jr. told me recently. "It was a case of mistaken identity. We were always having to explain who we were! It's really interesting when you have little children trying to tell adults that they — the adults — have been hoked by television!"

As for me, I had to evolve from a shy little Cajun kid who sometimes stuttered to a Latin look-alike of Desi Arnaz, trading my French background for a pseudo Cuban heritage. At a time when most children's identities are just being established, I had to jump from Keith Thibodeaux to Richard Keith to Little Ricky Ricardo with regularity.

On the set, I was Richard Keith, a star, mingling and working with four adults who were the hottest stars on the most popular TV show in the country. Off the set I was being chauffeured to and from the studio by Dad or picked up by a limousine.

At public appearances, I was Little Ricky Ricardo, a cute little lad fussed over by matrons who would pinch my cheeks and pronounce me adorable. I wanted to be an average, all-American boy and felt embarrassed when adults made a fuss over me.

At school, I was the smaller-than-average Keith Thibodeaux, constantly striving to win the approval of my classmates who could care less that I was Little Ricky.

At Lucy and Desi's mansion, I was Keith, family intimate and friend and playmate of Lucie and Desi Jr., surrounded by maids, servants, and a lifestyle far removed from the ordinary life I lived with the Thibodeaux family.

A lot of times I didn't want to go to Lucy and Desi's big house with servants running around. Most of all, I didn't like being away from my parents and the love and security of our family.

Mom, a stay-at-home housewife, did all the cooking and cleaning, took care of us kids, and managed the household. When Dad came home from work, we had dinner together and talked about the day's activities. After dinner, we took turns doing the dishes while Mom and Dad sat together, talking. In the evening, we watched TV, played games, or just sat around and relaxed.

At the Arnaz house, the kids did not eat with Lucy and Desi, and instead, we usually ate in a little breakfast room by ourselves. I never saw Lucy and Desi talking together about the day's events like Mom and Dad did at our house. To me there seemed to be a distance between family members at the Arnaz house.

As a child it was hard for me to understand why the atmosphere in the Arnaz household was much different from the scenes in the "I Love Lucy" show. In fact, "love" seemed to be the one thing that was missing at the Beverly Hills mansion.

Lucy and Desi were having marital problems, and even though I didn't yet fully understand what was happening, I could feel the tension between the two of them. It seemed strange to me because on television they were playing such a happily married couple. At home, however, the words they spoke to each other were not kind and loving.

Since I often spent more time with the Arnaz family than with my own, I began to feel somewhat detached from Dad and Mom and my brothers and sisters.

My brother Dwight and I shared a bedroom, and my brothers and sisters and I played — and fought — together. Still, as the oldest and because of my "job," I was the most important person in the household as far as the kids were concerned. Everything revolved around me, and I'm sure my brothers and sisters resented it. I was still punished like the rest of them and got the belt like anyone else when I needed it. On the other hand, I'd often receive special treatment.

For example, if I misbehaved, Mom would threaten, "Just wait 'til your father gets home!"

Then, when Dad came home, he would want to talk with me about the show or an event that was scheduled for me to do the next day; and my misbehavior would quickly be forgotten. Although my child star status did give me some leverage at home, I was far from your stereotypical, spoiled Hollywood brat.

If I wanted the latest style of clothes, I couldn't always get them because there were six kids in our family. Although I was a TV star on the set, at home I never felt like a rich kid celebrity.

My dad bought nice suits because he had to look good at work, but we never shopped at fancy Beverly Hills stores. All our clothes came from J.C. Penney, and Desi often kidded me about my J.C. Penney clothes!

I was constantly confronted by the fact that the Arnaz family was so rich, and my parents always seemed to be scraping financially, having just enough to get by. At times I felt as if I lived in two different worlds, going to the racetrack with Desi and Desi Jr., riding in fancy cars, and then going back to my house where, at times, it was hard to keep enough food on the table.

I don't want to give the wrong impression — our family wasn't starving or anything like that, but there was a stark contrast between our lives and the one I shared with Lucy, Desi, and their children. By our standards, Lucy and Desi were fabulously wealthy — I guess by anyone's standards, for that matter! Their wealth emphasized the vast differences between my life and theirs, even though our lives were so intertwined.

I would often overhear my parents talking about never having enough money, and subconsciously, that put more pressure on me. I felt I was the one with the potential to earn the most money for our family.

Added to all this was the mounting pressure that I felt on the "I Love Lucy" set. The pressure for me to perform was complicated by the ever-present knowledge that my family's livelihood depended in large part on my ability to perform in an acceptable way. Even though Dad worked for Desilu, I felt like the breadwinner in the family.

It was odd, but even then I viewed my early life in Bunkie, Louisiana, as the real world, and my time in California as the unreal world. Yet, Hollywood was the only world I knew.

4

End of an Era

I was a pretty healthy kid, but in November 1956, I stayed overnight at Cedars of Lebanon Hospital to have my tonsils removed. I remember very little about the operation, other than I was allowed to eat lots of ice cream after surgery!

About a week before the operation, I filmed the "I Love Lucy Christmas Show," which aired for the first time on Christmas Eve 1956.

The episode opens in the Ricardo home on Christmas Eve, with Ricky telling me that Santa won't come until I go to sleep. Ethel and Fred arrive to help trim the tree, and they reminisce, allowing flashbacks to previous episodes — like the show where Lucy breaks the news to Ricky that she's "expecting," and the show where Lucy goes to the hospital for the birth of Little Ricky.

In the end, Lucy, Ricky, Fred, and Ethel, dressed in Santa Claus outfits, are bewildered by a "fifth Santa" who shows up in their midst and then mysteriously disappears.

I only had two scenes in the show, a brief part where I talked with Lucy and Ricky before going to bed, and a Christmas morning scene, where I was able to play the drums — a Christmas present, along with a bicycle — that "Santa" leaves for Little Ricky. I enjoyed doing that particular episode, especially since I could play the drums.

As a special presentation, the show was not part of the syndicated show package that CBS-TV purchased. In 1989, after several brief clips from the Christmas special were aired on a talk show and during a tribute to Lucille Ball on the "Today" show, CBS started searching through its vaults to find this "lost episode."

A colorized version of the show aired again in its entirety for the first time in 33 years on December 18, 1989, on CBS and was the network's highest-rated show for the week ending December 24, 1989, testifying to the continuing popularity of "I Love Lucy."

The cover of *Look* magazine's December 25, 1956, issue featured a photo of me along with Lucy and Desi. Taken by Robert Vose, this cover photograph has always been my favorite of Lucy, Desi, and me. In the picture, Desi and I are both playing conga drums. (By the way, this is on the cover of this book.)

The lengthy feature story inside was accompanied by additional photographs, including one picture of Desi leaning down to listen to me during a script session with Lucy and the show's writers; another shows Desi Jr. and me on the set.

The same article reported that Lucy and Desi were so esteemed as marriage experts that *The New York Herald Tribune* invited them to be marital counselors at its 1956 seminar for brides. At the time, the public didn't know that the Arnaz's own marriage was experiencing difficulty. In fact, their turbulent relationship remained a well-kept secret for many years.

Fans and the media saw only the happiness of Lucy and Ricky Ricardo and assumed Lucy and Desi Arnaz had the same kind of marriage — another testimony to the way television blurs the line between acting and reality.

In TV-land in the 1950s, every family difference could be straightened out by the time the show ended. Family members loved each other; fathers were good dads; mothers took care of their homes; and kids were mischievous but not overtly rebellious.

In the case of "I Love Lucy," a big dose of comedy, along with great writers and a cast that jelled well together, set the show apart from other sitcoms of the day. By 1957, however, the fictional Ricardos held no relationship to what was going on in the real-life marriage of Mr. and Mrs. Arnaz. The more I was around Lucy and Desi, the more I realized they were actors doing a job.

I believe Lucy and Desi always loved each other, and I know they loved their kids. They tried to hold their marriage together, but there were incredible pressures on them. It was only later in life that

I began to realize some of what they must have been going through.

In 1957, Desi bought RKO Studios, a 65-acre studio complex where Lucy had begun her movie career. It was also the place where, years before, they had met and fallen in love.

Desi borrowed the down payment and bought the complex to further expand Desilu. The RKO Gower portion of the property was where Lucy and Desi used to work, and the RKO Culver portion was the site where Selznick Studios had made *Gone with the Wind.*

As the business grew, Desi worked even more, and his drinking escalated. I didn't understand all the business implications at the time, but life with the Arnazes, where I was treated like another child in their family, was starting to show the strain. Lucy worked hard as an actress, but Desi carried the bulk of the business responsibilities for the large, growing Desilu corporation in addition to his "I Love Lucy" acting and producing duties.

Even as a kid, I began to notice that Desi was drinking a lot. I later learned he would rationalize his drinking to others, saying he needed to get some relief from all the pressure he was under.

A favorite episode of mine, which was filmed in 1956 but aired in early 1957, was called "Little Ricky Gets a Dog."

In the show, I come home with a puppy given to me by a friend and decide to name the new pet Fred. When Lucy asks why I chose Fred as the dog's name, I tell Lucy, "I always name my dogs after my friends."

Landlord Fred Mertz arrives and reminds the Ricardos that their rental lease has a "no pets" clause. After learning that Little Ricky has named his dog after him, Fred relents, going to the basement to find a box for the puppy to sleep in.

After a sleepless night caused by the dog's howling, Ricky tells Lucy the puppy has to go. Lucy tries but can't bring herself to break the news to me.

Then a grouchy new neighbor arrives, demanding to know whether the Ricardos still have a dog. Lucy claims to have gotten rid of the dog. When the neighbor asks why she has dog biscuits if there is no dog, Lucy starts eating one, telling the neighbor, "I like dog biscuits as an afternoon snack."

In the end, the dog's presence is revealed, but Fred Mertz defends Little Ricky's dog, and the angry new tenant decides to move out.

During rehearsals for that episode, I fell in love with the little dog, who was actually a trained professional himself. After filming for the show was finished, I wanted to keep the puppy. I couldn't understand; if "Fred" was my dog on the show, why couldn't I have him and take him home with me?

"Daddy, can I have that puppy?" I pleaded.

"No, Keith, that's the trainer's dog," he replied.

"But Daddy," I persisted, "it's such a cute dog! I'd like to have it!"

Lucy was nearby and overheard us. "Tibbie," she said in almost a scolding voice, "you should get that child a dog!"

Lucy was a dog-lover and over the years had an assortment of poodles. Her favorite was a white toy poodle named Tinker. She also had poodles named Gigi and Fifi, too.

Desi had a dog named Junior that he got from the dog pound. One day Desi Jr. called me, crying, to say that Junior had died.

Not long afterward, Desi found another dog that looked uncannily like Junior. He named that dog Junior, too.

Shortly after the dog incident on the show, I got my first dog, a little black cocker spaniel that I named Susie. She became our family's dog, and I really loved her. When I came home from the set or from school, she always used to run out to meet me.

We ended up having Susie about a year before she disappeared in a strange incident.

Mom came home one day and told us kids, "Susie jumped out of the open convertible as I was driving down the road and disappeared."

I was heartbroken, and I couldn't believe that Mom had let her jump out of the car!

We later got another dog for the family, a poodle named Misty. Poodles didn't shed; they were sort of the proper "California dog." I always wondered if maybe my parents had actually given Susie away because they didn't like her!

"The Ricardos Visit Cuba," also filmed in 1956, still makes

me laugh when I think about it.

In that show, the Ricardos and the Mertzes go to Cuba for Ricky to perform and also to visit Ricky's relatives. Nervous about meeting Ricky's family, Lucy makes all kinds of mistakes which, naturally, are hilarious.

For example, Ricky tells her to keep saying "muchas gracias" (thank you) to his uncle, but Lucy mispronounces the Spanish words so that she actually calls Ricky's uncle a fat pig!

In the end, Ricky and I perform a drum and dance number, "Babalu," complete with me following Desi's dance steps as we both play conga drums.

Although I had never considered myself a dancer, during the dance scene with Desi it seemed to come naturally.

Hey, I thought, *it's okay, I really can move!*

Everything turns out okay for Lucy, too, because at the performance Ricky's uncle tells her, "Anyone who is the mother of a boy like that is all right with me!"

I enjoyed playing the conga although my hands were not conditioned for that type of drumming. Desi would pick his hands up high when he played the conga drums, but I kept my hands close to the drums because I was more oriented towards jazz and swing music styles.

One day Dad told me the drummer for Desi's orchestra was going to work with me.

"Let me show you some Latin beats you might want to use, Keith," the drummer said. He began to demonstrate different rhythms on the congas then stood aside and said, "Okay, let's see how close you can come to this rhythm."

I began to play the conga drum, beating out the exact same rhythms he did, adding some of my own embellishments.

Then he took back the conga, playing some single stroke rolls. Whenever he handed the drums back to me, I duplicated what he played, mimicking him.

Finally the drummer led me by the hand over to where Desi was standing on the set. He told Desi, "I can't do anything with this kid. He knows too much already!"

Desi laughed with that big, booming laugh he had, and smiled at me. "That's my boy! I'm proud of you, amigo!"

I said nothing, looking down at my feet shyly. I always felt embarrassed when Desi praised me.

In 1957, our family moved from Studio City to another house at 5533 Buffalo Street in Van Nuys, a Los Angeles suburb. At the beginning of 1957, which was midway through the sixth season of "I Love Lucy," — and my second season — the Ricardo television family also moved, forsaking their New York City apartment for a house in the suburbs — referred to on the show as "moving to the country."

Moving the Ricardos, and then the Mertzes, to Westport, Connecticut provided new story ideas as Lucy, Desi, and their friends explored suburban life.

It also gave me a playmate, at least on camera, because Ricky and Lucy's Connecticut neighbors, Betty and Ralph Ramsey, played by actors Mary Jane Croft and Frank Nelson, had a son named Bruce, played by child actor Ray Ferrell. Even though "Bruce" and I were playmates on these episodes, I don't remember Ray Ferrell being on the set that much. He was just another child actor to me, and I didn't really consider him a friend. Besides, I didn't relate well to child actors; they just seemed different to me.

When we filmed the episode, "Little Ricky's School Pageant," I was excited to learn that other kids would be on the show. Since I was usually the only youngster on the set, I looked forward to having some fun with these kids! But they were professional child actors who weren't interested in playing; they wanted to act. I was just the opposite. Acting was something my father pushed me into — something I had to do. I would rather have been outside, playing and being a kid. Although I did try to do my best, I never felt like an actor. Instead, I considered myself a musician and felt best about my abilities when I was playing the drums.

To make matters worse, I was particularly self-conscious about being short and so small for my age. Once, when Mom took me to a doctor's appointment, I asked the doctor, "What can I do to get taller?"

Since both of my parents are short, the physician just laughed and said, "Well, Keith, next time around, get different parents!"

To bolster my self-esteem, I tried desperately to please Lucy and Desi. Yet, when they complimented me, I was embarrassed because I always felt that I wasn't good enough.

Lucy was moody, and I learned to react to her moods. On the set, she didn't have much of a sense of humor. In fact, Lucy wasn't a naturally funny person without the scripts. Her personality differed greatly from the Lucy character she played, but onstage she dove into the part head first and made something great out of it.

I stayed busy with "I Love Lucy" in 1957, filming about nine episodes during the show's "Connecticut" period.

On the "Connecticut" set, Little Ricky's bedroom was upstairs. When the script called for me to race upstairs to my "bedroom," I ran up those steps and out of sight, but no second floor existed! It was all just a prop.

Although I knew we were filming for TV, in my child's mind, the "stairs to nowhere" seemed odd to me, and I often wondered why Ricky didn't have a real bedroom.

Some of the funniest "I Love Lucy" shows were filmed during this period, including "Lucy Does the Tango." In this episode, Ricky threatens to sell the laying hens that the Ricardos and Mertzes are raising to earn extra money because the hens aren't performing well.

Upset by Ricky's plans, Lucy and Ethel buy eggs and stuff them in their shirts and pockets, planning to hide the store-bought eggs in the hen house so Ricky will think the hens are laying.

When Ricky shows up at home unexpectedly to rehearse a tango number with Lucy, she's forced to dance with him. They dance along with no problems for awhile, but when Ricky pulls her to him, the eggs are crushed and splatter all over Lucy's shirt.

Real eggs were used in the show, which made the audience roar with laughter.

When Ricky discovers the truth, he vows to sell the hens. To keep that from happening, Bruce and I start hiding the hens, causing Ricky to accuse Fred of being a chicken thief. In the end I confess to taking the hens, and the hens are saved after all when they really do start laying eggs. As a city kid, I had a lot of fun with the chickens during that episode!

Madelyn Pugh Davis recalls that the writers built up the role of Little Ricky gradually the first year, with the 1957 season allowing me more dialogue in the scripts.

"Once we saw Keith could do it, we could expand his parts," Madelyn said, "although we were careful not to give him big, long speeches! Having Lucy and Desi move to the country in Connecticut gave us all new story ideas because we had a child who could do lines and a child who was a musician."

Madelyn laughs when she recalls that the writers didn't give Bill Frawley (Fred) long speeches either, believing he worked best with shorter lines that bounced off the other players. Fred sort of reacted to the other characters, and they tried to do the same with me.

When I told Madelyn that I remember Bill as being much like the Fred character — nice but sort of gruff — she laughed again. "Bill never had children and didn't know how to relate to a little boy," she told me.

To this day, Madelyn praises Lucy and Desi. "Lucy's comedy genius made the scripts click, and the fact that she was so supportive of what we wanted her to do, made her easy to write for." Although Madelyn had not written for other shows, and the other "I Love Lucy" writers were young, they were obviously very talented.

"I didn't realize until later how spoiled I had become by working for Desilu," she said. "We'd get an idea for an episode and go check with Desi, but neither he nor Lucy ever told us what to write. Desi was enthusiastic about our ideas and would pay for them!"

As a writer, Madelyn and her colleagues looked for the best stories possible; they didn't consider the actual cost of some of the stunts their scripts included. "Desi never said it was impossible or crazy or that it cost too much," Madelyn recalls. "Some of the stunts were expensive, but Desi seldom made changes in our scripts."

Lucie and Desi Jr. made their only appearance on the "I Love Lucy" show as extras in a crowd scene in "The Ricardos Dedicate a Statue," which became the last half-hour "I Love Lucy" to be made.

In the rerun, viewers won't be able to see the Arnaz kids

because the syndicated version edited the episode, cutting out the portion of the crowd that included Lucie and Desi Jr.

After a summer hiatus and filming started again in the fall of 1957, "I Love Lucy" ended as a half-hour comedy. Instead, Desilu decided to produce hour-long "I Love Lucy" specials featuring several guests stars. At the time, I didn't know the reason behind this decision but later learned that Desi wanted to lighten his "I Love Lucy" workload so he could concentrate more on running Desilu Productions. Doing fewer shows also meant that Lucy could spend more time with the children.

At the time, Desilu Studios was also responsible for programs like "The Danny Thomas Show," "Our Miss Brooks," and specials. In fact, by the 1958-59 season, an average of eight hours a week of filmed television time was filled by programs in which Desi either had a hand or from which he made a profit.

I continued working on the "I Love Lucy" hour-long specials, which ended in 1960, and I guest-starred in other Desilu produced shows.

My original contract was for seven years, calling for a high pay of $1,000 per week. Dad says my salary topped out at $800 per week before my Desilu stint finally ended.

Although some location shooting was done for these specials, the episodes in which I acted were all filmed at the new Desilu Studios (the former RKO Studios), which is now owned by Paramount Pictures.

We followed the same rehearsal schedule for the specials that we followed for the half-hour shows, but I'd usually be on the set for longer time periods. Many guest stars were used in these hour-long "I Love Lucy" specials, but only a few stand out in my mind.

I really enjoyed meeting and working with the great trumpet player and band leader, Harry James, in the show we did called "Lucy Wins a Race Horse." Harry James and his orchestra were one of the first bands I heard on the radio as a child in Louisiana, and I had always appreciated his trumpet playing.

Working with the great French star, Maurice Chevalier, in "Lucy Goes to Mexico" was especially exciting. I did a song and dance number with Chevalier and Desi, which was a lot of fun for me.

It was easy for me to identify with Chevalier because we both had French names, and I liked listening to him speak. His heavy French accent reminded me of the Cajun accents I remembered from my toddler days back home in Louisiana.

Lafayette, my birthplace, has a rich Cajun heritage and calls itself the capital of Acadiana since, in the late 1700s, the area became home for a majority of French refugees from the Acadia region of Nova Scotia. My ancestors, on the Thibodeaux side, were part of this French Canadian migration to America's deep south.

"Keith, your name is really Thibodeaux?" Chevalier asked me one day with a smile as we sat around the set between rehearsal times. "Are you French?"

"I don't know," I answered, unaware at the time that my Cajun ancestry had French roots. On the set, I had often heard my dad and the great actor converse together in French, but I didn't get the connection.

"I'm from Pa-reese," Chevalier announced in his warm and kind way.

"Where's Paris?" I asked.

"Well, eet is oh-ver the ocean," he said, smiling again. "You and your father must come and visit me there someday."

The attention he gave me made me feel special, and I never forgot his invitation to come to Paris. Unfortunately, we never took him up on it.

One of the "I Love Lucy" specials featured the principal actors of another Desilu hit television production, "The Danny Thomas Show." In "Lucy Makes Room for Danny," the story line had the Danny Williams family renting the Ricardos' Connecticut home while the Ricardos are away, but when plans changes, both families end up sharing the house.

Angela Cartwright, who played Linda Williams, one of Danny's kids on "The Danny Thomas Show" had a crush on me and followed me around the set! Later, when I switched to St. Jane Frances Elementary School in the fifth grade, I discovered that Angela also attended there.

In 1959, our family moved to what would become our last home in California, a single-story wood and stucco house on

Debbie Street in Van Nuys — three blocks south of Victory Boulevard, a major cross street in Van Nuys, and about 14 miles from downtown Los Angeles in the San Fernando Valley. A typical middle-class, California home of its day, it had four bedrooms, a two-car garage, a large kitchen, living room, den, and two bathrooms. We had a big yard and a common driveway that we shared with the house next door.

During the months when "I Love Lucy" wasn't being filmed, I was going to St. Victor Elementary School. Old report cards prove I was a good student, even though I tended to be a daydreamer in class. My third grade report card from 1958-59 shows final grades of all A's and B's, with straight A's for non-academic but graded qualities such as "courtesy and reverence, prompt and willing obedience, personal appearance, and perseverance."

Despite good grades and exemplary behavior in school, I wasn't always angelic! At seven or eight years old, a neighborhood girl and I would go out in the alley behind our house and pick up cigarette butts and sit around smoking them.

My second grade teacher, Sister Bernadette Marie, an Irish Catholic woman, told us she believed in leprechauns!

"Do you really believe in leprechauns?" we kids asked her, incredulous.

"Oh yes, I know there are leprechauns," she replied, in all seriousness.

I had seen a movie about leprechauns and the character Darby O'Gill, and the banshee character really scared me. Movies that had witches in them also really bothered me.

I was very aware of hell and knew at a young age it was a place of eternal torment. The Catholic church, however, also taught about purgatory, so I figured I could at least get that far! I thought you could forget about actually going to heaven unless you were a saint. Still, as an eight year old, I had a real awareness of God and wondered a lot about God and heaven. Spiritual things intrigued me.

Lucy and Desi's marriage problems were getting worse by the time we started working on the hour-long "I Love Lucy" specials. At one point, Desi moved out of the Beverly Hills mansion and stayed in the guest house out back. The problems in their marriage had become serious and frightening to us kids.

One day Desi Jr. and I were in the backyard playing when we noticed Lucy going out to the guest house. Suddenly we heard a lot of screaming, cursing, and the sounds of glass breaking.

We looked at each other and said, "There they go again. Let's get out of here!" Running as fast as our legs would take us, we got as far away from the commotion as possible.

Since I was considered a member of the family, nothing was held back when I was around. Lucy had a temper, and if she was upset about something, she'd go around slamming doors. Both she and Desi were very emotional, passionate people.

Like most families with problems, the Arnaz family would try to pretend everything was all right. Lucie, however, seemed embarrassed about her parents' fights and Desi's drinking binges. When her dad's temper exploded, she would withdraw into herself. Lucie now says she blocked out most of the negative things that were happening.

Desi Jr. would confide in me, but I didn't know what to do to help. The Arnaz kids looked to me as someone they could trust and talk to about more private issues. There weren't too many people they could take into their confidence.

I was supposed to be a part of it all even though I was not considered a member of the Hollywood elite. But I slipped into their world when I was with them, and I was expected to act a certain way.

Lucy was very protective of the kids, and I knew I had to act right around her. If Lucy didn't like one of Lucie's friends, she'd tell her daughter to stop seeing the friend and not permit her to visit anymore.

Lucy felt comfortable with me because she knew how I behaved, knew my habits, and knew I had been taught from a very early age to conduct myself properly.

I did act very differently at Lucy and Desi's house than I did at my best friend's home in the Valley. Sometimes, however, I did forget my manners and get Desi Jr. — and myself — into trouble.

One day Desi Jr. and I were in the kitchen at the Beverly Hills house when I noticed a cake that DeDe, Lucy's mother, had made sitting on the countertop.

"Hey, Desi. There's one of those cakes that DeDe makes!" I said, pointing toward the counter. "Let's have some!"

DeDe's cakes were the best I had ever eaten, and this one had marshmallow frosting with devil's food cake inside. My mouth watered just looking at it!

I was always a skinny little kid and could eat anything I wanted and not gain weight. Desi Jr., on the other hand, was pudgy as a kid and was supposed to be on some sort of diet. He looked at the cake and hesitated.

"Come on," I urged. "We can take the cake up to the roof of the guest house, and no one will see us."

We climbed up on the roof of the guest house out back, which wasn't very high, and together ate the whole cake.

Later than night, when I got home, Dad got a call from Lucy.

"Tibbie, Keith talked Desi into taking a whole cake and eating it," she said. "I can't have that kind of behavior with Desi trying to diet. I think it would be wise if Desi and Keith didn't see each other for a few months."

When Dad got off the phone, he confronted me: "Keith, did you eat some kind of cake over at the Arnaz house without asking?"

"Yes, sir," I admitted.

"Well, that's it. You and Desi can't see each other for a few months. Lucy was really upset about the whole thing."

I knew better than to say anything else to Dad, but inside I thought, *Boy, that's pretty harsh!*

I didn't think eating the cake without permission was a big deal, but I did feel sorry for Desi because he gained weight so easily. Unlike his sister — who was tall and lanky like Lucy — Desi Jr. was pudgy as a child, but he thinned down as he grew up.

When Lucie got mad at him, she'd call him "Tubs." That really cut Desi Jr. to the core, making it hard for him to stand up to his sister's verbal assaults.

Although, as brother and sister, they were close and loved each other, they would sometimes get into horrendous fights as kids.

To me, it seemed the Arnaz family was trying to capture happiness by surrounding themselves with wealth and expensive things, but there was very little genuine warmth in their home. I am sure Lucie and Desi Jr. had pleasant periods and affectionate times with their dad and mom, but generally the atmosphere in their home was tense — with no sense of being able to be yourself.

The Arnaz family wasn't always in turmoil. In fact, there were many interesting and exciting times.

One day when I was staying with them at the house in Palm Springs on the Thunderbird Country Club, Lucie, Desi Jr., and I were having a great time swimming in the pool. From their home we could look up at the majestic mountain range that seemed to tower over the skyline. Even as a kid, I remember being amazed at the natural beauty surrounding us.

When it came time for us to get out of the water, their maid brought out an armful of fresh towels. To this day, I remember the clean smell of those warm towels. As we came indoors to get dressed, Lucy told us there would be a guest for dinner.

"Who's coming, Mom?" Desi asked.

"David Janssen," Lucy answered.

"David Janssen? The guy who plays 'The Fugitive' on TV?" I asked, excited. Although I wasn't a big fan of "The Fugitive," I watched the show sometimes.

"Yes, so put on something nice," Lucy instructed.

That night I was a little nervous meeting David Janssen, who was soft-spoken and very polite.

Sitting next to him at dinner, I didn't have much to say. Although I don't remember what he and Lucy talked about, I do recall being fascinated by their dinner conversations. Unlike most kids, I enjoyed listening to adults talk; after all, I'd been around grown-ups since I was a toddler.

The famous columnist, Walter Winchell, who did the narration for the Desilu-produced hit TV show "The Untouchables," often visited Desi's beach house in Del Mar. He was an old man by then — or at least he seemed like an old man to me!

Desi Jr., Lucie, and I liked to ask him questions about mobsters and Al Capone and Elliott Ness. Mr. Winchell actually knew Capone and these famous gangsters, and his stories about them were fascinating.

Once the conversation drifted to nuclear war.

"Mr. Winchell, who will win if we have a nuclear war with Russia?" I asked.

"Son, I'm sad to say I think we'd all be losers. There wouldn't be any winners."

"If a nuclear bomb hit L.A., do you think anyone would survive? Would there be any place for us to go?" I persisted.

"Well, you'd have to go as far away as possible because if that happened, there would be bombing all over the United States," Winchell said.

"The first thing I'd do is go south, to Mexico," Desi interjected. "That would be the safest place."

While things were getting more difficult at the Arnaz house, Lucy kept busy working with the Desilu Workshop, a group of young, hopeful actors. Lucy had started the group to provide a steppingstone for young performers and worked with them for a couple of years.

Around this time, Desi Jr. and I put together a little Dixieland band and were invited to make a guest appearance on the "Dinah Shore Show" on April 3, 1960. I still have a telegram George Murphy sent to "Richard Keith," congratulating me on my appearance on the show and predicting Desi and I were on our way to stardom.

Nothing, however, could hide the fact that things were continuing to go downhill fast in Lucy and Desi's marriage. I knew the show would be ending soon since the decision had been made to film the last "I Love Lucy" special.

The last "I Love Lucy" special that I filmed also turned out to be the final episode using the "I Love Lucy" format.

"Lucy Meets the Mustache" featured comedian Ernie Kovacs and his wife Edie Adams as guest stars. The story line has Lucy planning an evening with the Kovacs because Ricky hasn't had any TV offers lately and Kovacs has his own TV show. Instead, Ernie Kovacs ends up offering a job to me.

I did a mini drum solo in the episode.

In the end, after Lucy's repeated attempts to "help" only make things worse, Kovacs asks Ricky to appear on his show.

Everybody knew it was the last "I Love Lucy" show, and the

sadness on the set was apparent. The fact that Lucy and Desi's marriage would soon end only intensified the somber mood of the cast and crew.

My father took me aside and said he had something to tell me. "What is it?" I asked.

"Lucy and Desi are going to get a divorce," he stated simply.

I didn't understand all the ramifications of the word "divorce," but I did know it would be tragic for my friends, Lucie and Desi Jr.

Later, when Desi Jr. and I were talking one day, he told me how his parents had taken him and Lucie to the Palm Springs house, sat them down, and told them about their plans.

"Throughout the discussion, they kept telling us how much they both loved us," Desi Jr. said.

Desi Jr. told me he asked his father, "But Daddy, a divorce? Isn't there some way you can take it all back?"

I tried to imagine what it would be like to have your family torn apart. The thought made me cringe.

I felt very sorry for Desi Jr. and for what was happening to his family.

After 19 years of marriage, Lucy filed for divorce not long after we filmed the last show. The divorce was final by the spring of 1960. Lucy got custody of the kids, with Desi having visitation privileges.

Even though their family's breakup saddened me, in a way it must have been a relief for the kids. When the family had all lived together, Desi Jr.'s room was located next to his parents, and he heard all their arguments. Shocked and upset by the shouting and harsh words, he must have been glad when the constant tension between them came to an end at home.

Lucy and Desi split their $20 million dollar Desilu TV interests, and each one kept 25 percent ownership in Desilu. Lucy also got child support, the Beverly Hills house, two cars, and a cemetery plot. Desi kept a country club membership, a golf cart, a truck, and some horses. He continued to run Desilu Productions.

Today, as an adult, I often wonder why Lucy and Desi Arnaz didn't get some sort of help or counseling for their marriage problems.

Lucie told me, "My parents didn't want to air their dirty laundry. Back then famous people were leery of counseling because they thought if the truth got out, it would ruin them. And confidentiality? In Hollywood? Forget it!"

I knew she was right.

In a way, I was kind of relieved when "I Love Lucy" ended since it gave me more free time to just be a kid. But my dad had other ideas.

After the show folded, Dad took me to audition for other shows. In spite of the fact that I had been a performer since I was three, I still dreaded the auditions. Once I arrived on the set, however, I found I really wanted to be chosen for the role I was trying out for! If I was interviewed and not offered the part, I got very upset.

When Dad told me auditions were being held for a part in the movie, *X-15,* starring Charles Bronson and featuring Mary Tyler Moore, I really got excited. In the film, which was released in 1961, Bronson played one of three test pilots in California who were preparing the X-15 rocket plane for a launch. The film's story line had Bronson killed in the test run and in the process saving the lives of his copilots. Done almost in a documentary style, with Lucy's neighbor Jimmy Stewart providing narration, the film gave special attention to aeronautic explanations.

I really wanted to do that movie and tried out for the role of Mike Brandon, the son of Bronson's character, Lt. Col. Lee Brandon.

This is my chance to be somebody besides namby-pamby Little Ricky, I thought.

Instead the part went to Stanley Livingston, who played one of Fred McMurray's sons on the popular television series "My Three Sons."

Not a particularly notable film, I don't recall hearing much about it when it was released. But I did want that part!

Hollywood producers seemed to like all-American kids with freckles, blond or red hair, or pug noses, and I didn't have any of those things. Still, I continued to act and did a number of episodes on various TV shows, including "The Shirley Temple Playhouse,"

"The Farmer's Daughter," "The Joey Bishop Show," "The Bill Dana Show," "Route 66," and many others.

In the fall of 1960, at the beginning of fifth grade, I switched to St. Jane Frances Elementary School in north Hollywood. My grades had started to drop by then. My fifth grade report card shows six C's, five B's, and only one A, in history. But I still got an A in conduct!

I remained friends with Desi Jr. and Lucie after the divorce and spent time with them, either at the Beverly Hills house or when they visited their father at his home. Desi eventually built a beach house in Del Mar and settled there, and I would often tag along when Lucie and Desi Jr. went to visit him.

Dad still worked at Desilu Studios and ran around with Desi a lot, often going with him to golf tournaments in Palm Springs.

Not long after the divorce, however, Lucy took the kids and moved to New York, where she appeared in a play called "Wildcat." I didn't see Desi Jr. and Lucie for about a year.

It was in New York that Lucy met a nightclub comedian named Gary Morton. They were married by Dr. Norman Vincent Peale in a private ceremony at Marble Collegiate Church in New York on November 19, 1961.

The changes taking place saddened me deeply. It was the end of an era.

Mom and I in the kitchen — 1963.

5

A Normal Kid?

Although I no longer appeared on a weekly television series, I continued to act in guest appearances on numerous television shows and also did commercials. Whatever push I had came from Dad. When I wasn't on an audition or rehearsing for a show, acting was the furthermost thing from my mind.

Other child actors went to acting classes and dreamed about becoming a star. Acting was their life. I dreaded interviews because of my fear of rejection. Having performed professionally since I was three years old, I was tired of it. I longed to be a normal kid, and between auditions and acting jobs that's what I tried to be. Sometimes, however, my desire for adventure took a wrong turn.

When I was about 12 years old, we were at Desi's ranch in Corona, where they had a pond with several ducks. Desi Jr., who often went hunting with his dad, had a .22 rifle. I don't know what got into us, but Desi Jr. decided to shoot the duck with his .22. When it wouldn't die, we took that poor duck and ended up banging it up against a tree. We even tried to drown it.

"Let's get a knife and cut its head off," I suggested, and Desi Jr. agreed. Just as we were about to do the dastardly deed, Desi came out of the house and stopped us.

"What's de matter wid you boys?" he shouted. "Are you crazy? Stop torturing that poor duck!"

He was really mad, and rightfully so.

The duck incident really bothered us. We were young and didn't understand until then what it meant to just kill something for sport. Desi Jr. was so upset that he actually had the dead duck stuffed, and kept it for many years as a reminder of what we'd done and how wrong it was.

I instigated it, but Desi Jr. went along with me, which, now that I think about it, was out of character for him. Always kind and sensitive, especially where animals were concerned, Desi Jr. hated to see them mistreated. When we would go horseback riding together, I liked to run my horse at full speed. Desi Jr., on the other hand, would get upset and slow down if he thought his horse was getting too sweaty.

In the sixth grade at St. Jane Frances Elementary School, I became close friends with a guy named Danny Sauer who lived with his family in Van Nuys, not far from our house. In fact, we've remained friends to this day.

With Danny, I could just be a normal kid. Hollywood didn't impress him nor was he enamored with Desi and Lucy, considering them to be just people, not idols or movie stars.

Tall, skinny, and freckle-faced, Danny was an all-American type of kid with reddish-brown hair. A natural athlete, he later pitched for the high school baseball team and played quarterback on the football team. Because he made the All-Star team, I looked up to him. Both of us played Little League baseball in different leagues, and we played on the school softball team together at St. Jane Frances.

One of seven children, Danny came from a traditional, stable, Catholic family. His father was employed by Pacific Bell for forty-three years, working his way up from cable splicer to regional superintendent. There was no big attraction to Hollywood in his family although some of his relatives worked in the show business industry behind the scenes with production crews. Danny had an interesting family; his grandfather, an inventor, had developed the idea for the brake shoe and automatic door locks for cars.

Danny and I had some great times together. One day we used hydrogen peroxide to lighten our hair and then told people the sun did it! My brown hair turned lighter, sort of blondish, while Danny's just got redder.

Danny would pedal all over town with me perched on the

handlebars of his bike, but we also liked biking together. Sometimes we would ride our bikes to the big observatory at Griffith Park toward downtown Los Angeles, then stop to buy big-stick popsicles, and keep riding to Traveltown, a place where they stored old trains.

Although I was much shorter and smaller than Danny, he used to let me push him around. In fact, I could talk Danny into anything.

A McDonald's restaurant was located right next to St. Jane Francis School, and we liked to go there after school for something to eat. A paper boy, and a very self-sufficient kind of guy, Danny always had money. I was lazy — and usually broke!

Danny would go up to the counter and order a milkshake, then look at me and say, "What's wrong, Keith? Don't you have any money? Why don't you get a paper route?"

"I don't have time for paper routes. Hey, Dan, come on, buy me some french fries and a Coke! I'll pay you back!"

Danny would roll his eyes heavenward, as he pulled his wallet out for more money to pay for my food. "Sure you will, Keith!" he sighed.

Danny always bought what I wanted despite his protests — still, he always protested! He later told me, "I let you boss me around just because I liked you."

Our admiration society was mutual because I felt a close kinship with him, too.

By this time, Lucy and her new husband, Gary Morton, had returned to Beverly Hills from New York with the kids. I had missed them and was happy they were back in California.

Desi Jr. and I resumed our friendship, and I introduced him to Danny. We all became friends, but Desi Jr. and I still spent time together on weekends or after school and, of course, during summer vacation.

Desi Jr. and I would ride our bikes all over the old RKO lot, now Desilu Studios, waving to all the workers as we pedaled furiously, leaving a trail of dust in our wake. We became a familiar sight to all the workmen there, who would wave back and smile at us good-naturedly as we zoomed past them. We treated the studio like our own private playground.

One of our favorite places to go was the prop department. We'd ride up to the big, three-level building, leave our bikes outside, and spend hours wandering inside. It was a fascinating place for a kid to hang out.

Every time we walked through the entrance, the first thing we saw was the huge, imposing replica of King Kong! Used in the original 1930s *King Kong* movie with Fay Wray, it gave me a jolt every time I saw it. Also fascinating were the many miniature, wooden airplanes used by the special effects people to "crash" in the movie.

We'd hang around the building for hours, exploring, playing, and just looking at all the props.

The whips and suits of armor looked so real to me that I turned to Desi Jr. and said, "Those things look like they could actually hurt somebody!" But like Hollywood, the weapons were all fake.

At the time, "Hogan's Heroes," "The Untouchables," and "Star Trek" were all filmed at Desilu, and we loved hanging around the sets where these shows were filmed. It was exciting to be able to actually go on the *Starship Enterprise* on the "Star Trek" set.

Desi Jr. was truly my best friend for many years. We especially enjoyed playing various sports together. Since I was older and could do things a little better, I beat him at most things, but he still liked to win.

Although we could both do things the other couldn't, our friendship was based on genuine good feelings for each other, and that continues to this day.

In 1961, Lucy started acting in a new TV show, "The Lucy Show," which ran from 1961 to 1968 and was produced by Desi Arnaz for Desilu Productions.

Lucy's character was Lucy Carmichael, a widow with two children. The show's cast included "I Love Lucy" sidekick Vivian Vance (who had played Ethel Mertz) as Lucy's friend, Vivian Bagley, and later, Mary Jane Croft, who had played Betty Ramsey, Lucy's Connecticut neighbor on "I Love Lucy."

Wilbur Hatch and his orchestra, the band who played for the old "I Love Lucy" shows, warmed up the audience for the new "Lucy Show" prior to the live-before-a-studio-audience tapings.

Desi Jr. was taught by his dad to play the conga drums, and I guess his drumming gave Lucy an idea. One day Lucy approached Dad and said, "Tibbie, I think it would be a good idea for Keith and Desi Jr. to do a little number for the show's warm-up."

When Dad asked me what I thought about Lucy's idea, I said, "Sure, that will be fun! Do I get paid?"

"Well, they said they'd work something out, maybe five dollars a night."

Such appearances had nothing to do with work or contracts; it was just a fun thing to do. I was usually in the audience anyway, so I figured I might as well do it.

Desi Jr. and I performed two big-band type tunes: "When the Saints Go Marching In" and "Satan Takes a Holiday." Sometimes we also played Dixieland-type melodies. Desi Jr. and I took turns playing both a set of drums and conga drums concurrently. Sometimes we'd flip a coin to see who would get "When the Saints Go Marching In" on the drum set, since it featured a drum solo.

"Here's Little Ricky and Desi Arnaz Jr.!" the announcer, Dick Martin, who later gained fame on television's "Rowan and Martin's Laugh-In," would proclaim.

Desi Jr. and I would run onstage, playing the two sets of drums for our two songs, accompanied by the show's orchestra. The audience loved it, roaring their approval.

As time went by and we still had not been paid, I asked Desi Jr., "When will we get paid?" He sort of shrugged. He never had to worry about money.

Finally, one day, we were given two envelopes with $75 each in them. I felt like someone had given me a thousand dollars! Back then you could buy a Coke for a dime, so $75 was a lot of money. Both of us were happy to get that $75, but that's the only time I recall being paid for our appearances.

In 1962, I started acting in a recurring role on another popular weekly television show that, like "I Love Lucy," was destined to become a classic television comedy: "The Andy Griffith Show."

I auditioned and won the role of Johnny Paul Jason, Opie's best friend.

Although I didn't have a heart for acting and lacked that inner drive to become a really successful actor, I did like the Johnny Paul character on "The Andy Griffith Show," which was more the kind of part I wanted to play if I had to act.

The part of Johnny Paul seemed more realistic, more of a "real boy" type character who played marbles and went fishing instead of dressing up in short pants and being polite!

It wasn't a big part, and I didn't appear regularly, but I stayed with the show until 1966, filming nearly a dozen episodes in all. Although the character of Johnny Paul Jason was mentioned in numerous episodes, I didn't always appear in the shows where his name came up.

"The Andy Griffith Show" starred Andy Griffith as Sheriff Andy Taylor, Don Knotts as Deputy Barney Fife, Ron Howard as Andy's son, Opie, and Frances Bavier as Andy's Aunt Bee Taylor — along with a host of other memorable characters. Running from 1960 to 1968, "The Andy Griffith Show" was about life in the sleepy, mythical southern town of Mayberry, North Carolina, and was based on the real North Carolina town of Mount Airy, where Andy Griffith was born.

The show was spawned by another Desilu hit, "The Danny Thomas Show," after Andy Griffith appeared in an episode as Andy Taylor, mayor of a small town called Mayberry. High ratings for the episode led to the spin-off of "The Andy Griffith Show." Besides acting in the show that bore his name, Andy edited scripts, oversaw each show, and became a millionaire in the process.

Every week, Andy and an assorted group of characters would get into some sort of down-home dilemma. Andy, a widower, was one of the few single parents on television in those days. Assisted by Aunt Bee, who lived with him and Opie, she took care of the house, cooked, cleaned, dispensed advice, and just generally acted like someone's nice old aunt.

Andy was Mayberry's guitar-playing sheriff and a homespun philosopher of sorts, as well as being a wise father to Opie. A good kid who was much more realistic than most television children, Opie was cast as a mini-Andy.

Barney, the skinny, bungling deputy sheriff, was childish yet lovable at the same time. It was like Barney was Andy's second child!

Before I came on the set as Johnny Paul Jason, the audience had never seen Opie's friend. Opie (Ron Howard) would have lines like, "But Pa, Johnny Paul says . . . ."

My first appearance put a face to the formerly invisible character.

When it was time for me to be in a scene, the assistant director would always shout, "Richard! Richard!"

I would think, *Why is he calling me Richard?*

Although my stage name was Richard Keith, to me I was simply Keith. It always sounded strange to hear someone call me Richard.

While many of the shows were incredibly funny, others were very poignant.

One of the funniest shows in which I appeared was an episode about Miss Crump's history class. Opie and I and the other kids in the classroom were acting bored as she tried to teach us a history lesson.

Later, Opie and Johnny Paul visit Andy at the Mayberry jail, where, in an effort to get all of us interested in history, the sheriff tells us a story about a war hero. The funny part to me was the way Don Knotts' eyes bugged out as Andy told the story — just like a boy our age would do.

Although I don't recall interacting much with Don Knotts on the set, I always thought Don's Barney Fife character was hilarious.

Out of character, Don Knotts wasn't crazy or funny; he was just a nice guy who came to the studio and did his job. When he took on the zany personality of Barney Fife, however, that was a different story, and he was hilarious! The looks he could get on his face said more than a thousand words of dialogue.

During one show, Barney was lecturing all of Opie's friends, saying, with all seriousness, "Listen, Opie. It's not fun being a delinquent."

As he talks, Barney backs into the jail cell and locks himself inside. The look of shock and embarrassment on his face is priceless!

Another of my favorite episodes involved a scene where the town bully gets all of Opie's friends, including Johnny Paul, to throw apples at street lamps.

Opie refuses, saying, "That's not right!" making Opie appear to be chicken. But after some words of encouragement from Andy and Barney, Opie stands up to the bully, and we soon take Opie's side.

Although Andy dispensed words of wisdom, his character wasn't syrupy but realistic. Andy, who was very much like the Andy Taylor character, basically played himself.

The show's executive producer, Sheldon Leonard, has been quoted as saying, "For the first time, Andy Griffith will be playing something he is — a semi-intellectual with a wry sense of humor."

Bob Sweeney, one of the show's directors, was also a funny, genuine, good-hearted man. Sometimes I would make suggestions to Bob about how I thought my character should say something.

Once, I told him, "This line just doesn't sound right to me, Bob. What if I said it this way?"

I repeated my line but with a different inflection in my voice. "Yeah, that's it!" Bob agreed.

Except for Ron Howard, most of my interaction on the set was with Andy. When I wasn't working I really didn't want to be around adults. I had been around adults most of my life, and now I was enjoying spending more time with kids my own age.

Ron Howard, known then as Ronny Howard, played Opie from age six to age fourteen. He and I became great friends on the set. Although I was about three years older than Ron, he immediately took to me because Miss Barton — my teacher on the "I Love Lucy" set and now Ron's on-set tutor — had told him about me. Ron told the writers to write more parts for me so I could be there to play with him!

Frances Bavier, who played Aunt Bee, was the typical working actress portraying a part. Between scenes, she would go to her dressing room, and I'd hardly ever see her on the set. I didn't really know her at all.

Howard Morris, the actor who played the town crazy guy, Ernest T. Bass — the character who was always going around trying to throw rocks at houses — was extremely talented. Morris, who had been a regular cast member on the popular 1950s television comedy, *Sid Caesar's Your Show of Shows,* also directed several of the "Andy Griffith" episodes.

Howard McNear, who played Floyd Lawson, the town barber, had played my music teacher on the "I Love Lucy" episode, "Little Ricky Gets Stage Fright." It was a pleasure to work with him again.

"Andy Griffith" was a great show — from the stories to the actual working relationships on the set. The laid-back and easy-going atmosphere was entirely different from the tense moments I'd experienced on "I Love Lucy." It wasn't unusual for the "Andy Giffith" cast and crew members to sit around playing checkers during breaks. The set had a real family feel to it.

Even though it was a top-rated hit show, the pressure, tension, and obsession with perfection I recalled from my "Lucy" days weren't present. Part of the reason for the reduced pressure was probably due to the fact that "The Andy Griffith Show" was not shot before a live audience, as "I Love Lucy" had been.

Although it seemed to me that almost everyone on the show was from North Carolina, in reality, Andy, Don Knotts, and Frances Bavier were the show's only North Carolina natives! Still there was a definite southern influence. In fact, one researcher noted that the show's scripts were much shorter — 30 pages instead of 45 — than the average TV situation comedy because the cast's North Carolina speech patterns were slower than those on city-based shows.

Before heading his own series, Andy was a standup comic and an actor in movies and television, appearing in both the Broadway and movie versions of *No Time for Sergeants*. Andy would bring his guitar to the set and sit around strumming it for the makeup men, cast, and crew. His relaxed, warm, and friendly manner made it seem as if he were just sitting on some North Carolina front porch with his friends.

I loved working on "The Andy Griffith Show."

One day in the early summer of 1962, I was playing in our backyard with a friend named Steve, who lived a few doors down from our house. For some reason, I decided to slide down our hanging clothesline pole. As I slid down the pole, I didn't notice a jagged piece of bamboo about ten inches long sticking up next to the pole, and as I descended, I slid my leg right into it.

"Owww!" I screamed as the bamboo went into my leg. "Steve, go get Mom!"

As I lay on the ground sobbing in agony, I could feel the bamboo deep in my leg. The pain was terrible.

"Keith Raymond, what have you done?" Mom shouted as she hurried over to where I lay on the ground. "How could you have done this?"

Mom's first reaction was anger at my pulling such a crazy stunt. As usual, Mom didn't ruffle, and remained calm despite my cries of pain.

"I'm hurt," I whimpered.

"I'll go get someone to help us," Mom said.

When she returned with a neighbor lady, together they loaded me into the neighbor's station wagon so I could lie down. We went to the doctor's office, not a hospital, where I was given a shot and the wound was cleaned out. The doctor said he had removed all the pieces and sent me home.

My leg didn't feel right to me, and I told Mom, "Something's still wrong."

A few days later, I began running a very high temperature and was so sick I could barely walk. I was taken back to the doctor, and x-rays confirmed that bamboo pieces were still embedded in my leg.

"Why does this have to happen to me?" I whimpered when I learned I would have to have surgery. I didn't want to have an operation, but I wanted to get well. After being admitted to the hospital, I underwent surgery to remove six inches of bamboo pieces. Later, the doctors told us that the bamboo had been embedded right between a major nerve and an artery. If the bamboo had hit a certain nerve, I would have been paralyzed.

While I was recuperating in the hospital, Desi came to visit me, creating a minor sensation among the nurses and hospital staff who oohed and ahhed over him.

"How're you doin', pardner? You going to get out of here soon?" Desi asked as he walked into my room.

"I think so," I answered weakly.

"Well, we're rooting for you, amigo. I know you'll be better soon!"

Dad was there that day, and Desi pulled him aside.

I heard him whisper to Dad, "Will he really be all right?" as Dad explained to him to the doctor's prognosis.

You can see what a warm and really caring side Desi had, to take time out of his hectic schedule to come by and see me.

After I went home, I remained indoors for the rest of the summer. As an active, outdoor kid, it was torture not to do anything physical. I was forced to stay indoors and entertained myself as best I could by doing paint-by-numbers pictures or watching television.

The year 1962 was also the year Lucy bought out Desi's interest in Desilu Productions and became president of the company. Desi also quit as director of the company and resigned his job as executive producer of "The Lucy Show."

At the time Desi was quoted as saying, "I quit the business because it got to be a monster. At the beginning, it was fun, but when you are in charge of three studios, with 3,000 people and 35 sound stages working all the time, the fun is long gone." He was tired of all the pressure and he wanted to retire, at least for awhile, to his ranch in Corona.

In those days, I didn't really think of Desi as an alcoholic, but that's what he was.

His drinking started as the pressures increased during the "I Love Lucy" days, and, over the years, his problems with alcohol worsened. Some people later said that the only time they could do business with Desi was in the early morning hours because he'd be drunk by noon.

Later, I learned that Desi had been hospitalized several times and treated for alcoholism. In the 1960s, there was little emphasis and education about alcoholism and almost no motivation for people to get help. I'm sure Desi was like many other alcoholics who deceive themselves into thinking they can handle their drinking themselves.

Desi wasn't close to a lot of people and was not really a public person. I thought he seemed uncomfortable in non-acting situations.

When he wasn't drinking, Desi was warm, affectionate, fun,

and a joy to be around. He was a big-hearted guy, and I loved him very much.

Lucie once described it well when she told me, "If actors are happy they dance around the room and overact; if they're mad, they slam doors and create havoc."

Adding alcohol to that equation can only make things worse. Actors, especially, tend to be volatile people anyway.

When I was with the kids at Desi's house, and we saw him get that bottle out, we knew to scatter fast and get out of there.

An alcoholic takes on a completely different personality; some change character when they get drunk. I know Desi did. First, he would get very moody and sit brooding in the dark. Then, all of a sudden, he would explode.

Although he never said anything harsh or unkind to me, I was scared of Desi when he was drunk. He'd get real nasty, becoming totally irrational and uncontrollably angry.

One time I was staying overnight with Desi Jr., who had a male summer tutor at the time. Evidently the tutor told someone else that Desi Jr. was a spoiled brat, and what he said got back to Desi. Desi Jr. and I were in bed asleep and the tutor was in the living room talking to some girl he had met on the beach. Desi, who had been drinking, found the tutor talking to the girl in his living room. I don't remember all the details of that evening, but all the commotion woke us up.

"What do you mean, calling my son spoiled? And what are you doing here anyway at this time of night?" Desi was yelling at the tutor.

Desi threw the guy out.

"What about my bags?" the tutor asked, as he was being forced out the door.

"We'll send 'em to you!" Desi shouted, slamming the door.

When things started blowing up, Desi Jr. and I had retreated to the maids' quarters. By this time, I was shaking.

"I'm going to hitchhike home," I told Desi, as I tried to keep from bursting into tears.

Desi came upstairs looking for us, and hugged both of us.

"I'm sorry about that fellows," he said.

We went back to our own beds, but I remained very frightened. Such acts of violence were foreign to me, and I wanted to retreat to the safety of my own family. There were six kids in our family and we fought between ourselves, but I never saw the kinds of things at home that went on at Desi's house. For the most part, my parents supported each other and were one voice, even though Dad did all the disciplining.

I was a very sensitive child, which I'm sure heightened all my feelings and fears. I always believed in God and was very aware of right and wrong.

Sometimes, when I was with my friends, I'd often gaze up at the sky and ask them, "Wow, don't you know there's got to be a God?"

Although I had a strong belief in God as the Creator, I also had some odd beliefs as a kid.

I believed in a last day judgment, and often thought about the Scripture that described the Lord's coming "as a thief in the night, on a day that ye think not."

Whenever I thought of the return of Christ, I got scared, so I figured out a way to remedy that situation: I didn't want Him to come back, so I always thought about His return! My reasoning was: If the Lord is coming back on a day "that ye think not" and I think about it all the time, then He won't come back!

In my young mind God and fear were entwined, and such unusual thinking seemed logical.

I saw Catholicism as very rigid, but I just accepted it as the way religion was meant to be. I remember thanking God that I was born into a Catholic family because I could have been like the kid down the street who was Lutheran or like another boy I knew who was Jewish. I was glad to be part of "the true church" because that is what I was taught.

When I went to church, I would stare at the statues of Jesus and Mary, thinking they resembled the Greek gods and goddesses, like Zeus and Diana, that I'd seen in movies. They fascinated me.

At first, nuns were scary to me, but as I got older I became more comfortable around them. In fact, when I became an altar boy, I considered that a big honor.

One day during a religion lesson in school, I asked a nun

about sin. She replied, "Before Adam sinned, we were inclined toward good more than evil. But since Adam sinned, we are now inclined more toward evil than good."

"Is that where we're stuck now?" I asked. "Can't we ever get inclined back to the good?"

"No. That's called original sin, and we can never get away from it," she replied.

I was left without any hope of salvation. The only way for me to deal with my sin was to go to confession and Mass every week.

Another frightening time during 1962 had nothing to do with God, religion, me, or the Arnaz family, but with the state of the world in general.

In 1962, the Cold War was at its height, and Communist Russia was viewed as the biggest threat to our national peace and security. It was also the atomic age, a time of bomb shelters, school drills practicing what to do in the event of nuclear war, and scary movies that fictionalized the end of the world should some world leader "push the button" and start a nuclear war.

In the fall of 1962, Russia began to move offensive weapons, including ballistic and surface-to-air (SAM) missiles, into Cuba, a small island only 90 miles from Florida. The Russian move precipitated a period that came to be known as "the Cuban missile crisis." This wasn't just another potential skirmish, or a threat of some minor war: This was a confrontation between the two giant atomic power nations, America and the Soviet Union, that brought the world, literally, to the edge of nuclear destruction.

That brief period of 12 days was truly terrifying and left a lasting impression on me, as it did for millions of others who lived through it. I was 11 years old at the time and turned 12 the following month.

During this time, I was shooting a commercial and would constantly ask the director, "How are things going with the missile crisis?"

The Central Intelligence Agency had confirmed, through photography done by U.S. spy planes, that Russia was busy building up an offensive nuclear missile installation in Cuba. Nuclear missile bases had been secretly established in Cuba, while the Russians proclaimed both privately and publicly that this would never be done.

But the pictures didn't lie.

The missiles were aimed at certain American cities. Government officials estimated that within a half-hour of the missiles being fired, 80 million Americans would be dead, and the world would be pushed into a nuclear holocaust.

I'll never forget watching President Kennedy's televised speech to the nation on October 22, at the height of the crisis. In the speech, Kennedy told the public what had happened. One part of the speech especially frightened me: when the President talked about the missiles themselves.

> "The characteristics of these new missile sites indicate two distinct types of installations. . . . Each of these missiles, in short, is capable of striking Washington, D.C., the Panama Canal, Cape Canaveral, Mexico City, or any other city in the southeastern part of the United States, in Central America, or in the Caribbean area," the President told the country somberly. "Additional sites are capable of striking most of the major cities in the Western Hemisphere, ranging as far north as Hudson Bay, Canada, and as far south as Lima, Peru."

I sat listening, spellbound and terrified at the same time. In perhaps the speech's scariest moment — at least to me! — the president confirmed that the United States would regard any nuclear missile launched from Cuba against any nation in the Western Hemisphere as an attack by the Soviet Union on the United States. If this happened, Kennedy said it would mean "a full retaliatory response" upon the Soviet Union from the United States.

Our family sat around the television set in hushed silence as the implications of what the president was saying slowly sank in. The idea of a possible nuclear war was staggering. I went to bed that night with my stomach in knots, and I didn't sleep very much.

I was deathly afraid of nuclear war.

Our family started stocking up with canned goods, and everyone in the neighborhood was talking about bomb shelters. During the days the crisis lasted, most conversation concerned preparing for war, bomb shelters, and how survivors of such a war would live afterwards. You could sense the fear in people during those frightening days.

I was especially terrified of radiation and nuclear fallout.

I remember thinking, *What good is stocking up on food going to do? We're only six miles from downtown Los Angeles. If a nuclear bomb hits there, we can just forget it! Those canned goods won't do us any good at all!* I wondered if I had a future at all.

After days of behind-the-scenes activity, Soviet leader Nikita Khrushchev finally agreed to dismantle and withdraw the missiles from Cuba. It was only later that the American public would learn all the details, details that truly showed how very close the world came to nuclear war.

I heaved a sigh of relief. Maybe my life would go on after all.

*Opie, me, and the gang with
the World's Most Famous Lawman.*

6

Where I'd Like to Be

Desi Arnaz married Edith Mack Hirsch in Las Vegas on March 2, 1963. Edie, as she was called, divorced her husband, Clement Hirsch, to marry Desi.

Edie's ex-husband, a wealthy man who headed the Kal Kan dog food empire, owned several race horses. Lucie, Desi Jr., and I used to joke, "If his horses don't win a race, we know where they'll end up!"

Edie's son, from her marriage to Hirsch, was named Greg but everyone called him Butchie. Although Desi Jr., Lucie, and I liked him, we harassed him mercilessly! His skinny frame, big glasses, and curly hair made him an easy target of our jokes.

Although Edie was a redhead like Lucy, that's where the similarity between them ended. Edie had more time to spend with us kids than Lucy did and was always eager to take us wherever we wanted to go — skating, bowling, or to the movies — and even joined in the fun.

In fact, we went bowling so much that one day Desi told Edie, "Buy the kids their own bowling balls!" and I was included.

After Edie married Desi, life with the Arnaz family became enjoyable again, especially the time we spent at the Del Mar beach house.

In the summer, one of our favorite pastimes was going grunion hunting at night. Grunion are little fish that look like sardines, and they came up on the beach every summer to lay their eggs.

Desi would check out his "grunion" books, to see when they

would be running, which depended on the tide, and tell us, "Tonight's the night!"

We would stay up late and then head toward the beach with our pails and flashlights. Using our hands, we dug around in the sand, searching for the grunions and scooping them up. Before long, we'd have a pail full of the squirming little fish.

The next morning, we would eat fried grunion for breakfast. They were delicious!

Some of my most memorable times with the Arnaz family came when Desi took us out on his big boat, *Mi Quierida* ("my love" in Spanish), to catch marlin.

On the morning of our fishing expeditions, Edie and Desi woke us in the middle of the night — probably around three or four in the morning. We got dressed, putting on warm clothes to ward off the pre-dawn chill in the air, and piled into his car, which would be crammed with all kinds of fishing gear, equipment, and ice chests filled with food and sandwiches that Edie had made.

After the 20-minute drive to San Diego, we launched the boat in the dark. By the time we were onboard, it still wasn't light yet, so we kids got a few more hours of sleep in the hull.

Desi then guided the boat out to the middle of the Coronado Islands, woke us up, and shouted excitedly, "All right, come on, get up, get up, the fish are ready!"

As our fishing instructor, Desi gave us specific directions on fishing for big game fish and always had us use lightweight test lines. He was opposed to heavy test lines that never break.

On every fishing expedition he would say, "Cheater fishermen use 'cheater' lines. Real fishermen — like us — fish with a real line!"

Strapping a safety belt around our waists, Desi usually had to help us get the heavy fishing pole in the water. But we weren't strapped to the chair like some big-game fishermen who literally anchor themselves and then put their fishing pole in a holder!

"You must hold the fishing pole yourself," Desi would say, although we knew, if we caught a big fish, he would help us reel it in.

During one fishing trip, Desi took us out in the *Mi Quierida* to a little island off the coast of Mexico. After sailing into a small harbor, Desi gave some Mexican boys chocolate candy bars to dive for lobsters. They came back up with huge lobsters, and we dumped the shellfish into big garbage cans with locked sides that Desi had brought along.

Lucie says today her dad always "pushed the envelope" when it came to lobsters because the large shellfish weren't supposed to be taken in territorial waters.

As we started back toward California, out of nowhere a Mexican gunboat appeared. Suddenly all these Mexicans in uniforms, with serious expressions on their faces, were pointing guns at us and speaking excitedly in Spanish! I had no idea what they were saying.

"Everyone just smile and nod," Desi whispered as the gunboat pulled alongside his boat. "If they catch us with all these lobsters, no telling what they'll do!"

We kids sat on top of the lobster-filled trash cans while Desi talked to the Mexican officials in rapid-fire Spanish. We did as we were told, nodding and smiling broadly at the men who were pointing guns at us, and tried to act very nonchalant about the whole thing. But inside my heart was pounding!

Whatever Desi told them must have satisfied the officers because they soon let us go. I sighed in relief as Desi revved up the boat's motor, and we headed back toward the safety of home.

Although I was really scared at the time, I later thought it would have made a great episode for "I Love Lucy!"

An excellent cook, Desi loved to make yellow Cuban rice and thick grilled pork chops or the fish we brought home from our deep-sea trips. The meal would be prepared to perfection, and we'd all rave about Desi's cooking. Everyone would be having a great time, but when I'd see Desi place the wine bottle on the table, my mood would change. An uneasy, fearful feeling would sweep over me because I never knew how Desi would react once he started drinking for the evening.

One night Edie took us to a drive-in movie in San Diego, and Desi stayed home in Del Mar. We were a little late getting home, and as we drove up to the house, I noticed Desi standing up on the balcony in his bathrobe, smoking a cigarette. The end of the lit cigarette glowed red in the darkness.

As we got out of the car and started toward the house, I noticed he was glaring at us. Lucie, Desi Jr., and I glanced at each other. No one spoke, but, I'm sure, we all had the same gut feeling: *Uh-oh, it's going to be one of those nights!*

After we kids all hurried up to the house to our rooms, Edie went to her bedroom, and soon we heard all sorts of banging around, yelling, and cursing. "Poor Edie," Lucie said. "Why does it have to be like this? We were only a few minutes late."

None of us understood at the time the effect alcohol had on a person. It didn't make any sense for Desi to get so mad over such an insignificant incident, but alcohol changed his nature. Desi had a temper anyway, and drinking exacerbated it.

Desi once fired his gun into the air because he saw someone sitting on his beach property. Terrified, the guy took off down the beach.

One day, when I was 13, Desi Jr. and I were at the Beverly Hills house, getting ready to go to a fair at his school, when suddenly we found ourselves in the library. I noticed a bottle of wine on the bar.

"Hey, Desi, want to drink some wine?" I asked.

Desi looked skeptical for a moment.

"You really think we should, Keith?" he asked.

I nodded yes, and then it only took Desi a moment to decide.

"Okay. Let's do it!" Desi agreed.

We took the bottle of wine, got drunk, and then decided to go ahead and go to the fair as planned.

As we walked around the fair, feeling silly and good at the same time, I felt our being drunk put us in some sort of secret society.

At the time I didn't view our getting drunk the way I saw it when Desi got drunk; we were kids, just having fun and acting silly. No one at the fair seemed to realize that we'd been drinking.

When we passed the fortune teller's booth, I noticed that a nun went inside. That seemed strange to me.

"Wanna get your fortune told?" Desi asked me, noticing my interest in the booth.

"Not me!" I was afraid of the future and didn't want to know what lay ahead.

One of the schoolrooms was set up for bingo, and a man was calling out numbers to the players as we wandered in and sat down. Desi and I started laughing uncontrollably and calling out numbers at random, completely disrupting the entire bingo game.

"Young men, you'll have to leave this room!" the bingo leader told us sternly.

We got up unsteadily, and I said, "Sure," as we exited the room together, still laughing.

We were still giggling as we walked away, but I think the nuns and the people at the fair just thought we were behaving like two dumb kids.

As I hit my teenage years, a lot of the guys in our crowd started experimenting with alcohol, and many of them smoked. Even though I had sneaked and smoked cigarette butts as a kid, as a teenager I was very much against smoking.

I don't remember why I felt that way, but whenever someone offered me a cigarette, I would say, "No thanks. I won't take one so don't even ask me!"

Because I was adamant that I wouldn't smoke, the other guys didn't tease me or ride me about it.

Danny and I started hanging around with two other guys, Chris and Tony, and the four of us would sit around in a barn behind Chris' house playing cards, talking, and drinking. The other guys smoked, but I didn't join them.

Although the age limit for purchasing alcohol was 21, we had no trouble finding someone outside a liquor store to buy it for us. One time I sneaked out of my house after everyone had gone to bed, met my friends to drink beer, and got so drunk I could barely stand up. I couldn't get home, so I stayed at a friend's house for the night.

The next morning when Dad found my bed empty, he called Chris' house looking for me. "Your Dad just called," Chris' father told me. I immediately ran outside, jumped on my bike, and pedaled home as fast as I could!

"Boy, am I gonna get it!" I said to myself.

When I got home, Dad was mad but he did not punish me the way I expected. In my mind, I had gotten away with murder and couldn't help but wonder why.

Mom never found out about the incident until much later. She told me, "I was never concerned about the 'fast life' in California. Taking care of six kids and running a house was about all I could handle. I always trusted your father to look after you."

Periodically, I still acted the part of Johnny Paul on "The Andy Griffith Show," but, at the same time, I was represented by an agency that sent me out on auditions for various roles.

I tried out for the role of Winthrop Paroo in *The Music Man,* released in 1962 by Warner Brothers and starring Robert Preston and Shirley Jones. Winthrop Paroo, the son of Jones' character, Marian Paroo, was a key role in the film.

As part of my audition, I had to sing the song "Gary, Indiana" as well as learn a few lines of dialogue.

The part ultimately went to Ronny Howard, whom I barely knew at the time since I had just begun working on "The Andy Griffith Show."

Dad later told me they wanted a more all-American looking kid for the role, and they certainly got that in Ronny Howard.

The Music Man featured Preston as a glib con man who stops in a small Iowa town and convinces the townspeople to start a band to keep local kids away from the "evils" of the local pool hall. He offers to sell them the band instruments and says he will teach the kids to play, but his real plan is to take the money and run. Things turn out differently, and he claims to have developed a new way to play music called "the think system" — all you have to do is "think" a tune and then you can play it!

The movie, perhaps best known for the popular song "76 Trombones," featured a lot of great music. The "Gary, Indiana" song I sang in the audition began a duet number with Preston and Ronny in the film.

I also auditioned for *The Sound of Music,* released by 20th Century Fox in 1965. The brilliant musical featured a score by Rodgers and Hammerstein and won the Best Picture Oscar for 1965. Shot on location in Salzburg, Austria, the interiors were filmed in Los Angeles at Fox's studios.

The heartwarming film followed Maria, played by Julie

Andrews, as she took on the job of governess for the children of Captain von Trapp, a man who had renounced warmth after his wife's death and was a strict disciplinarian. After a series of obstacles, Maria and the captain, played by Christopher Plummer eventually marry.

At the audition, I had to sing "Do Re Mi" as part of the interview for the role of the von Trapp family's second oldest son.

I was told I did not get the role because the producers wanted a blonde, European look for the role. Ironically, Angela Cartwright, a brunette who used to have a crush on me in grade school, won the role of one of the von Trapp daughters, Brigitta. Angela later went on to star in the TV series "Lost in Space."

I also did a screen test with Tony Randall for a role in *The Seven Faces of Dr. Lao,* released by MGM Studios in 1964. I would have played a main character in the quirky fantasy film — complete with excellent special effects.

During the screen test, I had to play some close-up shots with Tony Randall, and he had the worst breath! Maybe that came across in my reactions to him on film.

This film excited me more than any of the others and although I was told I "almost" got the part, I was especially disappointed to learn I had been rejected again.

Acting in a movie seemed more prestigious, as well as promised more money, so I made that my goal, but it never materialized. Even though I wanted to do a movie, I didn't experience a big let-down when I wasn't picked for a part.

In spite of the fact that I was now a teenager and a more experienced actor, I did not focus all my attention on becoming famous. When I wasn't at an audition or on a set, I seldom thought about acting.

Lucy had a private in-home theater where she often showed first-run movies borrowed from the various studios.

I'll never forget the night Lucy's husband Gary, a comedian himself, heartily laughed his way through Peter Sellers' slap-stick comedy, *A Shot in the Dark,* making it even more enjoyable for us kids. Inspector Clouseau's hilarious antics, and Gary's boisterous laughter had Lucie, Desi Jr, and me rolling on the floor in hysterics.

Lucy was also watching the movie with us, laughing just as hard as the rest of us. Lucy always appreciated good humor and enjoyed really funny movies.

Like most teenagers, I also enjoyed watching action films, like the James Bond movies that became popular in the 1960s. One night, Desi Jr. and some of his Beverly Hills friends and I watched *In Like Flint* with James Coburn over and over again!

Aside from adventure films, I also felt drawn toward movies with religious themes: Christians and the lions, movies about Jesus or the saints, or movies that emphasized spiritual things. Some of my favorite religious movies were, and still are, *Demetrius and the Gladiators, The Ten Commandments, Androcles and the Lions,* and *Spartacus.*

Although I had a strong interest in religion, I would sometimes get conflicting messages at school when it came to God and the Bible.

Once one of my teachers said some of the Bible's stories, like the story of Adam and Eve and the story of Job, did not really happen, explaining that they were just "illustrations."

I was so confused. Here were people who, in my mind, were supposedly the closest to God, telling me that the Word of God wasn't true! When I came home and told my mother what this teacher had said, she didn't believe me.

Nevertheless, the trappings of the Catholic church captivated me, and I was especially fascinated by the nuns who taught in my school. The fact that they would never marry intrigued me, and I used to wonder what motivated them to be "married" to God. I often wondered what life was like in a convent. Probably every Catholic boy who attends Catholic school considers being a priest at one time or another; and I was no exception.

One weekend, a group of boys from our school went on a retreat to a Catholic monastery. The dormitory setting made the experience seem like summer camp, and we made jokes, cut up, and tried to skirt all the rules.

Yet, when I got home, I thought, *Wouldn't it be nice to be a priest?* I made the mistake of mentioning my passing thoughts to someone, and the next thing I knew, a priest was calling our house wanting to talk to me about preparing for the priesthood!

At that point I started backing down, mainly because the more I thought about it, the more I knew I wasn't cut out for celibacy!

One of my teachers at Notre Dame High School, an all-boys Catholic school that I began attending in the ninth grade, was the most effeminate guy I'd ever seen. He had a high, falsetto-type voice and would stride into class, smiling at us while declaring, "You are all just a bunch of animals in the zoo, and here we are at the zoo again today!"

His mannerisms made him appear gay, and I believed that homosexuality was wrong.

Nuns, brothers, and priests were supposed to be people who were the closest to God in my mind. Something didn't seem right.

Although I was still working on television shows and Dad had a well-paying job at Desilu and drove a big Chrysler, our family never had much money.

In fact, I *never* had any money! If I wanted or needed something, I started stealing to get it. Danny and I were sort of partners in crime; when I wanted to shoplift something, Danny would do it, too.

One day Danny and I wanted to go to the beach, but I needed a new bathing suit. We decided to go to the May Company department store, where I tried on bathing suits and Danny tried on slacks.

I found a pair of swim trunks that I liked, put my clothes back on over them, and started walking nonchalantly out of the store. Danny took two pair of pants and was wearing them under his clothes.

I had gotten away with stealing before, but on this day we were both captured by a female security guard. She put Danny in a head lock and hauled both of us to the store's office.

When the guard started interrogating us, I did some great acting that day!

I started crying and pleading with the store personnel not to tell my dad. I could be very convincing when I wanted to get out of something, and I sure wanted to get out of that situation!

"Please don't tell my dad," I pleaded. "I've never done anything like this! I'll really be in trouble if you tell him. I don't even know why we did it, it was just stupid. We're sorry, and I promise, we'll never do it again!"

The store manager looked at me as if I were a very pitiful case.

"Well, we'll let you go this time," he said. "But if you ever do this again, we'll have no mercy. We'll call the police!"

We never shoplifted at that store again!

Getting caught, however, didn't stop me from stealing. I usually stole things I really needed, but sometimes I'd take stuff for fun.

Danny remembers one trip we made to Ralph's Grocery where I emerged from the store with a container of stolen chocolate cake icing and ate the whole thing!

Danny, who is four months older than me, had his driver's license before I got mine. At age 15, it was legal to drive but only without passengers.

One day we decided to go to Desi's house, and I talked him into letting me drive his little Honda 50 motorcycle.

"Come on, Danny, let me drive. You ride on the back," I said.

"You don't even have your license yet, Keith!" Danny reminded me. "A cop will take one look at you and stop us in a heartbeat!" But as usual, Danny gave in. He always protested, but he always gave in and I got my way.

Although I wasn't speeding, a policeman spotted us and pulled us over at the top of Mulholland Drive.

Deciding to give it my best shot, I started crying and acting scared and pitiful as Danny told the cop, "Look, officer, this is Little Ricky from the 'I Love Lucy' show, and we are on our way to Lucille Ball's house."

"Really?" the officer said. "Where's your license?"

Danny showed his driver's license to the policeman.

I stammered, "I left my license at home."

"Okay, let's go get yours," the officer said, looking at me intently.

I had to think quick. "Oh, I didn't leave it at my house. I left it at Danny's," I lied.

The next thing I knew, the policeman was taking us to Danny's house! When Danny's mother saw the two of us being escorted by a policeman, she couldn't imagine what we had done now. "Keith left his driver's license here, Mom," Danny lied to his mother, trying to protect me.

"Well, where is it?" the officer asked in an effort to get the truth out of us.

Finally, with Mrs. Sauer urging us to tell the truth, I confessed, "I don't have a license."

Once we told the truth, the police officer let both of us go with just a scolding.

Danny and I had no boundaries, and we liked to ride over to U.C.L.A. and play basketball in their gym. We often saw Kareem Abdul Jabbar, who was then known as Lew Alcinder, shooting a few hoops in the gym.

Sometimes we'd meet Desi Jr. and other friends at U.C.L.A.'s bowling alley, too. We kind of hung out there for awhile; it was the cool thing to do at the time! I pursued fun with a vengeance, but things took a turn for the worse on November 22, 1963, when President John F. Kennedy was assassinated in Dallas. It was a somber, sad time for our country and for me. Kennedy's death affected me deeply.

As a teenager, I had a normal curiosity about sex, but the church taught that sex outside of marriage was mortal sin, "a sin onto death," so I also had a fear of going to hell. But I didn't have to worry because I was so shy that sex just didn't factor into my life at that point!

I went to boy-girl parties where we danced, listened to music, and had little crushes on girls, but it never got into anything heavy or serious. As far as sex was concerned, I was really naive and learned what little I knew from my friends. I liked girls, but I didn't know how to relate to them. Even though he was younger than me, Desi Jr. had girlfriends from the time he was 12 years old.

I remember Lucie had a big crush on Ralph Hart, the boy who played Vivian Vance's television son, Sherman Bagley, on "The Lucy Show," and we all teased her about it. She liked to go to the show's set just to be around Ralph.

I still saw Lucy, mainly when I visited Desi Jr. at his mother's house or when we did our warm-up drum playing for "The Lucy Show."

Lucy's husband, Gary, a Jewish comedian, used to do comedy monologues for the studio audience before "The Lucy Show" was filmed. When Lucie, Desi Jr., and I were at the show, we would watch him and laugh because he always told the same jokes. We would tell the punch lines to each other before he did.

Gary was very protective of Lucy's kids and concerned about everything they did. Because Danny had his license first, he would often be called upon by Gary to drive us all around. Danny did it, but usually there were all these conditions attached to having Lucie and Desi Jr. go with us.

Gary always emphasized the fact that because Danny was the oldest, he should be "responsible." Danny just wanted to be one of the crowd and didn't like being put in a "responsible" position!

Gary also told Desi Jr. if he ever wanted to have a man-to-man talk about sex, just ask. Gary was the first "safe sex" person I ever knew; he advised Desi Jr. to always use a condom.

In spite of Gary's idiosyncrasies, he really cared about Lucy and her kids.

At Halloween, when kids came to Lucy's house trick or treating, she would open the door, smile, and say, "How about a trick instead of a treat?"

Lucie said, "Sometimes Mom and I would dress up ourselves, and do things like change the light bulb at the front door to a green light bulb. Kids out trick or treating would line up around the block to come to our house, and the guard at our gate would only send up maybe five kids at a time. We always tried to make it spooky and scary, and we'd do things like play horror music that you could hear outside."

Lucy frequently entertained her adult friends, and they would sit around playing cards or word games.

Sunday night dinner was a big event a Lucy's house. People in show business were invited, and the conversations were always interesting.

One guest, Mary Wickes, a character actress, made a career comeback of sorts in recent years, as the elderly nun in the Whoopi Goldberg movie hits, *Sister Act* and *Sister Act 2*. Other guests included comedians Jack Carter and Milton Berle.

The talk at dinner often turned to politics. No matter what the political discussion, Lucy always emphasized patriotism.

If someone brought up the president, Lucy would say something like, "Well, it doesn't matter if you voted for him or not, he's the president and we all have to get behind him!"

She was loyal to America the same way she was loyal to people she cared about.

At one dinner, Lucy asked everyone, "If you could live any place in the United States, where would you choose to live?"

Desi Jr. said Hawaii. I don't remember Lucie's answer, but I piped up, "I'd like to live in New England, or in some colonial-type or early American place."

Lucy smiled at me and said, "That's where I'd like to be, too."

I thought it was interesting that we both chose the same place.

Lucy had a buzzer on the floor under her foot that she used to summon the maids, who would rush in asking, "What can we get for you?"

Lucy's favorite foods included fried chicken, roast beef, and Yorkshire pudding, and they were often on the evening's menu. About half the time we kids would join the adult dinners; the rest of the time we would eat by ourselves in a separate room.

Even though I was a young teenager, Lucy still had tremendous pull in my life.

Many times she'd call Dad and announce, "I'd like to have Keith over for Desi Jr. this weekend."

If I already had plans with my other friends, I wouldn't want to go. A few times I actually cried — not because I didn't like Desi Jr. but because it meant changing my own plans!

But when Lucy called, I had to answer.

We did have a good time at Lucy's house. Lucie would have her friends over, and I'd be there for Desi Jr. We went swimming and watched movies, and sometimes the kids turned the garage into a kind of theater where Lucie would put on little plays; she was always into acting.

Lucy bought a jukebox for dance parties, and the kids would have swim parties at the pool. Their birthday parties were huge extravaganzas, a tradition Lucy and Desi had started when the kids were very little.

As Lucie and Desi Jr. got older, they liked to confuse the tourists who would drive through Beverly Hills looking for the homes of movie stars.

At times Desi Jr. would approach cars and say, "Hey, you got a movie star map there? That's an old one, they don't live there anymore. I know 'cause I live around here."

Then he would make up these crazy stories and tell the tourists, "Elvis Presley and Marilyn Monroe live down the street. If you like, I can get in the car and give you a real Beverly Hills tour for a buck!"

Lucie took a different approach and liked to sell "Lucy souvenirs" to the tourists. When they drove by, she would say, "Lucy's handkerchiefs on sale! Look, the lipstick marks are still on them!"

Lucie was always trying to fix me up with a friend of hers named Alice who also lived in Beverly Hills. Alice was nice, but she wasn't my type.

For awhile, Danny and Lucie had a boyfriend/girlfriend thing going, so when I'd go over to Lucie's house with Danny, Lucie would try to pair me up with Alice.

Lucie's friends also included MacDonald Carey's daughter, Teresa, and Hal Roach's daughter, Kathy. We all had a lot of fun together.

Danny, Desi Jr., and I sort of traveled in a pack, and several times, Lucy took a bunch of us kids to Disneyland for the weekend. Lucie always made sure there would be four boys and four girls, usually trying to pair me up with Alice!

It was great going with Lucy because, not only did she foot the bill, but she also got us sent to the front of every line. The Disneyland management knew if Lucille Ball stood in line like everybody else, pandemonium would break loose! Our entire group was escorted right past the long lines of waiting tourists and straight into each attraction.

We would arrive on Friday afternoon and spend the evening riding rides before heading back to the hotel to sleep. We'd repeat the process on Saturday, spend Saturday night, and have one more day touring Disneyland on Sunday before heading home that evening.

Around this time my interest in music started picking up again after going through a period where I didn't play the drums at all. I started playing in a couple of small rock bands, and for a while, Desi Jr. and I had a group we called "The Jaguars."

In February 1964 the music scene in America changed drastically with the arrival of the Beatles. A wave of British-influenced rock music that became known as "the British invasion" followed. The Beatles didn't just bring a new style of music to America, they brought different fashions, longer hair for guys, and a new lifestyle for American teenagers.

Like most kids my age, I thought the Beatles were great. Their music really grabbed me, the same way it grabbed so many others. The main attraction for me was not looks or lifestyle but the music.

I liked the Beatles and the Rolling Stones and later enjoyed a host of bands that evolved from that Beatles-influenced era, including the Yardbirds, the Leaves, Jethro Tull, Led Zepplin, and Canned Heat. Many of these bands had a strong blues influence, and I liked bands that played powerful music and not just pop songs.

The Beatles also influenced Desi Jr. Together with Dean Martin's son, Dino, who was 13, and a friend of Dino's, Billy Hinsche, also 13, Desi put together a rock band. The three-man combo — called "Dino, Desi, and Billy" — featured Dino and Billy on guitars and Desi on drums.

With financial backing, powerful parents, and savvy promotion — along with the novelty of Dino and Desi being the children of show-biz greats Lucille Ball and Dean Martin — they were signed to a deal with Reprise Records following an audition with Reprise president Frank Sinatra. The band had their first hit in the summer of 1965 with a pop single called "I'm A Fool."

Desi was only 12 years old, and suddenly his band was in great demand, playing to huge audiences of screaming teenagers. They even appeared in a 1966 Dean Martin movie, *Murderer's Row*. The group stayed together until 1968, releasing a half-dozen albums.

I wasn't great friends with Dino or Billy, although I once spent the night at Dino's house. In those days, I never related well to Dino. He seemed to have an attitude and acted sort of egotistical.

I had never seen a kid with so much stuff! He had everything a kid could possibly want, including big motorcycles, like a Triumph 650, and a real gun that he shot on a shooting range. A talented guy, Dino did a lot of things well.

When Dino, Desi, and Billy hit it big, Desi started going out on a lot of band tours, and we didn't see each other as much.

During that time, Desi was hit in the head with a surfboard in a surfing accident and injured badly. As a result, I was asked to substitute as drummer for one of the band's gigs and really enjoyed it.

Suddenly ambitious for a music career, I resented Desi's success with the band. Although Dino, Desi, and Billy were a talented group, I knew how much the family connections had helped the group in the beginning to hit it so big. I guess I was jealous and resentful that I didn't have the same opportunity.

When Dino, Desi, and Billy became popular, my envy of Desi Jr. grew. He was in a famous rock group; he had everything that money could buy; and he was very comfortable around girls. In fact, girls were really after him!

Desi's success in Dino, Desi, and Billy was sort of a role reversal for Desi and me. He had always wanted to be like me, and now I wanted to be like him.

7

Going Our Separate Ways

The British music invasion that swept America in the wake of the Beatles' popularity gave rise to a whole wave of imitators. People couldn't seem to get enough of anything related to England, whether it be music, hairstyles, or clothes.

One day on the set of the television show "Hazel," I met Davy Jones. A short guy like me, Davy was a good-looking British actor. In a feat of typecasting for that particular episode, I played the drummer for Davy's band.

During a filming break, Davy and I were sitting around in director's chairs when he mentioned, "Coming up in a few months, I have a part in a new television show, playing a guy in a band modeled after the Beatles."

Little did I — or Davy — know that soon he would be riding a huge popularity wave in both music and television as lead singer for "The Monkees."

The most popular of the Beatle-like music groups to appear in the 1960s, the Monkees was created by American television executives, no doubt trying to cash in on the Beatles craze. The band members played themselves, and the show was geared toward young teenage viewers.

Davy was the "cute" Monkee, much the way Paul McCartney was the "cute Beatle." Group members like Davy had to audition to be part of the manufactured group, but thanks to weekly television exposure, the Monkees went on to record hit record albums and play concert dates to halls filled with thousands of fans.

The incredible growth of the 1960s pop music scene inspired me and rejuvenated my interest in drumming and music.

Behind my love of music and good times, something more ominous loomed in the background. I knew about it, but it seemed very far away from my world: Vietnam.

I was still young, and Vietnam was far removed from my life in California. Besides, I figured the war would be over before I would be old enough to have to worry about being drafted.

Like the larger world in which I lived — one of continual change and upheaval — unknown trouble and pain were also brewing in the background of my personal world. On the surface everything seemed fine, but heartache and hard times for my family were simmering on the back burner. I just didn't know it yet.

With Desi Jr. often playing weekend gigs with Dino and Billy we didn't see each other as much but remained friends. When he was home, I would still go over to his house, so I often saw Lucy.

Even though I no longer worked on a show with Lucy, I had gotten used to being ordered around by her and Desi during my "I Love Lucy" days. So when I visited at her house, or at Desi's, it was always, "Keith! Get over here!" and I'd always respond. Even as a teenager, I was always polite to her and respectful.

Although Lucy always loved babies, she seemed to be more comfortable around adults than she did around kids who were older than babies, except her own kids or kids she knew very well.

I loved being a kid, but around Lucy I was like this miniature adult squeezed into a kid's body. That's probably why Lucy found it easy to relate to me.

Lucy was tough, straight, and honest. Being president of Desilu required a thick skin, especially for a woman back in those days. When Lucy took over in 1962, she was the first woman to head a major television production company.

A lot of Lucy's toughness probably had to do with her marriage problems and eventual divorce from Desi. People who knew Lucy when she was first married to Desi said she was much softer in her personality in those days. I think both of them always loved each other. In fact, even after the divorce and their remarriages, they stayed in touch with each other and remained close.

Lucy's new husband Gary appeared to me to be a "yes" man, but maybe that was his way of avoiding conflict in their marriage. Gary basically did whatever Lucy wanted. Although they got along well together, they didn't seem to have the passion in their relationship that Lucy and Desi had.

Desi's new wife, Edie, also went along with Desi and tried to avoid problems, especially when he'd been drinking.

In that way, both Gary and Edie were similar: They both just backed away and did not give Lucy or Desi a fight. Maybe that's why most people considered both Lucy and Desi's second marriages to be successful.

In 1965, Dad was still with Desilu Productions. Dad remained close to Desi, and often went golfing with him and Nick Nicoletti. Nick and Desi had been friends since the 1930s, shortly after Desi had arrived from Cuba and started playing with Xavier Cugat's band. Nick had been Cugat's secretary.

When Desi left Cugat to form his own band, Nick became Desi's band manager and they had remained close friends ever since. Nick's sons would often come to Desi's ranch in Corona, and we would have a great time with them! They were a little older than Desi Jr. and I, and we looked up to them.

Dad later said, "I knew Desi was an alcoholic," and recalled watching in amazement as Desi once drank a full glass of booze straight down like a glass of milk.

"Another time I watched Desi swigging vodka right before we were leaving together for Sunday morning Mass," Dad told me. "Desi never missed church in those days."

At the same time, Dad rationalized Desi's drinking. "Desi had so much pressure on him for so long that he deserved to use alcohol to relax," he once told me.

More than once Dad had to bail Desi out of some embarrassing situations due to his drinking, but he always defended Desi and was loyal to him.

Dad told me about one incident at the Indian Wells Country Club in Palm Springs, where he had accompanied Desi to a golf tournament. They were in the lounge area.

Dad recalls that Desi had been drinking and was "a little under the weather" on that particular evening. As Desi hurriedly walked into the room, pushing the double swinging doors of the lounge open, a well-known magazine writer came out. The door accidentally hit the writer square in the nose, causing it to bleed profusely. Immediately, a confrontation erupted between Desi and the writer.

"Desi wanted to whip the guy," Dad told me. "I calmed Desi down, urging him to leave the guy alone and come with me. I knew it would hurt his reputation if people saw him in that condition. I thought it was my duty to keep him out of trouble."

Like me, Dad knew it was not Desi's nature to hurt anybody, except when he'd been drinking.

"Desi was a wonderful person who helped his employees many, many times, and often doled out money when he heard someone needed assistance," Dad remembers.

Desi was a generous man and a big spender, and although Dad genuinely liked Desi, he also liked being included in the lifestyle of the "rich and famous."

Dad was loyal to Lucy, too. During some of the turbulent times before, and even after Lucy and Desi ended their marriage, Dad would sometimes accompany Lucy to public functions when she needed an escort.

He escorted Lucy to dinner several times and to the theater once. Dad said, "Your mother never minded. She knew it was part of my job and did not interfere with my business."

At other times, Dad would serve as an intermediary between Lucy and Desi.

During the waning days of Lucy and Desi's marriage, Lucy would often come to Dad seeking information about Desi and what he was doing. She knew that Dad was in a position in the company where he knew everybody and everybody knew him — both on and off the studio lot.

If Dad did know anything that might fuel Lucy's suspicions, he never told her. "I tried to keep them together," he told me.

Despite his relationship with Lucy, Dad also helped Desi cover his tracks in the days before the marriage ended.

Dad told me about one incident in Palm Springs when Lucy

asked him to go with her to the country club for a drink. While Lucy was in the lounge, Desi walked in with two women — one on each arm.

When Desi noticed Lucy at the bar, he took off! There were several "close calls" when Lucy would almost cross paths with Desi and some woman he was seeing in those days.

Drinking and partying weren't the only problems around Desilu, and Desi and Lucy weren't the only Desilu insiders to divorce.

Vivian Vance and her first husband were divorced in 1959, and she remarried a literary agent named John Dodds in 1961.

Ken Morgan, head of Desilu's public relations division and Dad's first boss at Desilu, and his wife, Cleo, Lucy's cousin, got divorced.

Madelyn Pugh Davis and her husband, producer Quinn Martin, split up. It was almost as if divorce was contagious at Desilu Productions.

The first time I saw Connie, Dad was still working at Desilu and invited her to a taping of "The Lucy Show," where Desi and I were doing our pre-show drum performance to warm up the studio that night. Connie was a young, slim blonde, and a secretary at Desilu. She was very pretty, about 21, and only six years older than me.

Dad described her as "a friend," adding that she was "a real sweet girl," and stayed busy escorting her around the set that night. After the show I rode with them as Dad dropped Connie off at her place on the way to our house.

As I sat in the car on the ride home, it seemed as though some sort of silent communication was going on between them. It made me uneasy and deep down in my heart, I had a sinking feeling that something was very, very wrong with their "friendship."

I was immediately jealous of the relationship Dad seemed to have with this girl. Dad kept urging me to be "extra nice" to her, but I sensed she was a real threat to our family.

The thought of what might be going on between Dad and Connie was burning me up inside, but I never told my mother or anyone else about these feelings. I tried to push the uneasiness from my mind, continuing to work on "The Andy Griffith Show" and hang out with Danny, Desi, and my other friends.

I liked being around Ron Howard on the "Andy Griffith" set, and we enjoyed playing football together. We were best friends on the set and had a good time together at work, but we didn't socialize outside the studio. Ron was younger than me, and I had my own friends. We ate lunch together, and he always hung around me even though there were other boys on the set.

Talented and likable, Ron was very down-to-earth, and his parents and home life are probably the reason he was such a stable, grounded kid. "The Andy Griffith Show" set itself also helped, since it, like Ron, was down-to-earth and fun. No one had a big star syndrome on that show.

Ron always seemed to have an interest in the behind-the-scenes stuff of the business even back in those days. His father was an actor who had also studied the ins and outs of the other side of the camera, and I'm sure Ron was influenced by him.

As a child, Ron used to do little amateur movies, experimenting with filmmaking. It didn't surprise me when he had such success as a producer and director as an adult. His hit movies, *Cocoon, Splash, Backdraft,* and *The Paper,* have proved his expertise in the film industry.

I continued on with my life, pursuing a good time and attempting to forget my suspicions about Dad. Although I tried to ignore the growing sense of uneasiness that I felt whenever I thought of Connie, one night it became painfully apparent that she was, indeed, more than just a friend to my father.

My mother's brother died, and Mom had to return to Louisiana for the funeral. After Mom left, Dad brought Connie over to take care of the house and the kids while Mom was away. Dad kept telling us kids what a nice person Connie was, warning us sternly, "Now ya'll be nice to her!"

Connie would stay with the kids during the day, and Dad would take her home to her house every night, leaving us at home alone. He would always be gone for a long time.

During the time Mom was away, Danny spent the night with me one night. We were coming out of my bedroom when I noticed Dad and Connie talking in low voices to each other in a darkened hallway. They didn't see us, but, as we passed by, suddenly they fell against the wall and into each other's arms. Then they were kissing.

I felt as though someone had stabbed me in my heart. Danny saw them, too, but I didn't say one word, and probably couldn't have if I wanted to because I was speechless. The scene was so traumatic for me that I didn't confront Dad. Danny and I just went back to my room.

Looking back, I think Connie and Dad had probably been seeing each other for about a year. The signs, in retrospect, pointed to a continuing affair.

I couldn't forget what I had seen, and it was a very difficult time for me. Other than Danny, no one knew about the scene in the hallway, and I told no one about it. I felt I had to be strong for my mother, for the other kids, and for my family. I kept my feelings bottled up inside.

To me, Mom was a gem — loving, sweet, and always there for me. All my friends liked her; she was warm, gracious, and hospitable to them when they visited the house. A great hostess, she cooked lavish Southern meals and always made sure everyone had enough food.

With six children, Mom had her hands full, but she always kept things running smoothly. At 15, I was the oldest child, and my youngest brother, Brian, was just three.

I kept hoping Dad's relationship with Connie would just go away.

One day Dad called home and said, "Come pick me up at work."

I knew right away that something was very wrong because the studio supplied Dad with a company car, a Triumph TR-4 sports convertible.

Why would he need to be picked up? I wondered.

As Mom and I drove up to the front gate at Desilu, I saw Dad walking out of the building with his briefcase tucked under one arm. He got in the car and said simply, "My job has been terminated."

Mom and I were both shocked, but when I asked him why, he mumbled, "I don't know." He never really gave me an explanation as to why he was let go.

I was really mad, madder than I had ever been, and that evening I called Desi Jr.

"Do you know what your mom did? She fired my dad!" I told him, my voice trembling with anger.

The tone of Desi's voice told me it was apparent that he knew nothing about it until I told him. The news seemed to totally surprise him, and he acted kind of mad himself. "Hang on . . . I'm going to go and talk to Mom!" he said, putting the phone receiver down.

After a few minutes passed, I heard him pick up the phone, and he came back on the line again. This time his voice no longer seemed angry. It had a different, quiet, almost subdued tone to it.

"I talked to Mom," he said. "Yeah, you're right, she did fire your dad. I'm sorry."

Desi Jr. gave me no reason for the firing. Although Dad had friends at all the major studios in town through his work at Desilu and was a likable guy, as far as I know he never worked at another Hollywood studio again. When Lucy fired him, it was as if Dad was washed up in the business.

It wasn't until much later that I figured out the reason.

Just before Christmas, in 1965, Mom, Dad, and I were driving home from a Christmas shopping trip when, for some reason, Mom opened the car's glove compartment to look for something. Inside she found a note from a mutual friend addressed to my father and Connie.

Dad tried to take the note away from her, but she wrestled it back from him. As she read, I heard her gasp.

"You (expletive)!" Mom cried. "Who is this Connie?"

"Oh, what are you talking about, honey? It's nothing, you're misunderstanding all this," Dad answered, trying his best to smooth things over. "She's just a friend."

"A friend!" Mom huffed. It didn't take much for Mom to put two and two together, and by the time we got home, my parents were in the midst of a terrible fight.

At home, there was more arguing, yelling, and finally Mom started screaming at Dad to get out of the house. "L.J., I just can't take this! This is the last straw. I want you out of the house now!" Mom screamed.

Dad kept insisting Connie was just a friend.

"Friend or not, I'm getting a divorce," Mom announced.

Dad started to cry at that point. I had only seen him cry once before, when his mother died.

There was more arguing, and finally Mom ran out, crying and heading for her car, a small Plymouth. I could see how upset she was, and I wasn't sure what she was going to do. Worried, I ran after her, calling out her name.

"Leave me alone!" she screamed out the window as she sped away in her car.

"How can you do this? Isn't there something you can do to straighten this out?" I asked Dad. "Isn't there some way to keep the family together?"

"No," he said, shaking his head. "We'll just have to go our separate ways. When you're older, you'll understand."

But I didn't understand. I couldn't understand. It was so wrong.

I resented Dad; this was all his fault. How could he do this to Mom? To us? I knew that talking to him further was useless. His Cajun, no ifs, ands, or buts about it, my-word-is-law attitude made me cautious about pushing the point. I didn't know how he would react.

By the time I got back to the bedroom I shared with my brother Dwight, I was crying. Dwight, who was almost 13, sat on his bottom bunk very quiet and didn't say one word.

Incredulous because Dwight seemed so calm, I asked him, "Don't you realize what is happening here?"

My questions were a desperate attempt to wrench a reply from him, but he didn't say one word.

"Don't you care that Dad won't be living with us anymore?"

He didn't answer me; he just sat there. A soft-spoken kid, Dwight always kept everything inside and never talked much as a kid. His way of dealing with the situation was much different than mine.

I was closest to my sister Katie, who was 14 at the time. There was less than a year between us in age, and she would listen when I needed someone to talk to.

She sometimes worked as an extra on "The Andy Griffith

Show" and, like Dad, had always been enamored with show business. As a teenager, her room was filled with teen fan magazines, and she had a crush on Desi Jr. for a period of time.

Leslie, nine years old at the time, was the quiet, studious one of the family and very much like Mom.

I told my brothers and sisters that our parents were getting a divorce. It was terrible for our whole family, but my sister Debbie was especially close to Dad and took the news very hard. Debbie, who was seven, loved and admired Dad.

Although Debbie had a tough exterior, she was a very sensitive child. When she did something wrong, all Dad had to do was talk to her and she would cry. The rest of us kids wouldn't cry unless we got the belt.

If one of us did something wrong, but no one would admit who it was, we would all get the belt. Before one such punishment, Dwight put on two pairs of pants and stuck a schoolbook in the back of his pants.

As usual, Dad lined us up in a row, telling everyone to bend over as he spanked each child. When he got to Dwight, he burst out laughing when he realized what Dwight had done.

"Dwight! Take that book out of your pants right now!" Dad ordered, but he was laughing so hard he could barely talk. It took the seriousness out of the whole incident very quickly!

After the big blowup that day, Mom finally came back a few hours later. By that time, she had gotten past the hurt and was angry. After several days had passed, Mom called us kids all together.

"You know that your father will not be living with us anymore," Mom began. "I hate for us to leave our home, but we have no way to afford this house anymore. I've talked to Aunt Rosalie and Aunt Leona, and they want us to come home to Louisiana."

As a housewife who had never worked outside the home, Mom would not be able to make it alone with six children. Although we had friends in California, she had no job and would need her family's support to start all over again.

As Mom told us what would happen — that we would move back to Louisiana after school ended for the year — the thought hit me: *I will be leaving my friends in California. I won't be able to go to Lucy's or Desi's, and I won't see Desi Jr. or Lucie anymore.*

Something told me that the good times were behind me, and I sensed a big chapter of my life was coming to a close.

With the breakup of our family imminent, to us kids, Dad was the arch villain who had brought all this upon us.

Dad moved out in January 1966, and our family began our last six months in California.

Mom never expressed to me all the rage, pain, and hurt I am sure she felt. Fortunately, she had many friends who helped her deal with the emotions and loss she was experiencing during those last months before we moved.

As for Dad, to this day I don't know for sure why he was fired from Desilu. We later heard that Lucy told him to straighten out his family life, and he told her it was none of her business. Soon after, he was fired. If that was the reason, it certainly made sense to me.

I talked about our family's breakup with Desi Jr., who had experienced his own parents' divorce and could certainly empathize with me.

I also poured out my pain to Danny but told him that my parents were only separated, adding, "You can't tell anybody about this, not even your mom and dad!"

In those days, the word "divorce" still carried an ugly stigma, especially in the Catholic community. People looked down on kids from broken homes, and I didn't want that.

Besides, I was ashamed for anyone to think I didn't have a father any longer, especially when Dad had been the dominant parent in my life. He had basically raised me, trained me, instructed me. We had worked together, traveled together, and lived together for years on the road without much of a motherly influence in my life.

Although I felt I no longer had a father, I couldn't accept the fact that he was gone. It was easier for me to deny his absence and hide the truth about our home situation.

I was just beginning to enjoy being a teenager. In addition to the Lucie/Desi Jr./Beverly Hills crowd, I had a lot of other friends in the Valley. The thought of leaving California saddened me.

On the other hand, I had always dreamed about someday going back to Louisiana where my relatives and my roots were.

My emotions were mixed: I was both fearful and hopeful.

I thought maybe I'd be safe in little old Louisiana, and I was hopeful that it would be a new start for me and my family.

William Frawley, who played Fred Mertz on "I Love Lucy" and had later joined the cast of "My Three Sons," died at age 79 of a heart attack in March, but things were so rough at home that his passing didn't affect me. I felt sad, but I was too wrapped up in my own life and in our family situation to be touched by his death.

Those last six months in California are kind of a blur to me. Somehow I finished out that school year. I don't recall any last good-byes or last meetings with Desi Jr. or Lucie or their parents.

In June 1966, my sister Katie and my brother Dwight and I prepared to fly to Houston, where relatives had arranged to meet us and drive us to Louisiana. Apparently, the airfare to Texas was cheaper than if we all flew straight to Lafayette. Mom planned to join us in August, traveling cross-country by train and bringing the three younger children with her.

Dressed up in a suit and tie, I boarded the airplane with my two siblings, whom Mom had also dressed in their Sunday best.

As the plane took off and began to climb into the clouds, my emotions churned. Leaving behind what had once been a kind of promised land for our family and returning to a place I had only known as a toddler filled me with pain, hurt, bitterness, nostalgia, and fear all mixed together.

When we got off the plane in Houston, I saw the smiling faces of my aunts from afar. My mother's three sisters — Aunt Wanda, Aunt Leona, and Aunt Rosalie — were all there to greet us.

As we walked from the plane toward our relatives, Aunt Wanda came over and hugged me and began to cry. She and her brother, Irvin, had lived with us briefly in California, so I felt as if I knew her better than I did my other relatives.

I glanced at Katie and Dwight, who were being greeted by my other aunts, and I suddenly felt very responsible.

I have to be the man of the family now, I thought.

But the problem was — I was only a boy.

8

Making Music

Leaving California ended my stint as Johnny Paul on "The Andy Griffith Show," but I didn't even care about that. To me it was Hollywood's fault that Mom and Dad's marriage had ended so painfully. I blamed myself because I knew our family had moved to California in the first place because of me. I looked at the whole Hollywood scene and saw it as the cause of my family's misery.

I'd had my fill of Hollywood. I was home now, back in the real world.

After we first moved back to Louisiana, I tried to put Hollywood, Lucy, Desi, and all the rest out of my mind.

My attitude about California and Hollywood could be summed up in two words: good riddance!

When I would overhear my relatives talking about the evils of Hollywood and how badly Dad had treated Mom, I felt torn. I loved Dad and didn't like them talking about him, but at the same time I knew what they were saying was true.

One day, probably in an effort to confront me with the truth, one of my aunts aimed her comments directly at me.

"Your dad is not coming back. He treated your mother badly, and he is not supporting you. We are," she said. "I want you to know that we love you and your brothers and sisters, and we'll do anything we can for you. But your dad is a fake, a Hollywood type, and he'll never amount to anything good."

I sat there, feeling helpless and trapped, saying nothing in reply. What was I supposed to say? I felt that some of what she was saying was true, but what could I do about it?

I knew life in Hollywood was superficial and that, over the years, Dad had changed. When Dad first arrived in California, he was a young man full of dreams. But the more enmeshed he became in the entertainment business, the more his old nickname of "Hollywood" fit him like a glove. He became totally wrapped up in the glamour and hype of show business.

I loved Dad and hated him at the same time. He had abandoned our family, and I felt hurt and ashamed.

From age 15 on, I felt as if I no longer had a father.

I blamed Dad; I blamed myself; but I also blamed God for the breakup of my family. I felt that God could have prevented it, and He didn't. It was the first time I could ever remember blaming God for anything bad that had happened in my life.

After Dad and Mom separated, my dad eventually left California and moved east. He and Connie lived for a while in Houston, where he started a talent agency called American Talent Management, Incorporated. His agency put together a summer show at the Houston Astrodome, a showcase event featuring a number of different bands.

Still hoping to capitalize on my Little Ricky fame, he tried to put together a rock group for me by circulating advertising flyers announcing that "Little Ricky" was looking for people to form a new rock and roll group. But nothing ever came of those efforts.

After my parents' divorce was final, Dad married Connie, and they eventually had two boys, Todd and Tate. Later Dad settled for a long period in Baton Rouge, where he operated an independent television station and broadcasting school.

Those first few months in Louisiana, I felt like a little frightened dog, cowering with my tail between my legs and licking my wounds. I was a has-been, a nobody. I had no father, no money, no car, and nothing going on in my life.

I was very bitter.

No one really knew how I felt because I kept my hurt and bitterness locked up inside. From that point on, my life took a gradual decline.

Dad sent Mom money, but the support wasn't regular, leaving

us at the mercy of Mom's relatives, who were very kind and helped support us.

At first our family had to be separated to accommodate all seven of us. Dwight, Katie, and I lived with Aunt Leona, while Mom, Leslie, Brian, and Debbie stayed with Aunt Rosalie. I don't know what we would have done if they had not taken us in.

I had always fantasized about going back to Louisiana and being a part of a big extended family, but reality was much different than my fantasies. We struggled, and life was difficult for us.

Before I left California, at the dentist's recommendation, my parents had braces put on my teeth. Now that finances were tight, we could no longer afford them. It was so humiliating for me to go to a local dentist in Lafayette and have my braces removed. Later, in my early adult years, I had braces put back on and paid for them myself.

In California we had lived in a large middle-class home and owned two cars; in Louisiana, it was as if we had nothing. Mom didn't have a car and had to borrow one of her sisters' cars when she needed to drive somewhere. We were almost totally dependent on Mom's family.

Our relatives tried to help us kids fit in and find friends.

One day my aunt invited Mike Comeaux, a younger guy in the neighborhood, to her house. He was the first person I met in Lafayette.

Mike introduced me to some other kids at the local Tastee Freeze, which was a teen hangout in those days. That day I met Jerry Romero, who became a close friend.

At first, Jerry and I attended Mass together at church, sitting in the back and kneeling down at the appropriate times but barely able to hear the priest. After a while, church became meaningless to me, and Jerry and I chose to spend that time at Hopper's, a local drive-in restaurant next to the university.

When Jerry discovered I had played Little Ricky, he sort of latched onto me and went around telling everyone, "Hey, Keith is the guy who played Little Ricky on 'I Love Lucy!' "

"You've got manager syndrome," I told Jerry because he acted as if he was my agent!

An outgoing guy, Jerry tried to talk me into going to a local television studio where they were doing some sort of charity telethon, but I refused! He was always pushing the Little Ricky connection.

That summer I also met Ricky Veron. His family lived a block over from Aunt Rosalie, and I spent a lot of time at his house. When school started, I bummed rides to school with Ricky and his older brother.

Among my friends, I was the only one who did not have my own car.

That fall I heard that Dino, Desi, and Billy were coming to play at the municipal auditorium in Lafayette.

"Hey, let's go see them!" Jerry urged. "You can introduce me to Desi!"

Jerry and I went to meet their plane. "Look! There's Desi!" Jerry said, pointing at the band members walking toward the gate.

I tried to get Desi's attention, but he didn't notice me in the midst of the screaming, shoving crowd. I quickly scribbled a note to him, folded it into a paper airplane, and launched it in the direction of the group. The paper plane landed right in front of Billy Hinsche, who bent down to retrieve it. Billy smiled as he opened my note and read it, then quickly handed it to Desi Jr. Desi scanned the note and looked up with a smile, his eyes searching the crowd for me.

"Hey, Keith!" he shouted as our eyes met. He pushed his way through the crowd to me and we made plans to get together after the show that evening.

California was beginning to drift further and further from my new life, but it was still good to see Desi again. I had missed him.

In January 1967, we were finally able to move to a place of our own — a rented, matchbox-like house on Blanford Street in Lafayette. The brick and frame house with three bedrooms was much smaller than the house we'd had in California. Now the seven of us shared one bathroom, and there was no air conditioning to bring relief from the sweltering Louisiana summers. A big ceiling fan helped move some air around in the tiny house.

About a year later, we moved to a house on Sorority Street with three bedrooms and two baths.

The room Dwight and I shared at that point was actually a converted garage with no separate heat source. On winter nights, we would huddle under electric blankets in our bunk beds, trying to stay warm. Sometimes the air in the garage would be so cold I would pull the blanket completely over my head, sleeping totally covered from head to toe.

We lived in that house until Mom was able to buy a comfortable brick ranch-style home in 1972.

Mom found a part-time job at Spencer Business College and went back to school. She ended up working there 10 years and taught typing classes and a course in business machines.

When Mom went back to work, one of her sisters took care of my youngest brother, Brian, until she got home from work. Later, Mom went to work for another company in town, Lafayette Woodworks.

I felt that I had to be the man of the house, but I certainly was a poor role model for my brothers and sisters.

When I began my junior year at Lafayette High School in the fall, my main objective was to fit into my new environment. Like any kid, I wanted to be popular; I wanted other kids to like me; and I wanted to have friends.

Lafayette was one of the fastest-growing commercial centers in Louisiana, and a lot of wealthy people lived there. Offshore oil drilling, natural gas companies, and the food processing industry drove the town's burgeoning economic development.

Despite its growing prosperity, Lafayette was pretty much a sleepy little town, and there wasn't a whole lot to do.

The popular kids at Lafayette High School were the kids with new Pontiac GTOs or Ford Mustangs, money, and social status — none of which I had. In fact, I felt lucky if one of my aunts let me borrow a car to drive.

My fantasy had been that I'd come back to this little southern town, and everyone would be star struck by my involvement with television. I saw myself being sought after by other kids and making friends easily.

The teenagers in Lafayette didn't care about Hollywood, and besides, they had their own cliques. I was just another kid to them — a shy boy who desperately wanted to fit in and be accepted.

Ricky Veron and Jerry Romero had passed the news to everyone at school that the new kid, Keith Thibodeaux, was Little Ricky — so that fact about me was known. But the facts that really mattered at Lafayette High School were who your family was, where your father worked, how much money he made, what kind of car you drove, and whether you were good in sports.

I felt as if I had nothing going for me.

I came from a divorced family with no father in the home at all, no car to drive, and my small physique kept me from excelling in sports. That left me with only one asset — my celebrity status.

Although I had spent the summer trying to push the Hollywood scene out of my mind, I decided to milk my Little Ricky fame for all it was worth to make friends. To do that, I not only used the Hollywood connection, but I became an incredible liar in the process!

Yes, I had played Little Ricky, Johnny Paul, and had acted in a lot of TV shows; and yes, I was good friends with the Arnaz family. But some of the stories I made up to get the other kids' attention were totally outrageous. I thought if I told the whole truth, it wouldn't be exciting enough, so I rationalized that I had to embellish on the facts.

For example, I told everyone I had seen the Beatles at the Hollywood Bowl, and they had come to Lucy's house, where I was able to meet them. When someone expressed skepticism about my story, I made up such a detailed account that soon almost everyone believed me.

"Wow, you must have made a lot of money in Hollywood!" a kid would exclaim.

"Oh, yeah, I probably made about a quarter of a million dollars," I'd lie in a nonchalant voice. "But my money is in a trust fund, and I don't get it until I'm 21."

It was true that a trust fund had been set up for me, but the amount was nowhere near $250,000. Before long, I had told that trust fund lie so often that I started believing it myself.

I didn't tell anyone about my parents' marital separation. Instead, I told everyone that Dad was still in Hollywood because his work was keeping him there. The more lies I told, and the more elaborate my stories grew, the harder it became for even me to know what was true and what was false!

The stories I concocted were really wild. When I was sick and had to stay out of school for a week, I bragged when I came back to school, "Oh, I had to go to Hollywood to appear in a guest spot on the *Green Hornet*," a popular television show starring kung fu expert Bruce Lee.

My old Hollywood connections were a novelty among the kids and kept my name circulating with the "in" crowd. At the same time, my pumped-up stories that combined truth with fantasy provided a dose of badly-needed self-esteem for me.

In high school, I was a get-by student. Math was my worst subject. I did like history, but I looked at school as a necessary evil. It was hard for me to focus my mind on school and homework because of everything our family had been through. I was restless and yearned to be out doing something; I liked being on the go all the time.

I realize now that my insecure family situation and the hurt I had experienced drove me to find ways to escape the reality of my life. I just wanted to have fun.

Eventually my claim to fame as Little Ricky started to wear off and lost its impact as an attention-getter. Television wasn't really a big deal to teenagers in those days. My most recent work had been on "The Andy Griffith Show," but older people liked it, not kids; it was not the cult classic then that it is today.

The only thing I had always been confident about was my drumming ability. Since I loved music, I decided that music would be the way to win friends and influence people. During my last two years at Lafayette High, I played in several different bands.

After awhile, I did make friends and found acceptance among a dozen guys who all hung out together, including Vince Vodicka. Although we became close friends, Vince and I were never part of the same band, but I admired his drumming ability. We also hung out with a group led by Jeff Pollard, which recorded the hit song, "New Orleans Lady." Jeff was the first person who ever talked to me about Jesus.

The first band I started was called the Sussex Six, which included guys I'd met in school: Gary Lamson, Robert Elwell, a guy I'll call Tony, and me. We played the popular rock songs of the day by artists like Paul Revere and the Raiders, the Beatles, the Rolling Stones, and the Byrds. We played at teen clubs and private parties. As a result, my social life began to revolve around the band and music.

With my dad no longer around to keep me in line, I started giving my mother a hard time. If I wanted to spend the night at a friend's and she said no, I'd tell her I was doing it anyway, and leave. I was too big to spank, so she really had no way to stop me.

One evening I got a phone call from a member of T.K. Hulin's band, a popular rhythm and blues group.

"Our drummer is sick," he said. "When we heard Little Ricky was back in town, we thought you might like the job."

"Sure," I replied, without hesitation.

That weekend I performed with them at Signorelli's Club in St. Martinsville, a town about 10 miles away.

Somehow Mom found out and hit the ceiling, "You're only 15 years old! They are just using you!" she shouted. "You're not going to play in a bar where everyone is drinking!"

Outraged, she called the club and told them, "I can't believe you would let an underage boy play in your club! Don't you ever call Keith again!"

Later, she told me I was the best-behaved child in the family.

I thought, *Wow, if I was the best, the other kids must have been really bad!*

I did try to help Mom by giving her some of the money I earned playing in bands. At one point, I was able to provide $25 a week to help out with the family's expenses.

My new friends and I viewed ourselves as the nonconformists at our school. In fact, in 1966, most schools had strict dress codes and rules about hair length, and our school was no exception.

Our group was always pushing the limits with hair and dress, testing the authorities. Although I had naturally curly hair, I had the barber straighten it so I could wear bangs combed down on my forehead.

We thought of ourselves as sort of the school hippies, but in reality we were just musicians. I dressed casually but neatly with sneakers, a T-shirt or a shirt tucked into my jeans.

Here I am getting a taste of celebrity status at age four. This was one of my appearances on "The Horace Heidt Show."

MEET YOUR NEIGHBOR

Above, talking to a caller on a local television show in Lafayette. At left, the self-taught three-year-old wonder.

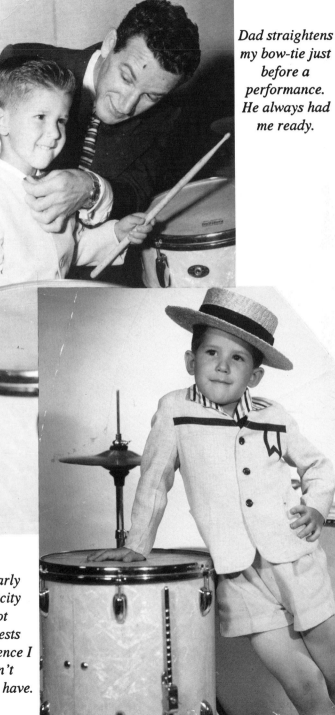

Dad straightens my bow-tie just before a performance. He always had me ready.

An early publicity shot suggests confidence I didn't always have.

The cast of television's most popular show: Desi Arnaz, Lucille Ball, Keith Thibodeaux, Vivian Vance, and William Frawley.

*In the Ricardo living room, Desi and I strike dashing poses.
This attitude wasn't fake on Desi's part — he treated me well
all the years I knew him.*

A rare photo showing me, Desi, and William Frawley (Fred Mertz) on the "I Love Lucy" set. This is the episode in which we had a boat on the soundstage. Real-life fantasy for a little boy!

Birthday parties were always a festive event at Lucy and Desi's house. In the photo above, I'm polishing off some punch with Desi Jr. and Lucie. My aunt and uncle, Terrell and MayBelle Thibodeaux, enjoy the moment with us. At left, the Dynamic Duo, Keith and Desi Jr., show off the attitude that made women swoon (most of the time).

More birthday memories . . . . In the photo above, I watch as Lucie blows out her candles. Below, Lucy lets her hair down as she snaps photographs. I was always struck by how beautiful she was — makeup on the set or not. She was always a lot of fun at these parties.

*My skills blended pretty well with Desi and Lucy. She seemed
to come alive as a comedienne the minute the camera came on.
Desi couldn't hide his charm and sophistication behind silly
costumes, and we had a lot of fun in these sketches.*

Lucy had the best "cry" this side of Stan Laurel. In this sketch, I appear disinterested, but it was really my great acting ability in action!

Two shots from the day Lucy presented me with my own brand-new dressing room. We were getting ready to shoot, and she really did have this expression on her face when she announced the big surprise. I even got my own director's chair.

Richard
Keith

*Here I am jamming away with Santa Claus in the
"Lost Christmas Special."*

Playing Johnny Paul Jason, Opie's best friend on "The Andy Griffith Show." I am second from right.

The musical years. In the photo above, with Genesis in 1969. At right, with the Lively Stones in 1990.

David and the Giants in 1985. Left to right: Rayborn and Clayborn Huff, Keith Thibodeaux, David Huff.

Kathy in her element — as an award-winning ballet dancer.

Tony, a very likable and talented guy who was humorously eccentric, became my best friend. His father was a doctor, so Tony had money, cars, and a lot of nice-looking girlfriends.

Everyone thought Tony's father was a really cool guy because he had some very open-minded ideas. In fact, he got the American Civil Liberties Union involved in a dispute about the length guys could wear their hair at Lafayette High!

Gary Lamson's dad worked in the oil industry and also came from a well-to-do family. Gary wore his hair long like the rest of us, but he was sort of halfway between a hippie and a jock. A lively kind of guy, he was always in motion and had a constant smile on his face. Our common ground was music; he played the guitar and was lead singer for the Sussex Six.

Gary always encouraged me. If I was feeling particularly down, Gary would smile and say, "Keith, you're a great drummer; you're a good-looking guy; you can be anything you want!" With my low self-esteem, I craved praise and sopped up any positive reinforcement like a sponge.

Throughout my junior year, I had a terrible crush on Jan Simmons. Considered the most gorgeous girl at school, Jan was a cheerleader with long blonde hair, nice legs, and a great body. I idolized her from afar.

Gary's girlfriend was Jan's best friend. One day Gary called me and said, "Jan wants to go out with you."

"You're kidding," I said, finding it hard to believe.

"No, really," Gary said. "In fact, let's double date this weekend. We can go to a drive-in movie."

I was ecstatic!

The night of the date, I sat next to Jan in the back seat, petrified to be in the same car with my idol. I didn't know what to say — so I didn't say anything! I knew I was blowing my big chance with this beautiful girl, but I didn't know what to do to salvage the evening.

All four of us were drinking wine, and I was sort of out for the rest of the evening. Jan eventually got drunk, too, and fell asleep.

That was my first and last date with the girl I had idolized for so long!

The crowd I ran with drank, so I drank, too, but I don't remember any drugs at my high school, except maybe for a few kids who sniffed glue to get high.

In the summer of 1967, my friend Tony and I took a trip to California to visit Danny and Desi Jr. The trip had nothing to do with Dad; I was just going to see my friend. I don't even remember who paid for the trip or how it worked out that we could go, but I was really looking forward to it.

We flew to Los Angeles, and Danny, Lucie, and some other friends picked us up at the airport.

Desi Jr. was leaving that day to do some concerts with Dino, Desi, and Billy and would be flying out of the same airport. As we walked out of the terminal, I saw Desi Jr. open the door of a big limousine and he ran over to hug me. "I have to do these dates with the band, but I'll see you in a few days when I get back," he said. "You can stay at our house for awhile."

Tony and I stayed both at Danny's and Desi's during our two-week visit. I think even Tony had doubted some of my stories, so going to California allowed him to see for himself the places I had told him about. He could tell that Desi Jr. and I were indeed buddies.

One day Danny, Tony, and I planned a tuna fishing trip with Desi Jr. on Desi's yacht, which was docked at the Kona Kai Yacht Club in San Diego. "Meet me at the dock," Desi Jr. told us, "I have something special I have to do first."

We said, "Okay," and went down to the dock, where we waited and waited and waited. Desi Jr. never showed up.

Finally Danny, who knew what was going on with Desi Jr., tracked him down at a hotel.

"Desi's having an affair with a woman old enough to be his mother," Danny told me.

Desi Jr. eventually showed up, and we did do some fishing, but I couldn't forget what I had learned. After all, Desi Jr. was only 15 years old.

I had enough Catholic teaching in me to worry that sex outside of marriage was a mortal sin. And on top of that, the fact that Desi Jr. was involved with a grown woman really bothered me.

"I can't believe you're having an affair with this woman," I told him, not hiding my shock.

"Promise me you won't tell anyone," he begged. "Just don't tell anyone!" Desi Jr. kept repeating, obviously concerned that someone would find out.

During our stay in California, we went to Desi's house in Del Mar where Tony, Desi Jr., Danny, and I met some girls on the beach one night. Soon a big group of us were sitting on the sand in a circle around a bonfire we had made, listening to one of the guys strumming a guitar.

Soon the music stopped, and the guitar player pulled out a marijuana cigarette. The next thing I knew, the joint was being passed around the circle of people.

Tony and I had never seen anyone smoke pot, and I was horrified to watch as Desi Jr. sucked on the joint.

Later, I came down hard on him.

"What do you think you're doing?" I yelled. "Don't you know how dangerous this stuff is?"

"It's cool!" he said, shrugging off my concern. "Why don't you try it and see how much fun it can be?"

Tony took a few drags on the joint, but I didn't join in with the pot smoking.

I was very disillusioned with Desi Jr. During the year since I'd seen him, it was obvious he had been exposed to a lot more than I had, probably as a result of his playing with Dino, Desi, and Billy.

But I play music, too, I thought, *and I don't use drugs.*

The shock I'd felt at seeing Desi Jr. smoke a joint wore off once I was back home in Lafayette. Soon I was thinking about trying marijuana myself, just to see what all the fuss was about. Seeing Desi Jr. smoke pot had subconsciously made me very curious about drugs.

During the first semester of my senior year at Lafayette High, Tony and I smoked some marijuana in his bedroom. We didn't have to worry about getting caught because Tony's parents knew we were smoking dope.

In fact, his dad, the nonconformist, actually smoked marijuana with us a few times. All the kids thought Tony's dad was cool, and his favorite motto was: "No problem!" Tony's mother, who was more old-fashioned and mild-mannered, didn't even try to enforce any kind of household rules about pot smoking.

Something about Tony's family situation bothered me, and I couldn't help but think: *A kid wants his dad to be his dad — not his drug buddy.* I felt sorry for Tony — and with good reason. He was later busted for marijuana possession and spent an entire summer in jail.

Soon we were having regular marijuana parties at Tony's house, where music, people, and plenty of pot abounded. I began to notice that when I smoked marijuana, the music sounded more alive to me. For some reason, I could listen to just the bass or just the guitar, making the rhythm or the melody more enlightening.

I remember telling myself, *I'm only going to do pot; I won't do other drugs!*

One night Vince, Jerry, and I went to the Yarc Club, a favorite teen dance club in Lafayette where I noticed a girl with long, auburn-blondish hair and was immediately attracted to her.

"Who's that?" I asked Vince.

"That's Jan Simmons' younger sister, Nancy," he replied.

I stared at the girl and wondered if Jan had told her sister about our disastrous date.

"But she doesn't look anything like Jan," I said, noting that Nancy was smaller than her sister and more cute than pretty. Since there were about 2,000 students in our high school and Nancy wasn't part of our senior class, I had never met her.

Nancy and her friends called themselves the "Nutty Buddies" because they liked to act crazy, silly, and boisterous.

Mustering my courage, I telephoned Nancy, and we talked. Then I asked her out.

"Yes," she replied, obviously delighted.

At the keg party, both of us were drinking. The beer must have loosened my otherwise quiet nature, and I found myself sharing with her about Mom and Dad, my family, and my feelings — things I had not told anyone. Nancy had some problems, too, and told me that her folks were always arguing. Both of us were empathetic to each other's feelings, and I felt I could be myself around her. Nancy captured my heart, and soon we were a steady twosome.

There was only one problem: her upper middle-class parents didn't like me. They said I was too old for Nancy, but it was more likely because I came from a broken home and lived on "the poor side of town."

Nancy and I had to sneak around to see each other. I would get Jerry to pick her up for me, and then she and I would get together.

During my senior year, I phased out of the Sussex Six and joined another band called the Persian Market, which became quite popular. The group included Lee and Brad DeHart, who were brothers, along with Tony, Doug Cochran, Doug Begnaud, and me. The group did cover tunes, but we also recorded an original song, a single called "Flash in the Pan," that became a regional hit.

We had two managers at different times, Ben Skolnick and Eddy Raven. Eddy, a songwriter who later became a famous country music singer, was a great pal and our first manager. A talented Lafayette native whose real name was Eddy Futch, he was always making demo records in an effort to get a big hit song. Our group often played background for him on the demos he recorded at La Louisianne Studios in Lafayette. Buckwheat Zydeko, who later gained national fame as a Cajun accordian player and musician, often joined us on the demo sessions we did with Eddy.

Eddy's first album, "That Cajun Country Sound," was released in 1969 and kicked off an active regional career that lasted until he moved to Nashville in 1972 and signed with a major record company there.

Our second manager, Ben Skolnick, had the words "Persian Market featuring Little Ricky" painted on the side of the band's van. Once somebody threw eggs at the van, and I wondered if that was symbolic!

By that time, I didn't want to be Little Ricky anymore. At only 5'6" tall, I was very sensitive about my height and didn't want to be called "little" the rest of my life! After all, I was 16 years old.

As the band performed in more and more places, some people seemed impressed with the fact that I had been Little Ricky; others weren't.

Ben operated a store at the local college recreation center and always seemed to have plenty of money. To portray his big-shot image, he liked to take the guys in the band out to a restaurant for a meal and announce loudly, "You guys order whatever you want!"

Later he'd take the cost of the meal out of everyone's pay!

"I got you guys an audition at the Vapors," Ben told me one day. "Let's you and me go down and check the place out."

"Sounds great!" I said. Ben made a great manager.

The Vapors Club was an 18-and-over club that attracted a predominantly youthful crowd. All the big-names played there: Chuck Berry, Aaron Neville, B.J. Thomas, Little Richard, Jerry Lee Lewis — even Jimi Hendrix.

When we walked into the club, a group called David and the Giants was onstage. The Vapors also showcased the best regional groups, and David and the Giants performed as the club's house band. Popular in Louisiana and Mississippi, the group played some original music but did mostly cover tunes and backed up some of the big acts that played at the club.

We listened to the group play until the club's owner approached David, the leader, and said, "Let this kid sit in on the drums for one song."

I could tell he was hesitant. David later told me he thought I was about 11 years old and wondered if my foot would even reach the drum pedal. "Okay," he agreed anyway, and I climbed onstage and sat down behind the drum kit.

"Well, what do you want to play?" David asked.

"Anything," I replied smoothly.

From the look on his face, I could tell he thought I was just being a smart-aleck with my answer. But I wasn't.

David picked the hardest song the group knew, but I blended right in with the band and tore up those drums that night!

After awhile, David quit singing and stood to one side of the stage and watched me play the drums. Later, we were formally introduced, and David learned I had portrayed Little Ricky on "I Love Lucy."

At 23, David Huff was a full-time musician and the nicest guy I had ever met. The band included David's younger identical twin brothers, Rayborn and Clayborn, and I liked all three of them immediately.

"You're the best drummer I've ever seen," he told me sometime later. I didn't know at the time how much our meeting that day would change all of our lives.

9

Giants in My Life

I stayed on the go my senior year, combining school with playing in the band, music, dating Nancy, and hanging out with my friends.

Dad came to visit us a few times during my last two years of high school, but the visits were not memorable.

Once I was awakened from a sound sleep with him yelling at me to get up, but I didn't want to get up and see him.

I remember thinking, *You're not really my dad anymore; you're never here.*

The only thing I remember about those years was that I coveted his car — a red Buick Skylark convertible.

I once asked, "Dad, do you think I could have your car for my birthday?"

"I don't know, Keith," Dad said slowly. "It's the only car I've got!"

For some reason, I felt that Dad had money but was not providing for us. He had a nice car and always dressed nicely, yet he said he had no money.

When Dad came to visit, he tried to act cool, witty, and charming. I felt as if he was everything I wasn't.

I didn't regard him as my father and still felt betrayed by him.

In 1967, Desilu Studios had been sold to Gulf and Western Industries, who had owned Paramount Pictures since October 1966, for $17 million in a stock exchange deal. Whatever was left of Desilu was now just part of a big conglomerate company. Lucy, who had controlled 60 percent of Desilu, netted $10.2 million in Gulf and Western Stock.

After the sale of Desilu, Lucy had formed her own production company, Lucille Ball Productions, naming her husband Gary as vice-president and herself as president. Gary was also serving as executive producer for her new television comedy, "Here's Lucy."

In her new comedy, Lucy played Lucille Carter, a widowed working mother, still playing the zany Lucy character with two teenage children — her own Lucie and Desi Jr. The show launched Lucie and Desi's acting careers, and I thought they were good in the episodes that I watched.

During my senior year of high school in 1967-68, the Beatles made a much-publicized trek to meet with an Indian "holy man" named Maharishi Mahesh Yogi. Their visit ushered in a new interest in meditation, eastern religion, and spiritual things among westerners. So-called "psychedelic" music — rock music that combined electric guitars and electronic synthesizers with drug-influenced lyrics and music that symbolized getting high — became the latest rage. Popularized by artists like Jimi Hendrix, the Doors, and Jefferson Airplane, their music impacted an entire generation of teens and young adults.

A preoccupation with eastern religion affected both fashion (Nehru jackets, beads, tunics) and music (eastern sitar music). Drugs were increasingly viewed as a way to "find truth" as well as just a way to get high.

Although I had yet to view drugs this way, I was still using pot to have fun and help me shed some of my inhibitions and insecurities. Unfortunately, my relaxed state of mind led me to do things I would later regret.

One night several friends and I went to the house of a mulatto woman who was a notorious prostitute. About 35 years old and unmarried, she had a couple of kids and ran her own little "business" by herself, right in her own home.

I don't recall what precipitated our visit. We all knew about her, and someone suggested going to her place. Sex was a big mystery to me, so I guess nobody had to really pull my arm to get me to go along. We were all drinking, and the idea was to get drunk and have some fun that night.

I remember that she did a little dance for us. One of the guys who went with us was seriously dating someone, and he was amazed that we wanted to go there! He waited in another room of her house while several of us took turns with her.

I don't know where my fears about mortal sin had gone, but I guess they went to the same place that my fears about drugs had been dumped! I didn't even think about what I was doing that night; I just did it.

After the incident, I developed a terrible fear that this woman had given me some sort of venereal disease. That never happened, but the fear was there for a long time, later leading to serious hypochondriac behavior. Maybe it was a reaction to guilt that I was not even aware of at the time.

Everything we do in life is a stepping stone. Murderers don't grow up thinking, *I'd like to kill people when I grow up.* They start by doing "little" wrong things and rationalizing their actions to themselves. Their behavior escalates to worse acts, and they finally end up murdering someone.

When we continue to sin, our conscience becomes hardened and numb to sin.

I had been shocked by Desi Jr.'s affair with an older woman, yet I went to a prostitute; I was upset by his smoking marijuana, then I started using drugs myself. It didn't make any sense, but sin isn't logical.

The nature of sin is escalation, which is why it's so deadly. It always starts with one step over a self-imposed line and then builds from there.

Nancy and I were a romantic item throughout my senior year in high school although we tended to have an on-again, off-again kind of relationship. I really cared about her and respected her. We kissed, and I felt that I loved her — the way a 17 year old loves someone — but we never had sexual relations.

David and the Giants played in Lafayette several times after our Biloxi meeting, and I always enjoyed going to see them when they were in town. I kept pretty busy playing in my own band, but

I liked going out to hear other groups play whenever I could.

My drug use continued to escalate that year.

One day I was at Tony's when a friend came over to his house with these little plastic packages that turned out to be LSD.

"Man, if you think marijuana is good, wait'll you try this!" he said, urging Tony and me to have some.

So we added LSD to our already growing use of alcohol and marijuana as ways to get high.

My crowd, the guys I was going to school with and hanging out with, smoked cigarettes, drank beer and wine, and now we were using more potent drugs. But whenever any doubts or concerns about drugs crossed my mind, I would think, *Keith, these are your friends!*

We considered ourselves some sort of special, cool, select group. Not a lot of people knew about drugs, but our crowd did, so we thought we were "the in-crowd." Marijuana represented one level of this secret society, and LSD meant we could jump up to another level. I was one of the "special few," I thought, who knew what these drugs were like.

When I first started doing drugs, there was a part of me that said, *This is terrible, don't do this!* But another part of me answered, *Who cares? Your life's not that great anyway.*

Drinking and drugs gave me confidence, so I could open up and talk to people more freely. I was still immature emotionally, very shy, and couldn't express myself well. I rationalized that drugs helped me be freer and loosened me up. Drugs and alcohol also somehow symbolized being a man to me, despite what I had seen alcohol do to Desi Arnaz.

Many times in later years, I heard parents wonder why their kids, kids who knew better, would be foolish enough to use drugs. I think the answer is pretty simple: deception.

Modern "just say no" anti-drug campaigns don't take into account the total effect drugs can have on young people. It gives kids a tremendous camaraderie with their drug buddies. Drugs can take the place of food, sex, and everything else, and can quickly become all-consuming. It's not just the high a person gets from using a certain drug; it's the whole drug lifestyle. That's why they call it a subculture.

The first year I did drugs, it was incredible — not horrible.

Kids don't see the dangers at first because they're too busy having a good time and enjoying the companionship of friends in drug-shared experiences.

In the summer of 1968, shortly after I had graduated from high school, I had a chilling LSD trip that was a foreshadow of things to come.

Tony and I decided to drop some LSD one night before going to see the movie *2001: A Space Odyssey*. The movie became a landmark film, combining an interest in outer space with special effects that capitalized on the drug counterculture. Science fiction fans liked it, but it was also a popular movie among drug users. The "in" thing to do was to watch the movie while stoned or tripping.

That night the acid gave me a heavy feeling inside, and I wasn't really understanding the movie, which, with all its symbolism, is difficult to figure out on a normal day. After the show, we walked to the lobby where I noticed a lot of people milling around.

I saw my girlfriend Nancy, and she smiled at me and said, "Hi, Keith."

I went over and said, "How're ya' doing?"

I talked to her for awhile, then told her I had to go and left the theater.

We had walked to the theater from Tony's house and had to cross a busy street to get back home. In our condition, it was a miracle we even got across the street without being hit by a car!

The next day I called Nancy.

"How did you like the movie?" I asked.

"What movie?" she quizzed.

"Oh, come on," I laughed. "You know, *2001.*"

"I didn't go to the movies last night," she said, obviously confused by my statement.

"Oh," I mumbled. "It must have been someone who looked like you."

Suddenly, I realized I had experienced a drug-induced hallucination. A chill went down my spine. Nancy and those faces in the lobby had seemed so real the night before! It scared me to think that none of what I had seen had been reality. It was the first time I could remember being frightened after taking LSD.

In the fall, I enrolled at the University of Southwestern Louisiana, a 735-acre campus in Lafayette. Established in 1898, Southwestern Louisiana, with its large, sprawling campus filled with moss-draped oaks and native cypress trees, is home to thousands of students.

With the help of Dad's old Desilu friend, George Murphy — who later became a U.S. Senator — I was able to obtain a grant to pay for my college tuition. Believe it or not, I started out as a pre-law major, a ridiculous goal for someone who was only a get-by student during his last two years of high school. In fact, it was a miracle that the university had even accepted me.

I didn't do well because the courses required work and studying, and I was just into partying. Later I switched to a music major.

I had no idea what I wanted to do with my life. Going to college seemed to be the next step for me to take, but I was never really serious about my education. To me college was a place to socialize — not a center for academic advancement.

All I cared about was playing in bands and drinking in bars with other guys. I really "majored" in drinking beer, playing pool, and skipping classes.

College was "trappings" to me, something you did for appearances' sake. My thoughts were colored by Dad's way of thinking; he was always impressed by the trappings.

My friends Jerry Romero, Vince Vodicka, Lee DeHart, Brad DeHart, and Tony all joined me at Southwestern Louisiana University. Gary Lamson went off to Louisiana State University, and we slowly drifted apart. I was still close to Tony, who was a very bright guy and made dean's list grades in college.

My life was wrapped up in my friends, drinking and drugs, partying, and music. After the scary LSD experience at the *2001* movie, I still did acid but remained a little wary of it.

At a place called the Stump Gallery, we'd have endless musical jams. Sonny Landreth, a talented blues guitarist who later played with John Hiatt, often joined our jam sessions. Lafayette was home to many talented musicians. All the good musicians in town would get up onstage and play, high on acid or some other drug. Our lives centered around music and drugs.

Big Steve, a 6'7", 300-pound drug dealer kept our group of friends supplied with drugs — for a price, of course. One night I was tripping on acid and watching Big Steve play the guitar when he actually bent the guitar neck. At the same time, in my drug-induced state, dozens of colors swirled in front of me, creating an incredible sight.

Another time during one of our jams, I was playing the drums when little colors appeared in the air in front of me. It distracted me somewhat from my drum playing because, in my mind, the colors were like drums that I could hit with my drumstick. The colors, of course, were all just drug-induced hallucinations.

In those days, every musician I knew got high. Drugs were everywhere; bands were all over the place; and it seemed as though the world was doing drugs.

One night, after we had played at a club, a bunch of us piled into Big Steve's car on our way to more drugs and more partying. A Cajun girl named Ferdie had been hanging around our group that night, and she really seemed attracted to me. I liked her, too, but not romantically.

While I was sitting in the car out in the parking lot, Ferdie opened the car door and got in, trying to kiss me.

"Leave me alone," I said, just wanting to enjoy my drug-induced high.

I kept ignoring her advances, until she got very angry.

Ferdie jumped out of the car, slammed the door hard, and, as she left yelled, "Keith Thibodeaux, I hope you die!" She spat out the words at me.

Her words dug into me like a knife.

Ever since the *2001* experience, I had been afraid of dying and had become very cautious when it came to using acid. I didn't want to do LSD too much because I was afraid I'd overdose. When the effects would sometimes last a long time after I had taken the drug, I would get really scared thinking, *This is it!*

Although I obviously knew about the euphoric feelings and had experienced the colors, sights, and hallucinations common to LSD users, I was unaware of the drugs serious side effects.

Complications, such as depression, anxiety, and mental disturbances that doctors term "psychosis" plagued me, but I never connected them with LSD at this time.

I knew about flashbacks and that the drug could be dangerous, but even my fears were not strong enough to stop me from using LSD and other drugs.

One night I was at Tony's house doing acid with his younger brother, Don, who was also a musician. In fact, he later played with several nationally-known blues rock artists.

Don and I were looking at the television screen when both of us saw a conductor conducting an orchestra at the same time, even though the television set was turned off!

We looked at each other at the same time and asked, "Hey, man do you see what I see?"

The mind-altering capacities of LSD were incredible.

So much was happening in the world that it actually assaulted your senses; I couldn't take it all in. The Vietnam War was still raging, and in March 1968 President Johnson announced that he would not run for re-election, his support erroded by continuing opposition to the war. In April, civil rights leader Martin Luther King was assassinated, and in June, John Kennedy's brother, Robert Kennedy, who had become a U.S. senator and was competing for the Democratic Party's presidential nomination, was felled by an assassin's bullet. Although I was shocked by the King and Robert Kennedy assassinations, they did not affect me the way John Kennedy's death had. Their deaths just seemed like two more terrible things that happened on top of a growing list of terrible things happening in the world.

In the summer of 1969, the big Woodstock music festival was held. Some of us talked about going to New York to the festival, but we never made it.

On July 20, 1969, a friend and I planned to go to Nancy's house to watch the moon landing that was being broadcast live on television. He was dating a friend of Nancy's, and the four of us planned to watch it together.

Before we left for Nancy's house, we decided to get high. I took what I thought was THC, but later learned I had actually taken a drug used as a horse tranquilizer. It was really powerful stuff that caused me to be stoned out of my mind.

When we arrived at Nancy's house, I was so out of it that I barely remember watching astronauts Neil Armstrong and Buzz Aldrin as they collected dirt, rock samples, and walked on the moon.

Nancy knew about my drug use and had been worried about me. When she saw the condition I had gotten myself into, she started crying and warned me, "Keith, you're going to kill yourself if you keep on doing this!"

I knew she was hurt by my selfishness and scared, too, but still it wasn't enough to stop me. Eventually we drifted apart.

I dropped out of college and decided to move to a town not far from Duke University, North Carolina, where Tony and some other guys were planning to start a blues band.

A blues musician named Mel drew us there with promises of great dope and big-time music opportunities. We lived in a little rented house out in the middle of nowhere because we thought it would be a safe place to do drugs.

Tony and the guys who planned to start the band were all from wealthy families and were being supported by their parents. I had no money when I moved there, so I sort of hung onto their coattails.

We decided to call our band Red Scud, after Panama Red, a type of marijuana, but our plans quickly deteriorated into one long drug party. We spent a lot of time reading books about Indians and other groups who used hallucinogenic drugs, and Tony read about this guy who was experimenting with peyote. It was during this time that I added mescaline and other drugs to marijuana, LSD, and alcohol.

Looking back, I realize we were using drugs as part of our search for spiritual enlightenment instead of using drugs for kicks. Like the others, I was deceived into believing that drugs were helping me to expand my mind.

One day during an LSD trip, I knew I was freaking out and went into the bedroom to lie down. Suddenly, my whole life started flashing before me: I saw my dad, I saw the things I had done, and I hated myself. I was so ashamed of the life I had lived; I felt as if I were dying.

It seemed as if there were no restraints on my mind and no limits as to where my mind could go. The only problem was I kept seeing all the terrible things I had done, and they were magnified a hundred million times!

Time and reality are distorted by LSD, so I had no idea how long the trip lasted, but it seemed like a very long time.

I remember glancing at Tony, and his appearance — in my mind — sent chills down my spine. His face was turned upward toward the ceiling, and he had a maniacal expression like that of the madmen I'd seen portrayed in movies.

In my mind, my life kept rushing past me, and I kept thinking, *I'm dying, I'm dying, I'm dying.* It was mental torture.

Finally, I stumbled into the other room. "I need help, man!" I said to one of the guys. "Have you got something I can take? I'm freaking out!"

"Take these," he said, tossing me some downers. "They'll calm you down."

After a while, reality returned, but I was so terrified by the whole experience that I never used LSD again.

From that moment on, my mental state slowly started to deteriorate. I became so introspective that I was paranoid about myself, my actions, and my thoughts. I felt like a mental and physical cripple; I couldn't think, and I had no energy.

To keep going I took uppers but had to quit because the "down" afterwards was so bad! Uppers also took away my appetite, and I figured I didn't need to get any skinnier. At that point, I was 5'6" and only weighed 115 pounds.

After that horrible night, I just wanted to go home. My life was a mess. I had dropped out of school, the band had folded, and I was disillusioned with everything. Nancy and I had broken up. I had nothing.

After we returned from our ill-fated journey to North Carolina, I visited Tony at his house. It scared me to see that his mind was almost gone. He eventually got to the point where he couldn't even communicate with anyone.

I was afraid, because I thought, *Gee, if Tony is losing his mind, my mind must be just as bad!*

I heard stories about how Tony would sit in the middle of his front yard, just staring at nothing and acting weird. Later I learned that he had to be committed to the state mental hospital.

As an escape, I turned again to the only thing I knew — music — and started playing with a band at a place called the River Oaks Club in Lafayette. The band's organist turned me on to amphetamines in the form of diet pills, and I'd take them and stay up all night, unable to sleep. The pills tore my system down, but I kept taking them anyway.

One night Big Steve and I were riding around in his car, smoking some Acapulco Gold, when a police car pulled up and started following us.

Big Steve sped up, and I yelled, "Take a right here!"

We rounded the corner, tires squealing. With the cops right behind us, I was able to throw the dope we had out on the street. It was so dark they didn't see me, but the cops stopped us and made us get out of the car and walk a straight line.

I was released, but they took Big Steve off to jail.

During this time, David and the Giants stopped by the River Oaks Club to watch me play.

One day in December 1969 I got a phone call from David. "How'd you like to join our group as the drummer?"

"I thought you had a drummer," I answered, trying not to sound too excited.

"We do. But we'll let him go if you agree to join us," David said. "Besides, we've got a contract with Capitol Records."

"Sounds great!" I answered, thinking this could be my ticket to the big time. Besides, I was glad to have a way out of Lafayette, where my name was becoming known to the local narcs (narcotics officers). I had just turned 19.

David Huff and his brothers Clayborn and Rayborn were country boys who grew up in Raleigh, Mississippi, with parents who took them to the local Baptist church. The Huffs were poor, but they were a close, loving family.

Their father was a logger who later worked in the oil industry. He loved country music and bought David and his sister Dorothy musical instruments when they were just kids.

With David on the guitar and Dorothy on the piano, they

started playing country music and were soon featured on a local Saturday radio show. By the time he was 13, David was playing music in honky-tonks and bars.

"After being up all night, I'd go to the Baptist church and fall asleep in the middle of the preacher's sermon!" David once told me. "It was hard going to church because the preacher preached against bars and honky-tonks, and I felt as if the preacher was preaching right at me. I didn't like it!"

David had made a profession of faith in Jesus Christ at age 12, but nothing really came of it. Many people who grow up in church make "a decision for Jesus" without really knowing God or committing their lives to Him, and unfortunately, that happened to David and his brothers, too.

David's younger twin brothers, Rayborn and Clayborn, had little interest in music until Beatlemania hit America. Then, within a year, they had formed a band and were playing for high school dances, with Rayborn on keyboard and Clayborn on bass guitar.

David moved to Laurel, Mississippi, after high school to attend Jones Junior College and formed a rock band called the Twisters. He started playing in rock clubs while still going to school. When the band decided to change their name, someone suggested calling the group David and the Giants, and the name stuck.

David's band played in some rough places in those early years, including a spot called the White House in Laurel, where fights were frequent among the patrons.

"One night I saw a guy get shot in the arm," David told me. "Another time someone tried to bomb the place with dynamite! Eventually the club was destroyed by a fire."

Rayborn and Clayborn joined David and the Giants just as the band was offered a job on the Gulf coast in Mississippi. At the time I came on board with the group in 1969, none of the Baptist-raised Huff brothers did drugs, drank, or smoked.

"David and the Giants don't do drugs. That's a big no-no," the band's sound man, Big Jerry, warned me. "They don't drink either. But if you want to drink, that's okay. But doing drugs is definitely out!" That was fine with me because, at that point, I felt I would just as soon not do drugs anymore anyway! But that decision proved to be short-lived.

The first place I played with David and the Giants was the Crazy Horse, a big club on Canal Street in New Orleans.

David ran the band much differently than any I had played with in the past. He was such a nice guy, and we all got along so well that I really enjoyed working with him and his brothers.

In a way, however, the Huff brothers puzzled me. They had long hair, but they didn't use drugs. And, although David was married at the time, he always had women around him — as did Rayborn and Clayborn, who were single. I couldn't figure it out. *Why do this, and not do that?* I wondered.

One night at a club a girl offered me some marijuana. I really wanted to enjoy it, yet I didn't want to. Even as I gave in to the urge, I felt I was somehow being untrue to myself.

Before long, my drug patterns started all over again.

Guilty and paranoid about resuming my drug use, I lived in fear that David would find out.

The band was based in Laurel, so I moved there and lived with the band's light man and road manager, who also used drugs. I developed a pattern of doing drugs, feeling guilty about it, and trying to keep David from finding out about it.

There were times I would get away from using marijuana because it seemed like a kind of junior LSD at times, and I wanted nothing more to do with LSD because of my experience and because of what it had done to Tony.

Since I had freaked out on LSD, the drug culture was like a brotherhood that I once belonged to but no longer enjoyed. Yet for some reason, I still believed that there was "truth" in drugs, and that drugs helped me be a better musician. Since drugs supposedly brought out "the real you," I thought it would help me to be more real.

I mainly used downers like Quaaludes during this period, taking anything that would keep me from feeling any kind of emotion. I even used a muscle relaxing drug, which I got from a friend who had a prescription to use it. Using downers made me depressed, but at least I wasn't in a state of paranoia. The main drugs I used were alcohol, downers, and some marijuana.

When we were home in Laurel, David lived with his wife, and Rayborn and Clayborn had their own place out in the country.

I became close with the twins, and one night at a club I talked Rayborn into trying some beer. Before the night was over, he was drunk.

We were on our way home on a rural country road when Rayborn announced he had to go to the bathroom. I stopped the car while Rayborn wandered out to the middle of a nearby field. When he didn't come back, I got out of the car to look for him.

I found him in the middle of the field, sprawled on the ground where he had passed out! Somehow I was able to get him back to the car and take him home.

Soon Rayborn talked Clayborn into taking a drink, and I had my drinking buddies in the band.

I remember urging Rayborn to try pot, but he was very hesitant.

"I don't know, Keith," he drawled in his slow Mississippi accent. "If David ever finds out . . . ."

Rayborn and Clayborn were deathly afraid of David.

"Loosen up, man," I told them. "You need to quit being so afraid and experience life."

"Well, just this once," Rayburn said as he took the smoking joint from my fingers.

Like I once had done, they had vowed never to drink or use drugs, but soon, like me, they broke their own vows.

Everyone in the band was drinking and using drugs, except David.

He was the straight one — for awhile.

10

Pleasure for a Season

Shortly after I joined David and the Giants, a matter of very serious concern loomed on my personal horizon: the draft.

About this time, President Nixon started a policy called "Vietnamization," which called for a gradual replacement of American soldiers with South Vietnamese troops. The idea was to eventually phase-out American involvement in Vietnam, letting South Vietnam fight its own war.

By the summer of 1969, 25,000 American soldiers had come home, but there were still 500,000 U.S. troops in Vietnam.

Even though the war was supposedly winding down, the draft was still in effect. Having registered for military service at age 18 as required by law, I was now really worried about the draft. The last thing I wanted to do was serve in Vietnam.

As a draftee, I would be required to give two years of my life to fight in a tiny, far-away country, in a war that I didn't even understand. Besides, I had known several guys who came back in body bags. The thought of going to war totally terrified me.

One writer later observed that avoiding Vietnam was "a generation-wide preoccupation." I know it preoccupied my every waking moment!

Post-war studies revealed that huge numbers of young men avoided duty in Vietnam through special deferments or physical exemptions. In fact, one survey estimated that 15 million draft-age men who did not see combat — about 60 percent — "helped fate along." A third of all Selective Service registrants were exempted for physical, emotional, or mental defects. In some southern states, the rate of exemptions approached 50 percent.

I am certainly not proud to admit it today, but I was among those who avoided service by "helping fate along." If I had been drafted, given the emotional state I was in at the time, I believe the outcome would have been disastrous. But that does not make what I did right, nor does it make me feel good today about my actions.

By the time I became eligible for the draft, the government had instituted a lottery system to assign men to military service, a sort of Russian roulette way to decide who would go to war and who would not. The lottery numbers went up to 366, and if you drew a low lottery number, military service was pretty much inevitable. When my lottery number came up, it was low, around 100 or less.

The day I received my notice to report to the induction center, I panicked. I went through the physical exam at the induction center, passed it, and received my assignment to Fort Polk, a well-known departure point for Vietnam. When the sergeant handed me instructions about the service, I suddenly realized I was actually going!

I'll call David, I thought. *He'll know what I should do!* Because he was older and, to me, much wiser, I often turned to him for advice. Besides, everyone knew that David had married to get out of going to Vietnam, so I figured he could identify with what I was facing.

"What am I going to do?" I asked, explaining the situation.

He hesitated for a moment before answering. "I know a doctor who will give you a medical excuse," he said thoughtfully. "Let me give you his number."

At one of the band's concerts, David had met a Biloxi doctor who told him not to hesitate to call him if he ever needed help "for anything, anytime."

I went to see this doctor, and he gave me a note to take to the induction center stating that I suffered from acute bronchitis.

When I reported to the center, note in hand, the sergeant briefly glanced at it before quickly handing it back to me. "This isn't good enough, son," he said. "You've got to have a chronic condition to be exempted from military service. If you can get a note saying you have a chronic condition . . ." his voice trailed off.

I went back to the doctor who documented that I had chronic bronchitis, which rendered me unfit for service. The induction center accepted the second note, and I was exempted from the draft.

My relief at that moment was so strong that I actually sighed heavily, as if a tremendous weight had been lifted from my shoulders.

Later, emotions that combined guilt and shame would almost overwhelm me. Only drugs helped numb the ever-increasing load of negative emotions that were piling up inside me. I often found myself thinking about the young men who were sent to Vietnam. To this day, what I did still troubles me.

Once the shadow of Vietnam was eliminated from my personal life, I breathed easier, tried to forget what was happening overseas, and went on with my life in the band.

Before I joined them, David and the Giants had a couple of regional hit tunes like "Superlove" and "Ten Miles High." They continued to be a hot group on the club and party circuit, and we played at smoke-filled bars and clubs, private parties, fraternity parties, college auditoriums, and concert halls. Our primary gigs were in southern states like Mississippi, Louisiana, Florida, Georgia, and North Carolina, but we were also a popular act in the northeast and in the Chicago area. Sometimes we opened concerts for big-name bands.

Although David signed record deals with both Capitol and MGM Records at different times, nothing really happened with our music. The Capitol Records deal I had been so excited about when I first joined the group fizzled out. I don't know if it was lack of promotion or what.

Wrapped up in my own problems, I didn't seriously question what happened with the record contracts and, instead, just went along with the flow. I felt powerless to do anything except complain to David about the music we did.

David liked what I called "bubblegum" pop music. David was a good writer, but he tried to write songs that were too commercial, songs that would sell. I guess he thought the bubblegum-type stuff was what people wanted.

As I spent more time playing with the band, I became

increasingly frustrated with the kind of music we were doing. My tastes leaned toward everything from Miles Davis to Jethro Tull and Yes, preferring their aggressive and more challenging music.

When anyone asked what kind of music I liked, I usually replied, "All kinds and styles that are played well. I can appreciate any kind of music — except Hawaiian!"

I kept urging David to have our band do only original music, but we mostly played songs made popular by other groups like "Crystal Blue Persuasion" by Tommy James and the Shondells, a medley of the Supremes' hits, or songs by the popular group Chicago.

Money wasn't the issue with me. We made a good living and had plenty of work to keep us busy, but I felt by covering other artists' songs we were living off their talent and fame. It seemed we were either backing famous artists or playing their songs in some club. I became more and more disappointed with our music, which added to my growing disillusionment with the way my own life was going.

Before I joined the band, my life had no direction. Now I felt like a rat on a treadmill in a cage, furiously running but never really getting anywhere. In spite of the fact that I was making a good living playing music, I seemed to be spinning my wheels.

I didn't see much of daytime in those days. When I went to bed it was usually dark, and when I'd get up the sun was going down.

We'd start playing around eight or nine at night and continue until two or three in the morning, depending on the venue. I usually stayed up all night because, after the show, we'd go out partying or, if another club was still open, we'd go there and listen to whatever band was playing. I rarely got home before dawn, and then I'd go to bed and sleep until four or five in the afternoon. When I woke up, I'd have dinner, then go to the club or concert hall where we were playing, and the cycle would start all over again.

During this time, my shyness around girls started to disappear because I didn't have to do anything to attract them — they started coming to me. Being in a band, the charisma, the energy of the music, or whatever, attracted women.

At the clubs, girls would give us the eye, with a come-hither look on their faces. Dating a band member provided them with a sense of notoriety. The guys I knew in bands took full advantage of this attraction that girls seemed to have for musicians and music.

Often I'd see a girl smiling at me with a knowing look while I was playing onstage. During a break or after the show, I'd go over to her, ask if she wanted a beer, and we'd take it from there. It was obvious which girls were available.

Some of the girls hanging around the band were incredibly gorgeous, but they seemed to have no respect for themselves. Most of them were groupies, party girls who were out to have a good time, and that was fine with us guys. Some were very aggressive and not at all shy about letting you know in graphic ways or terms that they wanted you.

At first their boldness and lewdness shocked me. But it didn't take long for the shock to wear off as I fell into all the patterns that were the unwritten rules of the rock and roll lifestyle.

This sounds terrible to say now, but most guys felt these girls weren't worth anything, so we didn't have to care about them as people. Then again, the guys in the band weren't any better than the girls we ran with — and it was every man for himself in those days!

One time a girlfriend of one of the other guys in the group came on to me. Taking advantage of her approaches, I agreed to go to her apartment to be with her one morning when he wasn't there. He never knew about it, and I wasn't about to tell him!

I got to the point where nothing really surprised me anymore although an incident in Biloxi, Mississippi, stands out in my mind.

When we were out of town, playing at a gig, two guys in the band would share hotel rooms. It wasn't unusual for one of us to be in one bed with his girl, while another guy would be in the other bed in the same room with a different girl.

One night, I got up to go to the bathroom. As I groped my way back to bed in the semi-darkness of the hotel room, I heard a soft voice addressing me by name, "Keith, honey." It was my friend's girl. "Anytime you want to come see me when you're in Biloxi, you're welcome to," she whispered in her most seductive, southern voice from the other bed.

I glanced over at her. Her bare shoulders were visible above the sheets, and she smiled at me. I realized she wanted me to know that she was available to me, too, even though she'd just slept with another band member. I didn't answer her, and crawled back into my own bed.

Despite the partying, the sex, and the fact that all of us were sleeping in the same room, I was shocked that she would offer herself to me while still in bed with another guy!

I did meet a few nice girls in those days, like Barbara from Laurel, whom I dated for awhile. When our relationship didn't work out, I tried to avoid getting serious with anyone.

Most of the girls at the clubs used drugs. Even in my warped state of mind, I knew I didn't want that kind of woman for a wife! I also had decided that when I did get married, I wanted my life to be much different from the way I lived now.

My life had quickly become a tangle of all the excesses associated with the rock lifestyle. Sex, drugs, and rock and roll — that described my everyday existence.

When I first joined David and the Giants, I shared a place in Laurel, Mississippi, with the group's sound man and light man. Later I lived with Clayborn and Rayborn, who were renting a house out in the country. We dubbed it "the shack." A little frame house at the end of a long dirt road, it became a party center for the band.

Looking back, that house was like Satan's den. Parties took place almost nightly.

Whenever a bunch of drunk or drugged people get together, the atmosphere can deteriorate very quickly, and it often did. Fistfights were common, and a few times knives were drawn.

It was a very wild, crazy way to live.

Those years seemed endless because the days and nights blurred into each other. Every day was a round of sleeping, eating, playing a gig, picking up girls, and partying all night long.

The band only rehearsed once in a while — usually when we were working up new songs for our act. Rehearsals, which should have been top priority, were far down on our list of important things to do.

In December 1971, I turned 21 and finally received the money from the trust fund that had been established for me in my "I Love Lucy" days: it came to $8,000. Not a huge sum of money and certainly nothing like the quarter-million dollar fantasy trust fund

I'd bragged I'd receive, but $8,000 would stretch a lot farther then than it would today.

The money had been invested in bonds, and they had matured. I never received any accounting of the funds, and at the time I didn't really care.

I sat at the bank for nearly an hour, signing papers to redeem the monies owed to me. When it was all over and I learned it was only $8,000, I was disappointed, but simply assumed the amount was correct. Later I wondered why it was not more and tried to get in touch with some of the banks in California responsible for the fund. But trying to go back so many years to find answers proved futile.

Instead of doing something sensible with the money, like investing it or buying a house, I went out and bought my first car — a brand new, yellow Datsun sports convertible that cost $3,900. A friend of mine in North Carolina had one, and I had often dreamed of owning a Datsun just like his. Being able to buy that car gave me a sense of importance that I'd never had before.

David asked if I could buy some new sound equipment for the band, and I agreed; then I bought myself a new set of Pearl drums. The rest of the money I blew on clothes, drugs, and whatever I wanted. I went through the whole $8,000 in about two weeks. That's how long it took for the legacy of my child star days to evaporate.

I loved that little sports car. After years of borrowing other peoples' cars, it was great to finally have a car of my own. It was nothing for me to rev that car up to a hundred miles an hour as I careened down the back roads of Mississippi! I was always a pretty wild driver, and later wrecked some cars and had several close calls.

When I got the trust fund money and spent it, it was nice to get a car and to have some real money for a change. But something was still missing from my life.

I was becoming increasingly discontent, and I remember thinking: *I would give any amount of money to stop the gnawing pain I feel inside.*

It was a pain that music, women, drugs, or sex was not able to erase. As the days passed, the anguish increased, but I never stopped to analyze my life or to sit back and question how I was living. I just longed for something to come along and zap me and somehow change my life into something fulfilling.

David told me later what he thought at the time: "When I'd see you so strung out on drugs and so unhappy, I figured that the breakup of your family, coming back to Louisiana from Hollywood, and all that had happened put you under a shadow."

That described my life pretty well. I felt like a dark cloud surrounded me, and there was no way for me to crawl out from under it.

"You were so fragile emotionally," David went on to say. "You were like a little kid who expected someone else to take care of you."

David was right. In fact, I often looked to him as a father figure the way I had looked to Dad. Growing up, I had never learned to take responsibility for my own life.

On the "I Love Lucy" set, people had fawned over me and catered to me, and Dad took care of everything in my life for years. But then he was ripped from my life.

I was searching for a father, for purpose, for meaning in my life, but it wasn't until years later that I became consciously aware of the source of my insecurity. At the time, I just kept hoping that somehow my life would suddenly change!

I didn't have any contact with Lucy, Desi, or the Arnaz kids during those years. They were busy with acting and performing, and my touring with the band didn't send us to California, so I had no reason to seek them out.

When I graduated from high school, Desi had sent me a nice card and $200. I received a telegram of congratulations from Lucy.

At the time I didn't think much about the $200 I received from Desi. I probably blew it pretty quickly. But as I reflect on it today, here I was, away from the whole Hollywood scene for a few years, and someone like Desi Arnaz had still found time to make me feel like I mattered. It was typical of his genuinely giving nature. He was one of the biggest-hearted men I have ever known.

Even though "I Love Lucy" was part of a long-ago past, like a ghost, Little Ricky continued to hover over my head. At times I'd be talking to a girl at a club, and one of the guys in the band would tell her, "Hey, do you know you're talking to Little Ricky?"

Sometimes the girl would be enthralled by that revelation, but if she wasn't excited about it, I'd feel like crawling under the table.

When I did think about Little Ricky and "I Love Lucy," it was with bitterness, not at Lucy or Desi or anybody, but because I blamed my involvement with the show and Hollywood for causing my parents' divorce.

Mom knew I felt this way and would insist, "Keith, your dad could have done what he did anywhere." Of course, Mom was right, but in my mind, I convinced myself the family breakup was my fault.

During the time that David and the Giants were playing from town to town, Clayborn married a beautiful and seductive Cuban girl named Sonia. With black hair and a dark complexion, she had a kind of smoldering sensuality about her. Although she loved Clayborn and he loved her, it didn't surprise me when they were divorced after three years of marriage.

Sonia liked guys, and she particularly liked guys in bands. One weekend she went to visit her parents in New Orleans, went to a club there, and met a drummer playing in the club's band. When she returned home she told Clayborn she was leaving him. She ran off with the drummer she'd met, and that was the end of the marriage. With his heart broken and his pride shattered, Clayborn was devastated. We all hurt for him.

David's marriage also eventually ended in divorce. During the time I had been involved with the band, David had never acted like a married man. Like the rest of us, he pretty much did what he wanted.

The mentality of our rock and roll lifestyle made it almost impossible for any marriage to survive.

Even during those partying days, I dreamed about settling down and getting married one day. I had a desire to find a girl I could really love — and someone who would really love me.

My parents' divorce had scarred me deeply, and I didn't want my marriage to end the way my parents' had. When it came to marriage, I had an ideal in my mind and felt particularly strong about being faithful to my mate once I was married.

I had broken most of the promises I'd made to myself by this time, but I still had certain lines — sort of my own code of ethics and morality — that I vowed not to cross. But cross most of them I did, and with each crossing, my conscience became more and more seared.

I still thought certain things were wrong, but pleasure pushed away most of my guilt. The Catholic teaching I had received as a child was always in the back of my mind, and one of the lines I had not crossed involved adultery.

That was until one night when I met a girl who was married, and she invited me to her house. "My husband's not here, he's out of town. Please come over, Keith!" she urged.

I struggled with whether I should go, but in the end, I accepted the invitation, went to her house, and slept with her while her husband was away. It was a line I never thought I would cross, and the guilt I felt was incredible.

Why? I don't know. After all, I was involved with many, many girls, but sleeping with this one married woman seemed like the most terrible thing in the world! It was all wrong, but up until that point, I had been able to tell myself that at least I wasn't having an affair with someone who was married.

Maybe my strong feelings about not getting involved with a married woman stemmed from Dad's affair; I hated what he had done to Mom and to us. Now I had crossed the line and had been partner to committing adultery. For some reason, being with this married woman was a turning point for me, a dividing line in the downward spiral of my life.

I could pretty much be talked into anything, which is also probably why I eventually ended up with a married woman. I had no power in me to say no to anybody.

The guys in the band always called me "Thibodeaux," not Keith. As a joke, one of them would say, "Hey, Thibodeaux, you look terrible." I would believe anything anybody told me, and before the day was over, I'd be in bed!

To deaden my feelings as much as possible, I buried myself further in the music, the party lifestyle, and in drugs. After that terrifying LSD trip in North Carolina, I never used acid again, and instead depended on alcohol, pot, and pills. Still, I never thought of myself as a drug addict, nor did I ever associate any of my growing mental and emotional problems with my drug and alcohol use.

Since Tony had gone over the edge because of LSD, the thought of losing my mind constantly haunted me. My mental and emotional state continued to deteriorate, and once, when Clayborn and Sonia were still together, she urged me to see a psychiatrist because I was so down all the time.

I never smiled; nothing made me happy. At times, I would crawl into my own little shell, my own little world, and isolate myself from other people. I only felt good about myself when I was onstage with the band.

It was really hard for me to get through daily life, and the band was the only thing that kept me going. I was very lonely, despite all the people and the partying that surrounded me.

Many times, sitting onstage behind my drum kit and pounding out the rhythm to a high-energy song, I would watch as people out on the dance floor laughed, danced, and seemed to be having a great time. I'd look at them and think: *Why can't I have a good time like that? Maybe I need more drugs.*

Other than numbing my mind and helping me to escape, drugs no longer held a feel-good attraction for me. They were something I now did out of desperation.

One time, when I went home to Lafayette to visit Mom, I tried to talk to her about my growing depression. Late one night, as we were sitting at the kitchen table, I tried to make her understand what I was feeling inside.

"Mom, I really think I need to see a psychiatrist," I said, desperation clinging to every word. "There's something really wrong with me."

Searching her face, I could see she didn't understand my cry for help.

"Oh, Keith," she said, shrugging off my confession, "you just need some rest. There is nothing wrong with you. Only crazy people go to the psychiatrist."

I kept insisting, "Mom, I've got a problem, and I don't know what to do about it."

"Everything will be fine," she smiled, patting my hand.

Mom didn't want to acknowledge what was going on in my life. She could never accept that I had such severe problems, and to this day, insists she never suspected that I used drugs. Maybe it was a form of denial on her part, refusing to believe anything bad about one of her children.

The only thing that bothered her was my long hair and my hippie-like appearance. She'd shake her head in exasperation, telling me, "Keith, go look in the mirror. Do you really think you look good like that? You look like hell!"

She was probably right.

One day Dad, who was living with his new family in Baton Rouge, called and asked me to meet him for lunch. Still angry and bitter, I don't know why I even agreed to see him, especially since we seldom had any contact. I still had not forgiven him for leaving.

As we sat across the table from one another, he stared intently at me for a long time before saying anything. My appearance must have shocked him. With wild, long hair, I was unhealthy, skinny, and sick-looking, and in the midst of deep depression.

Finally he spoke, in a slow, quiet, very serious voice. "Keith, I can tell you're at the end of your rope. If you don't do something about your life, we'll be burying you, and I'd hate to have to bury you."

His frankness shocked and scared me, but I wasn't about to admit that to him! I had a tremendous fear of death, and his talk about burying me dug deeply into my heart.

My feelings of anger and, at times, hatred, toward Dad made it impossible for me to admit that he was right about my life and my state of mind; I'd die rather than agree with him!

I brushed aside his words and tried to act as nonchalant as possible when I answered him. "Oh, no, I'm doing okay. Everything is cool, Dad."

He shook his head and sighed. Everything wasn't cool. He knew it, and I knew it. I was having a nervous breakdown.

The Bible says there is pleasure in sin for a season, and I was at the end of my season. I knew something was seriously wrong. I had to have a miracle in my life.

11

Silencing the Turmoil

I rolled over wearily, glancing at the clock on the night stand beside my bed. It was 8 a.m., and I had only been in bed a few hours. The window shades were drawn tight to keep the sun from streaming into my room and adding to my sleeplessness.

My head throbbed. My mouth was dry, and my gums ached. Why bother getting up? I had been tossing and turning, but I still needed to try and sleep; I had to play again that night.

I sighed. Should I stay in bed and try to go back to sleep, or get up and walk around? It didn't make any difference. No matter what I did, the depression was still there. *If I can just get to sleep, I can escape for a little while,* I thought.

Sleep was one way of escape from the relentless pain of my life. I stayed up as late as possible so I could sleep longer. If I woke up and couldn't get back to sleep, I'd prowl around the house, restless, and do whatever I could to make myself sleepy.

When I was sleeping, I didn't have to think.

I turned my face against the pillow, willing myself back to a fitful sleep.

It was 1974, and I'd be having a birthday soon.

In December, I'd be 24 years old, but I may as well have been a hundred. I felt like I'd already lived several lifetimes. At a time when most people my age were starting out in life, excited about their dreams and goals, I felt like my life was already over.

My day had come — and gone.

I had tried it all, and nothing helped ease the constant loneliness that I now felt. Whether I was with people or alone, whether I slept by myself or had some girl with me, the loneliness and sadness never left. It felt like the weight of the whole world was crashing down on my shoulders. Depression had settled on me like a thick, heavy fog, and the weight of it seemed almost physical.

For a long time, the band had been the only thing that kept me going and preserved my sanity. The rhythm, the beat, and my ear for music were all instinctive. I had never taken a drumming lesson or a music lesson in my life. Drums were like an extension of my body, not some separate part but part of the whole. Playing the drums was as natural as breathing for me. Music was my passion, the one constant in a life tossed by change and upheaval.

The band and music kept me going, but I was getting weaker with each day. It was a constant struggle just to get through daily life. Looking back, I had all the symptoms of true clinical depression: a sense of hopelessness, failure, and inadequacy; resentment and bitterness; self-pity; and deep, deep loneliness that just ate away at me.

At the time, I didn't know anything about symptoms. I only knew that my depression seemed insurmountable and unstoppable. I got to the place where I couldn't carry on a normal conversation with another person because my concentration was so bad. I never laughed or had any kind of joy. At times, I had periods of utter desperation.

When my desperate feelings subsided, to be replaced by the now-familiar chronic sadness, somehow I could never work up the motivation to see a doctor or to try and get some help to fix what was wrong with me. I kept drinking and popping pills, desperately searching for a way out, for truth.

Nothing was working.

I still didn't think of myself as a drug addict. Drugs were something I used to try to deaden my inner pain.

The drugs I had used can have some terrible side effects. The amphetamines I'd started taking in Lafayette — those pills that kept me up all night and gave me increased energy — also can cause paranoid thinking, confusion, irritability, and depression, all of which I had.

Quaaludes have a tendency to cause people to think they're

losing their minds, which probably only added to the fears I had already that I was losing mine!

Mescaline, a naturally occurring hallucinogen derived from cactus plants or produced synthetically in a lab, can cause intense self-absorption.

Experts say that long-term marijuana users often have diminished drive and lessened ambition, introversion, and many other symptoms — all of which described me!

At the time, I didn't fully understand the role that drugs might be playing in my mental, emotional, or physical state. It never dawned on me that drugs were causing my problems not alleviating them.

When I first started using drugs, they got me high, lifted me up, and made me feel good. They provided a sense of euphoria and well-being. Now I used drugs to try to find peace and some relief from the pain of my life. Instead, my own mind began to turn on me.

The more paranoid I became, the more my depression grew. I used amphetamines because I was so down emotionally and had no energy. Uppers were how I got through the night for a period of time.

The world seemed as troubled as I was. A peace treaty was finally signed in 1973 calling for withdrawal of American forces from Vietnam, but the war was still dragging on as negotiators talked.

Because the band played at night, I was home a lot in the daytime. When I couldn't sleep, I watched television. The infamous Watergate hearings were topping Vietnam as the big news story, and there was nothing on TV to watch except the hearings. I sat home for days on end, taking in all the drama.

As I watched the hearings, incredulous at what was happening in the country, with all the talk about a cover-up, spies, possible CIA involvement, the FBI, and so on, it only reinforced my depression and paranoia. It was a depressing time to be alive.

I'd sit staring at the TV, shaking my head in wonder and thinking, *You can't trust anybody anymore!*

In addition to my depression, I was very unhealthy. The rock lifestyle of weird hours, junk food and poor eating habits, drinking, and drugs obviously doesn't contribute to good health! I didn't have much of an appetite and was mostly just skin and bones. On top of that, I had a terrible case of gum disease.

One possible side effect of amphetamine use is retraction of gum tissue, but I never linked my gum problems to my drug use.

My gum problems got so bad, I turned into a hypochondriac and decided I had cancer. Hypochondria is defined as "mental depression accompanied by an abnormal preoccupation with imaginary physical ailments," which pretty much described me at that point! Although I did have some real physical ailments, they were all greatly magnified in my mind.

One day when I was visiting an aunt, I complained aloud, "My gums are killing me. I can't stand the pain."

"Let me see," she said, and I showed her my mouth. My aunt was a dental hygienist.

"Keith, your mouth looks terrible!" she exclaimed. "Why didn't you tell me about it before?"

Her reaction finally sent me to a dentist for treatment, who told me I had the worst case of gum disease he had ever seen!

I went home and prayed to God in desperation because I was still convinced that I really had cancer and was going to die.

Bargaining with God, I prayed, "God, if You heal me and let me not have cancer and let me get better, I'll serve You."

One night I was awakened from a sound sleep to hear the sound of beads rattling noisily.

In the house where I lived in Laurel, we had strands of brightly colored, plastic "love beads" — made popular by California hippies — hung up in one room between a doorway. They would rattle whenever someone walked through them from one room into the next.

"Hal! Hey, Hal! Are you here?" I yelled. Hal Leach was one of the guys who lived in the house.

No one answered.

Terrified, I suddenly felt a heavy, oppressive presence in the room. I could actually sense evil. My hair stood on end.

When we first rented the house, we used to joke about it being haunted because we heard that someone had died there. Once we asked the Ouija board if there were ghosts in the house, and its marker pointed to "yes." We joked about it, but I always felt a weird, eerie feeling in that house.

To make matters worse, in my search for inner peace, I had begun to investigate the occult. I started getting into astrology, Ouija boards, tarot cards, and began reading books on witchcraft. But the more I read and searched, the more true peace eluded me. Now the darkness seemed to be closing in around me.

I ran out of the room and found Hal in another part of the house. There was no one else in the house and no breeze that night. I knew those beads hadn't made all that noise by themselves.

I tried to laugh off the rattling beads incident with Hal, but that night I couldn't sleep at all. The fear was overwhelming, and it began to rule my life. I didn't even know what, exactly, I was afraid of. The fact that my fear was unreasonable didn't make it any less real to me.

Desperate for relief from this constant fear, I did something I would live to regret. I had heard about people selling their souls to the devil and how he had given them what they wanted, so I decided to try it. Thinking he would give me back my mind and my body, I asked Satan to come into my life.

The next day I started having my first thoughts of suicide. In fact, I started thinking about suicide all the time and wondered if it could be a way out for me.

Racing my little convertible up to 120 miles per hour, I would see a tree and fantasize about hitting it. Or, I'd be careening down the highway, rubber burning, revving up that car as fast as it would go, and suddenly a voice in my head would seem to whisper, "Why don't you just throw yourself out?"

"Man, I think I must be going crazy for sure," I told the band's sound man, Jerry Langford, one day. "I'm thinking about suicide."

I knew I startled him, but I was crying out for help.

With a serious, concerned look on his face, all Jerry could say was, "Keith, just be strong. You gotta' be strong."

If I could have gotten over what was tormenting me that easily, by just being strong or by positive thinking, I certainly would have done it!

Everyone knew something was terribly wrong with me: the band members knew it; I knew it. It was as if we were all playing some sort of stupid game by pretending things were not as bad as they really were. I didn't want to admit that I might be going crazy — that the depression was so incessant and overwhelming I felt I had no reason to live.

The guys in the band had no idea what to do for me or how to help me. When we had problems, the only thing any of us knew to do was drink a little more, do more drugs, or party a little more. Everybody in the band had problems with women, drinking, and drugs, but the depression I had was an entirely different dilemma.

Much of that time remains a blur to me, although David tells me I did things like drive the band truck on sidewalks. It's a wonder any of us lived through those days!

I started thinking a lot about the past and would try to remember times before I had started feeling this way — times before despair ruled my life. I even visited some friends from those days and tried to recapture some of the old times and old feelings with them. But it didn't work. They were fine, and I was not. I felt completely lost.

My life was such a long way from Hollywood and eons from Little Ricky Ricardo and "I Love Lucy." How do you top stardom at age five in the most successful television series of all time? How do you deal with believing your life is over at age 23?

That little boy back in Hollywood, a child star whom people oohed and ahhed over, the kid who hung out with Lucy and Desi and their kids and rode around in limousines and expensive cars, seemed like someone else. It was as if I could stand back, removed from myself, and see that past life in the far-off, dim recesses of my mind. It was as if that kid was another person, not Keith Thibodeaux. The problem was that I had no idea who Keith Thibodeaux really was!

Tommy Aldridge, who later was the drummer for several famous rock bands, including Whitesnake and Black Oak Arkansas, often played in the same clubs where our group played. One night after we finished playing Tommy and I took two girls out. Tommy's girlfriend had brought along a friend who liked me, but I didn't like her.

After a late night of playing, they were ready to party and have some fun, but I just wasn't interested. I was so tired and so messed up, all I wanted to do was go home, crash, and sleep. Even partying didn't hold the old attraction to me that it once had.

I looked around, and it seemed as if the whole world was going to hell and I was, too. Nothing mattered to me anymore.

Although I hadn't been to church in years, I started going to Mass again and to confession. I would play until two in the morning, go home and try to sleep a few hours, and then get up to go to Mass at six o'clock in the morning. I started going to church to confess and pray, but it wasn't enough. I was trying to get rid of the guilt that was weighing me down.

I prayed to God to save me and I confessed to the priest about my drug use, thinking God would heal me of the bad memories, the terrible thought patterns, and the depression. I confessed everything I could think of that I had done that might be wrong!

Going to Mass helped a little in that I was at least trying to take some action, to do something to help myself. But going to church wasn't the answer.

I needed more than church — I needed power to change my life!

In the midst of my search, I had a very strange dream one night. In the dream, my sister Katie and I were in Louisiana, near a river and a bayou area where we could swim. While we were swimming, a huge snake came up behind us and started chasing us. I swam as fast as I could, trying to escape the snake, when suddenly it changed into a huge, serpent-like monster. It had become a terrible dragon-type creature. I made it to shore and somehow had a bow and arrow in my hand. I shot an arrow into the dragon, but it was as if I had stuck a small needle into this big creature.

Suddenly, I woke up with the thought: *God's going to have to fight the dragon, not me.*

For a long time, I was obsessed with this dream, but, oddly enough, it gave me hope. To me, the dream symbolized that I was going to get away from my problems — I wasn't going to go crazy or die.

My mother, at the invitation of a friend, had started attending services at a little Catholic church way out in the country, 20 miles from Lafayette in Grand Coteau, Louisiana. Whenever I would visit, Mom would tell me about what went on at these church services.

"The church hosts Charismatic prayer meetings," she told me exuberantly.

I didn't even know what "Charismatic" meant, but I listened to her, curious and fascinated at the same time.

Mom seemed different to me. There was an aliveness about her, and she had much more joy in her life. Since she had never remarried, Mom had struggled as a single parent, raising six kids alone. Added to her burden was the stigma of divorce. Now she seemed changed somehow — more understanding and loving.

"People from different denominations come to these services," she told me. "Some speak in tongues, and there are healings and miracles."

At first I was very skeptical. "Sounds like voodoo to me," I scoffed.

Then I remember what Dad had said months earlier. I was at the end of my rope and I knew it.

I need a miracle in my life, I thought. Nothing else I tried had worked.

Mom kept urging me, "Why don't you go to church with us and see what's going on at the meetings?"

I finally agreed to go and see for myself. I was so desperate, and Mom seemed so at peace with herself that it intrigued me. Going to that meeting was a last-ditch effort for me. I really felt as though I were at the point of death.

I laugh every time I remember that drive to church: There we were, me, a rock band drummer with long hair and a hippie attitude, riding along with Mom, my 12-year-old brother, and three little old ladies to Grand Coteau! The old ladies, friends of my mother's, were praising the Lord in the car the whole way there!

When we walked into the church, I was immediately impressed by the music. At the front, a group of young people was playing acoustic guitars, and everyone was singing and clapping their hands to lively songs. *This sure is different than the music from my old Catholic church days,* I thought.

All kinds of people were there: young people, middle-aged

people, old women, old men. All of them seemed to have a great joy about them — and in them. They were praising God and lifting their hands in the air in worship. I had never seen anyone do that before.

This is weird, I thought. But, at the same time, I wanted to lift my hands, too, but I felt silly about it.

Unlike a traditional church service, everyone shared in the meeting. Someone would stand up and read a Scripture from the Bible; then someone else would have a song to share.

It was so different than anything I'd ever experienced before.

When the people talked about God, they really believed what they were saying; I could sense it. They talked about God as if they actually knew Him. Others spoke of having a relationship with Jesus Christ, and they talked as if they knew Jesus as a person, not as a religion.

One lady was so radiant that her whole face shone like an angel's.

For the first time, I sensed I was seeing the love of God.

As opposed to just going to church, where we were always told what to do, how to do it, and when to do it, Mom said these people were trying to be "led by the Spirit of God."

I didn't really understand what that meant, but I knew one thing: These people knew the person they were worshiping. They were worshipping someone who was living; it wasn't just some dead ritual.

It surprised me to see a few priests and nuns at this meeting. I always thought nuns and priests were so high up on the spiritual ladder that they just automatically knew God. Yet, here they were, searching for God just like the rest of us. I suddenly realized that in the Lord's eyes, there was no rank or difference between people.

I went to the church several times.

One night a man gave a teaching and drew pictures on a chalkboard with God on the top, Jesus in the middle, and mankind down at the bottom.

He explained, "When you commit your life to Jesus, God doesn't see you, He sees Jesus. He sees us through Jesus."

That was a new concept to me. I had thought we had to make our way to God on our own.

In these meetings, the emphasis was on establishing a "personal relationship" with Jesus, another term I had never heard before. The concept that Jesus was actually here, and not in some far-off, distant place where He had nothing to do with me or my life slowly started to sink in and take hold.

One night a priest who was attending the meeting said, "I would like to lay hands on everyone present, pray for them, and let the Holy Spirit minister to them."

My younger brother was with me, and we both went to the front of the church for prayer.

As the priest prayed, my brother and I fell to the ground. Later, I learned this is called being "slain in the Spirit."

Everything seemed dark, and as all the prayers around me faded away in a babble of voices, I could see a great darkness and then a light far in the distance. I kept gazing at the light, and as it kept getting closer and closer it also became larger.

Finally the light seemed to actually hover above me, and in its center was a person. Somehow I discerned that this person was Jesus Christ of Nazareth, the one who had died 2,000 years ago. There was no doubt in my mind about whom I was now seeing. It wasn't a physical "seeing," in that I could not make out His physical characteristics; it was all spiritual, and it was very real.

More love than I could ever describe or imagine was coming from Jesus. It was as if Jesus was wrapping His love around me. Understanding, compassion, and more power than the universe could contain, all of these were evident in the person of Jesus. It was awesome to realize that I was actually in the presence of the Creator of the whole universe!

Throughout this experience, my mind was going through all my sins, all the things I had ever done wrong.

In my mind I was thinking: *Well, Lord, what about this?*

My sins seemed too great. I had always thought God was off in the distance somewhere, ready to clobber me with a hammer when I did something wrong!

It was as if my whole life passed in front of me, all the bad things I had done. Then I confessed my sins to Him. In the middle of it all, I sensed He had empathy for me and for each one of those sins that had come to my mind. I felt so unworthy that He should even be there, and that I should be in His presence!

In the vision, all I had to do was think a question, and He answered. I didn't hear an audible sound or voice, but I knew I was asking, and I knew His answers.

I asked, "What about all my sin, and all the guilt?"

"That's the reason that I died," He replied.

In the vision, I realized that Jesus Christ actually experienced the shame and guilt of every one of our sins on the Cross. He actually felt each individual person's sin! I thought: *He became sin for us.*

All of these truths were suddenly being made real to me in this vision. Jesus Christ, the Son of God, had died on the Cross for me, and He had become sin for me! He had actually become sin, and in doing so, had paid the penalty for mankind's sins.

Jesus had paid the penalty for my sins. The thought was staggering in its implications!

"Lord, are You really like this?" I asked, still incredulous even in the midst of the vision.

He just said three simple words in reply: "Yes, I am."

When He said those words, that was the greatest moment in my life!

Slowly I sensed that the vision was over. Once again, I could hear the voices of people around me praying.

I have no idea how long the experience lasted, but I knew I was forever changed.

I went home that night and immediately began to read the Bible. For the first time, I could understand the words of Scripture.

In my vision, the fact that Jesus had become sin for us became real to me. Now I actually read those very words for the first time in the Bible: "For he hath made him to be sin for us, who knew no sin, that we might be made the righteousness of God in him" (2 Cor. 5:21;KJV).

I also read another passage that seemed to describe what had happened to me perfectly: "Therefore if any man be in Christ, he is a new creature: old things are passed away; behold, all things are become new" (2 Cor. 5:17). I was a new person; the old had passed away, and my new life had just begun!

Before this experience, the Bible had meant nothing to me; it could have been written in Egyptian for all I knew! Now I started devouring the Word of God and had an incredible desire to read it. It was my hope, my faith, and my lifeline. The Bible opened up to me like some treasure that had been hidden in the earth for many years.

Whenever I read some new revelation, I thought: *Has this been here all this time?*

In Galatians 3:13, I read: "Christ hath redeemed us from the curse of the law, being made a curse for us."

The words, filled with truth and life, jumped out at me.

I had been under a curse, but I had done it to myself. I deserved "the curse of the law" because I had been in gross sin and had totally turned my back on God. Starting with my parents' divorce, I blamed God for all that was wrong with my life and had turned a deaf ear to His voice.

I read in John 10:10 where Jesus said the thief — Satan — comes to steal, kill, and destroy. I knew that had happened to me. Satan had tried to destroy me with drugs, with pain, and with sin; he had tried to steal my sanity; and he had tried to kill me with thoughts of self-hatred and suicide.

In contrast, Jesus said in John 10:10, "I am come that they might have life, and that they might have it more abundantly."

Life! Life! That was what I had been searching for!

Not just the promise of eternal life — although God promises that, too — but life in the here and now. An abundant life!

I learned that the word "gospel" means "good news," and I well understood that message, for the Word of God was such good news to me!

I've heard some people describe God as "the God of second chances." To me He became the God of a thousand chances!

All my problems didn't disappear overnight. Some of my weird mental quirks and the destructive patterns I had formed in life were not yet broken.

But I also had, for the first time, peace. The inner turmoil that had tortured me for so long was finally silenced.

Soon I learned that this new life would not be easy.

12

On the Road Again

Finding the reality and truth of life, as embodied in Jesus Christ as the Son of God, was the turning point in my life. Knowing that God was real and that He cared about me provided the missing link. The piece of the puzzle I had searched for so long was finally in its rightful place.

An interviewer once asked me how I knew Jesus was "the real thing."

I replied, "To me, finding Jesus was like finding a treasure chest full of gold, rubies, and silver. People might try to tell you that you didn't find that treasure chest, but you know that you did!"

That's how I felt when I realized that Jesus Christ was real and that the Bible was true. Jesus actually came and dwelt within me.

I was changed — there was no doubt about that — but I was a baby Christian. To make matters worse, I found myself alone with my faith. At the time, I didn't know about the importance of what the Bible calls "fellowship," or being with other believers.

Instead of surrounding myself with mature Christians, people who were strong and could encourage me in my walk with God, I went right back to the rock and roll world. I went back on the road and back to the clubs with David and the Giants because it was the only job I had. It was all I knew to do.

I still needed to be freed and delivered from drugs and the way they had affected my mind. Relationships with people still scared me, and I had a real paranoia about giving of myself, for fear that I would be hurt. Everyone I had ever cared about had let me down, gone crazy, or died.

At that point, I didn't have enough teaching to know what the body of Christ could give me. I was really afraid of getting involved with the "wrong church," and I kept praying and asking God to show me which church was the right one.

I'm not saying this to excuse any of my actions; I'm just trying to explain the reasons why it took me so long to settle down in my Christian faith.

Yes, my spirit, my inner man, the real Keith Thibodeaux, had been born again, but I had the same old carnal mind!

I didn't yet understand the importance of what the Bible terms "renewing your mind," which means allowing the Word of God to erase the old thought patterns and old ways of doing things. I didn't understand these truths then; I was too young spiritually, a real baby in the Christian faith. I just tried to hang on.

As I clung to my Bible, I tried to share what had happened to me with the other guys in the band.

"The Bible is true, man! It's got the answer to life!" I told them.

When they showed little interest, I tried appealing to them from a marketing aspect. Maybe they would be interested in God if music was involved.

"We need to start playing godly music. Hey, we could do original music with godly lyrics. Nobody is really doing that!" I suggested. "Instead of songs talking about drugs and going to bed with women, we can just change the lyrics to godly lyrics!"

"Who in the world would we play for?" David scoffed. "How could we make any money doing that?"

David, Rayborn, and Clayborn weren't particularly desperate at that point in their lives, and my pleas fell on deaf ears.

"Keith, all the songs we do have 'Oh baby, baby' in them. I can't imagine singing, 'Oh Jesus!' " David said, obviously amused by my suggestions.

They probably thought "crazy ol' Keith" had flipped out on drugs or that I was off on some new "religious trip." The Jesus movement was going strong back then, and there was a lot of talk about God and Jesus even among drug users.

I would later learn that my words had not fallen on deaf ears.

David told me, "After you came to Christ, I felt guilty about the life I was living!"

That surprised me since, on the surface, he seemed not the least bit interested in what had happened to me.

I started carrying a little green New Testament in my shirt pocket all the time. During breaks from playing the band, I'd sit around reading my Bible.

In spite of my lack of Christian fellowship, I could see changes taking place in my life. I became a more giving person.

Every day I used to see this black guy walking down the street. After I was saved, it dawned on me that he was walking because he didn't have a car. I immediately felt compassion for him.

I had an old Austin-Healy Sprite convertible, so one day I just walked up to him and said, "Hey man, you want this car?"

For a moment, he stared at me in disbelief, but I continued, "I don't know why I'm doing this, but this is from the Lord for you!"

He was all smiles as I handed him the keys. The car needed some work, but he got it fixed. Later, I saw him drive by with that little car packed with people! Wearing a beret, he smiled and waved at me.

I knew God was working in my life.

God began to deal with me about lying. From the time our family moved back to Louisiana from Hollywood and I had started making up incredible stories to win acceptance from people, I had become a habitual liar.

One day I read in the Bible that Jesus said the devil is "the father of lies," and I sure didn't want Satan to be my father! I determined not to tell any more lies, and my lying stopped. It was as if the Lord just took it away from me.

When I read the verse from Ephesians 4:29, "Let no corrupt communication come out of your mouth," I quit cursing, even though I was surrounded by it all the time.

In spite of these immediate changes, I found myself gradually slipping back into the old patterns. I was walking in two worlds, trying to learn the Word of God all by myself and living in the rock world.

I quit doing drugs for awhile, but I drank because I didn't see anything wrong with that. Soon I found myself slipping into the old drug habits, too. The girls that hung around the band were still available, and, when they would approach me, at times I would be strong. But at other times, I'd find myself falling back into sin — back into the same old partying patterns.

One day I came across Romans 7:18-19 from the Amplified Bible: "For I know that nothing good dwells within me, that is, in my flesh. I can will what is right, but I cannot perform it. I have the intention and urge to do what is right, but no power to carry it out. For I fail to practice the good deeds I desire to do, but the evil deeds I do not desire to do are what I am (ever) doing."

When I read those words, I knew they described me, but I still didn't understand the solution. I started rationalizing that if I sinned, I could ask God for forgiveness and He would forgive me.

It wasn't until much later, when reading Romans 6:1, that I realized that this was the wrong way to approach sin because that verse says, "What shall we say then? Shall we go on sinning so that grace may increase?"

As a struggling Christian, without any fellowship, without a body of believers to teach, support, and encourage me in my new life, I rationalized my sin. I finally had peace within myself because I knew that Jesus was the answer, but my Christian conversion didn't mean that I automatically let go of all the sin that had troubled me for years.

In retrospect, I think the Lord just had mercy on me because my emotional state was still so fragile. Like the apostle Paul said in Romans 7:18-19, I really wanted to do the right thing! But often my good intentions didn't blend with the reality of my situation.

When I did fall, I felt terribly guilty and immediately asked God for forgiveness, but I didn't have instant deliverance. Accepting Jesus as Saviour was my beginning, but because of ignorance about spiritual things and the lifestyle around me, it was a very rocky take off!

I talked to the twins about the Lord a lot, particularly Rayborn, but they could not grasp what had happened in my life. My own spiritual development was so weak, they probably couldn't see a lot of Jesus in me!

The band was having problems, so finally the twins and I decided to leave and form our own group, a band we called Angel. David got some new "Giants" and continued playing while we moved to Gulfport, Mississippi, and struggled to get our new group on its feet.

It wasn't long before I started taking drugs again.

One night I decided to take the band truck and drive home, but I was high and in no condition to drive. Our road manager, Doug, was with me. When Clayborn found out we had taken the band truck and left, he took off down the road after us.

I came to a red traffic light and slid the truck right through it, winding up on a curb! Meanwhile, Clayborn was following us, blowing his horn in an effort to get us to stop. But I kept driving even as a policeman started following us, siren going and lights flashing.

As I watched the police car in the rear view mirror, it suddenly dawned on me that I did not have my driver's license.

"Doug, I don't have my license with me. Get over here quick and pretend you were driving!" I yelled.

Doug, who was also high, agreed. As I pulled over to the side of the road, we quickly changed places. When he told the police he was driving the truck, they arrested him and put him in jail overnight.

The next day, when Clayborn went to the jail to bail Doug out, Doug told him, "Tell Thibodeaux he owes me some money!"

Doug had to pay a fine and stay in jail — all because of me. I felt guilty about my behavior and realized it had hurt my Christian witness, but I didn't have the power to stop sinning.

I stayed with the new band about six months, but things just weren't clicking with the group. We weren't getting the work that we needed, and our cash was running low. Things got so bad that I sold my blood to a blood bank for money.

Finally, I decided I'd had it with music and started considering doing something I had never done in my life — manual labor.

I had never had a real job. All my life I had lived in a fantasy world of acting or playing music. Everyone was always saying I needed to get a real job, so that's what I decided to do.

My cousin Gaynelle's husband, Jackie, worked for a big oil

company at the time, and through him, I was hired by the same company in 1975.

My first job was on an offshore oil rig about 120 miles off the coast of Louisiana. I was hired as a cook's helper, but I made beds, worked as a dishwasher, and cleaned toilets.

I had been attracted to the job partly because I figured there wouldn't be any drugs or alcohol way out in the Gulf of Mexico. Boy, was I wrong!

I thought: *Man, I can't get away from it no matter where I go!*

I still remember talking about the Lord to this alcoholic guy who was working on the rig as he sat right beside me having tremors.

While I was out at sea, I pretty much kept to myself. Still suffering the effects of my drug use, I was very insecure and in constant emotional turmoil. The loneliness I felt was overwhelming at times.

The only solace I had was my Bible. Many nights I would lie alone on my bunk, reading my Bible and thinking about my life.

One day as I was cleaning toilets, I remember thinking: *So this is what my life has become. I wonder what people would say if they could see me now — Little Ricky washing dishes and cleaning toilets!*

A few of the co-workers knew I had been Little Ricky, and they would rib me, saying, "If you're Little Ricky, what are you doing here?"

I'd answer them sharply: "Just trying to make a living like anybody else!"

After about four months, the isolation was really getting to me, and I found myself emotionally unable to handle it. I resigned and took a boat back to land.

Before long, I found a job as a roustabout, or a roughneck's helper, working on a construction crew that was building a gas plant to be shipped to Venezuela. I made a few friends on the job site and even talked to some of them about Jesus.

The company had a rule that employees could not leave the property during working hours. One day another fellow and I decided to eat our lunch together in his car where we could talk. When we returned to the site, both of us were fired on the spot.

My attempts at holding "real jobs" had lasted about six months.

Tired and unemployed, I moved back home to Lafayette to live with Mom. I was really at loose ends by this point.

Mom had drifted away from the Charismatic meetings and was firmly entrenched in the traditional Catholic church again.

While I was in Lafayette, trying to decide what to do next, David called. The twins had their own band, Magic, and David had his own band. One day he called me.

"Hey, man, how ya' doing?" David asked in his usually friendly manner.

"Could be better," I said, somewhat despondent.

"Look, I've got a new band going and thought you might like to be my drummer."

With no prospects for another job and no real direction, I said, "Why not? Sounds good to me."

Back in the rock world, my life started sinking again. I began drinking and using downers, and I was especially weak when it came to women.

On my strong days, when the guys would go out after a gig partying with girls, I would stay home and read my Bible. If I was having a weak day, I'd end up with some girl again. I would even witness about Jesus to the girls I took to bed! I knew what I was doing was wrong, but I somehow consoled myself with the thought that God would forgive me.

The new guys in David's band would occasionally break out cocaine and heroin. I should have known better, but I tried both drugs. I used heroin only once or twice, sharing a needle with the other guys, and soon saw why people called it "the drug from hell." The high I got from heroin was an incredible body high, not a mind high. No wonder it's so addictive. I snorted coke a few times until I had a chilling experience with it.

One night after snorting cocaine I was unable to sleep. By the time dawn broke, I was still awake. As I listened to the birds singing and chirping, I heard the birds talking to each other, and they were talking about me!

Immediately, I started praying, "God help me!" It was a

desperate plea as much as it was a prayer! Birds talking?

I have to be losing my mind, I thought.

Then, I heard one bird say, "Shh!" while another bird proclaimed, "He is a servant of the Most High God!"

After this, the birds continued to chirp, ushering in a new day, but I heard no more voices. The nightmare ended, leaving me shaken, and I didn't use cocaine again.

One day in 1976, I got an unusual phone call. "Keith Thibodeaux?" the voice asked.

"Yes," I answered, somewhat cautiously.

"This is the producer of the 'Mike Douglas Show,' " the man said, and I immediately knew it had something to do with Little Ricky.

"Desi Arnaz has written his autobiography and will be appearing on Mike Douglas' talk show to promote the book," the producer continued. "Desi Jr. will also be on the show. We'd like to fly you to Philadelphia, where the show is taped, as a surprise for Desi."

"Sure," I agreed.

Afterward, I was terrified. I hadn't seen Desi since I'd returned to Louisiana. I'd last seen Desi Jr. seven years before during my brief summer trip to California.

Instead of anticipating some sort of cozy reunion with Desi Jr. and his dad, all the old feelings and the old pressure I had experienced as a child started to rise up in me again. It would be my first time on TV in years, my first time back in that world again.

It was as if I could hear Dad's voice still echoing in my brain: "Keith, I want you to do good!" The desire for acceptance, for esteem, all welled up in me again.

I talked David into flying up to Philadelphia with me. On the plane, a battle raged inside of me as my emotions churned in anticipation of this "reunion."

During the flight, I sat next to a sailor who was a Christian and confided my fears to him.

"Just keep your eyes on Jesus and you'll be all right," he advised.

His words calmed me down somewhat.

As the plane headed toward Philadelphia, David and I talked and got to know each other better during that trip.

That day I wasn't stoned, but David, who was heavily into drugs at that point, smoked pot in the limousine the show sent to pick us up from the airport.

When I arrived at the studio, I ran into Desi Jr. in the men's room, and we hugged each other warmly.

I didn't see Desi until they brought me onstage as part of their "surprise." Desi's hair was solid white, and he had aged a great deal.

When he saw me, I could tell he was shocked by the way I looked. Still skinny with long, wild hair, I wore a print, open-collared shirt and bell-bottom blue jeans.

To this day, I shudder to think about how I must have looked — not only to Desi but to the entire television audience.

For me it was a nightmare experience.

When Mike Douglas asked me where I was living, and I replied almost sarcastically, "I'm living in Dixie."

Although I tried to portray a Joe Cool image, I was so nervous I made stupid comments without thinking.

"I play drums in a rock band," I said, trying to act as if I had it all together.

I sensed Mike Douglas couldn't wait to get me off stage! Even Desi seemed embarrassed by my performance.

Everyone probably thought I was stoned even though I wasn't.

During the commercial, the producer said, "We need to make room for the next guest, so you can just slip off-stage now." I had the feeling he just wanted to get me out of there.

David stayed backstage in the Green Room, watching the show in disbelief.

Years later, he told me, "I wanted to run onstage and put my arms around you and tell you everything was all right." That's how pathetic I must have appeared.

The actor Barry Newman was also a guest on the same show, and I thought: *Man, this guy really thinks he's something!*

For some reason I had gotten the impression that everyone was looking down on me.

After the taping, we were standing in a hallway when Barry

walked by. He walked about 25 feet down the hall, abruptly turned around, came back, shook hands with me and said, "Good luck, man."

When he did that, I felt so guilty for the bad thoughts I'd had about him!

After the show, the four of us — Desi, Desi Jr., David, and I — stood around talking in a studio hallway.

Desi said, "We're taking a helicopter back to New York. Why don't you come along, and we'll all go out to dinner."

"Thanks. It's nice of you to offer," I said, "but we have a plane to catch."

In reality, I didn't want to go because I felt I had been such an embarrassment to Desi.

As we were leaving, Desi Jr. looked at me and said, "I love you, brother."

On our way back to the airport, David turned to me and said, "That's the first time I have ever heard a man say, 'I love you' to another guy. I can tell that Desi and Desi Jr. really care about you."

"Yeah, but I really messed up today," I said. "I was such a jerk." All I could see was that I had performed terribly and embarrassed myself and everyone else. I just wanted to get out of there and go home.

The summer of 1976, I was back living in Laurel with the band members. Feeling more lonely than ever, I started pleading with God for a wife. I really desired someone I could love and who would really love me. I thought marriage would bring stability to my life.

The band had a week booked at the Red Lobster Supper Club in Jackson, out by the Jackson Reservoir. This was no rock and roll joint but a nice supper club with an upper level, candlelit tables, and a dance floor in the middle of the room.

On the fourth of July night, I noticed two girls entering the club. One I knew was Patty Huff, a cousin of David's.

Wow! I thought. *Who is that with Patty?* Tall and slim, with long, straight, dark brown hair that streamed below her waist, she was the most beautiful girl I'd ever seen. During a break, I went over to their table and Patty introduced me. "Keith, this is my friend, Kathy Denton. I brought her to hear the band."

Looking into Kathy's beautiful face, I was suddenly aware that I was 26 years old, skinny, and had braces on my teeth.

"Kathy attends the University of Southern Mississippi," Patty continued, trying to fill the silence left by my awestruck behavior.

"Oh," I responded. "What are you studying?"

"I take dance and theater classes," Kathy replied sweetly.

"She's a ballet dancer," Patty explained. "In fact, she's the star of Ballet Mississippi."

I didn't know what to say, so I got straight to the point.

"You probably have a boyfriend, don't you?" I asked bluntly.

"No," Kathy replied in a quiet voice.

I later learned she had recently broken up with a longtime boyfriend, a Joe College sort of guy she had dated for five years.

Although she was quiet, Kathy was friendly and easy to talk to. At 19 she had an assurance about her that I found very attractive.

I guess I wasn't the only one because I soon learned that all the guys in the band wanted to go out with her.

Later, I learned that David told her, "Don't get involved with Keith. He's too moody."

But I was determined to date her.

A few nights later, Kathy came back to the club, this time with a date. As she danced in front of the band with this guy, an incredible jealously overtook me. I hardly even knew her yet, but here I was, feeling all this jealousy because she had a date with someone else!

One evening, as I was sitting on a couch in the club's foyer, feeling very alone, Kathy walked in. When she saw me, she immediately sat down next to me and asked, "What's wrong?"

I mumbled some answer, and we continued to talk for a while.

Then, mustering up my courage, I asked," Will you go out with me?"

Evidently she saw something in me, something beyond the braces, the wild hair, and the moodiness, because she very sweetly said, "Yes."

There was a strong attraction between us from the beginning of our relationship, and the first time I kissed Kathy, I knew she was the girl for me.

One of four sisters, Kathy comes from a very proper, middle-class family. Her youngest sister, Amy, at 16 was killed in a car accident the same summer that Kathy and I met.

One night, Kathy brought her mother, who was divorced from her father, down to the club to meet me. I probably was not her first choice for her daughter, but we got along.

Her father, who was a little on the gruff side, seemed to have the attitude that nobody was good enough for his little girl, especially some musician!

I guess we did seem like the proverbial odd couple: a struggling, still-confused young musician and a star ballet dancer from a conservative, rather sheltered home.

David later told me, "I thought Kathy and you were mismatched at first, but after being around you for awhile I could see that you were actually a perfect match."

We were definitely opposites, but opposites attract, and besides, both of us were artists, Kathy in dance and me in music.

Fortunately, Kathy did not have an artist's temperament. The moodiness I experienced is somewhat typical for artistic personalities, but Kathy was and is the sweetest girl I have ever known. That's not just my opinion, but the opinion of everyone who knows her.

A former manager of Ballet Mississippi once told a newspaper reporter, "Kathy has none of the temperament you associate with a ballerina. The other girls love her. There's no jealousy because she's such a lovely person."

A ballet dancer since age eight, Kathy was asked to join the Jackson Ballet at nine, making her the youngest dancer in the company. As a champion swimmer in high school who held the state record for the butterfly stroke, Kathy had also considered a career as a competitive swimmer. Ballet always took priority, however, and was her great love. She danced all through her high school years, and by age 19 was performing as the principal dancer with Ballet Mississippi.

One reviewer said Kathy was "born to dance" and I agree. Even though I found her easy to talk to when we first met, sometimes she finds it difficult to express everything that she feels inside. Through dance, what's inside of Kathy clearly shows through, in her facial expressions, her movements, and even her spirit and soul.

Kathy had been raised in the Methodist church and went to church every Sunday as a child, but by the time we met she was no longer going to church. She knew about God, but she didn't know Him. She believed in God, but that was about the extent of any religious faith on her part.

We began dating, and I started talking to her about the Lord. I'm sure it seemed a little odd to Kathy because I certainly wasn't living an exemplary Christian life! My life wasn't settled yet. I was still drinking and having emotional battles.

One night when the band was playing at a club in Laurel, I was drinking so much that I couldn't even continue playing. Kathy was with me that night. "I'll drive you home, Keith," she offered in her usual sweet way.

As we were getting into the car, a policeman stopped me. "Thibodeaux, you're under arrest for public drunkenness," he announced. "Please get in the car with me."

"Let go of me!" I screamed angrily, as they handcuffed me and stuffed me in the back of the patrol car.

Poor Kathy didn't know what to do; when we got to the station, I fought back. Three cops had to hold me as I walked up the stairs to jail. Then one of them, a big, bruiser type of guy, hit me in the ribs.

When I was placed in a cell at the jail it was dark, and I couldn't see very well, plus I was very drunk. I sat down on a single bed with a bare mattress without sheets and just cried out to the Lord. I prayed aloud.

"I'm so sorry, Lord. I know I shouldn't be living like this," I said, sobbing into my hands.

The next morning, a more sympathetic policeman was on duty. He came by and stopped, peering at me through the bars of the cell. "Keith, you ought not to be in here at all. You're not the type of person who should be in here," he said.

"I know," I answered quietly.

That morning David came down to the jail and bailed me out.

I knew I had to do something to straighten out my life. Even though I wasn't living as a Christian should live, I still had a heart toward God.

I kept talking to Kathy about the Lord, but when I talked about topics like the baptism in the Holy Spirit and knowing Jesus as a real person, she didn't really understand. But she knew there was more to God than what she had learned in church.

I loved Kathy, and I wanted to marry her. But I had to be sure that marriage was what God wanted.

One night I told Kathy, "Let's ask God whether we should get married or not."

Kathy later told me she thought, *Me, married at 19?*

When she met me, her previous five-year romance had just ended; in fact, the guy kept calling until I finally told him one day, "Hey, we're going to get married so leave her alone!"

I knew Kathy loved me, so despite any misgivings or doubts she may have had, she agreed to pray with me.

As we held hands and bowed our heads together, I sensed the presence of the Holy Spirit in that room as we asked God for His direction. "Lord," I prayed, "You make the decision for us. We just want Your will."

We had a Living Bible, a paraphrased version of the Scriptures, and we decided to close our eyes, open the Bible, and let it speak God's answer to us.

Kathy took the Bible, put it in her lap, and we closed our eyes and prayed again. Kathy opened her eyes, and opened the Bible, reading where it had fallen open, from the Book of Ruth: "It is I, Ruth. Make me your wife according to God's holy law."

We stared at each other, amazed.

Looking back, it was like playing Russian roulette, but I believe that God once again was having mercy on us, directing us through His Word despite our naiveté and ignorance! God honored our childlike faith. We had asked God for an answer, and He had given it.

We eloped that night and were married by a justice of the peace on October 26, 1976, after a whirlwind three-month courtship. Finally, I had someone I truly loved and someone who truly loved me. Maybe now I could really start living, with God's help and with Kathy's love.

13

Gone with the Wind

When Kathy's parents learned of our marriage, I suspect they weren't pleased but the deed was done. They pressured us to "marry again," in a formal ceremony to sort of solemnize our marriage, and so all our relatives could be there.

We agreed, and on November 15, 1976, went through another wedding ceremony at Kathy's grandmother's condo. My parents came to the second ceremony, as did Kathy's, plus a bunch of aunts, uncles, and other relatives. But to this day, we celebrate our elopement date of October 26 as our anniversary.

We moved into a small, furnished trailer out in the country in Laurel, Mississippi, to begin our married life. Kathy had dropped out of college and found work teaching ballet classes at a new ballet school that had just opened in Laurel. We didn't have a honeymoon because I immediately had to go back on the road with the band.

Proverbs 18:22 says, "The man who finds a wife finds a good thing; she is a blessing to him from the Lord" (TLB).

I had definitely found a blessing and a good thing when God gave me Kathy, but I had totally unrealistic expectations about marriage. I loved Kathy very much, but I had this fantasy idea of a home life and being married and having the ideal wife.

Kathy quickly learned that she had married someone who was moody and unstable. I was not an easy person to live with. Kathy says that when I was sweet, I was really sweet, but when I was mean, I was really mean!

My extreme jealousy forced me to discourage her from

coming to the clubs where I played. I knew how I had lived, and I knew what it was like in the rock world. I knew the guys at the clubs were like sharks circling their prey! Because she was so beautiful I knew the guys there would be hitting on her. Deep down, I guess I was afraid Kathy would meet someone else and leave me.

One night we were playing in some club, and Kathy was sitting at a table near the stage, watching the band. A guy came up to her and started whispering something in her ear. From my spot onstage behind my drum kit, I could tell he was drunk. As soon as the number was over, I raced to the table, grabbed the guy by the hair on his head, and started shaking him.

"What are you doing?" I screamed at the guy. "Don't you ever talk to my wife like that!"

I was yelling at the top of my lungs, and everything in the club just seemed to slow to a standstill.

"Where are you from?" I yelled.

"Iran," he replied, looking as if he just wanted to get away from me as fast as possible. The poor guy may have been drunk, but he didn't want to deal with a crazy man!

"Then why don't you just go back to Iran?" I screamed.

I continued shaking him, and everyone was watching us. He was bigger than me, but I didn't care. He had a terrified look on his face because I was so mad. Finally, I let him go, and he got out of there quickly.

That night Kathy and I checked into a local Holiday Inn, but I couldn't sleep, thinking about how I had overreacted.

"I'm sorry, honey," I said, apologizing to Kathy. "I should never have acted like that. Can you ever forgive me?"

It seemed I was still doing things that I felt bad about afterwards.

One night I wanted to call Desi Jr. and decided to take some Quaaludes because they seemed to loosen my tongue and help me talk easier.

"What do you think about me coming out to California and us starting a band?" I asked Desi Jr. over the phone.

"Sure, yeah, let's talk about it," Desi said.

Desi's acting career was going pretty well at that point, and

I'm sure he was just humoring me. But I felt as if I had to get away to straighten out my life.

I called my Uncle Irvin, Mom's brother, and his wife Lil, who lived in Orange County, and arranged for us to stay with them. Kathy and I packed our bags and headed for California.

We met with Desi Jr. in Beverly Hills and later visited him at his home. Dorothy Hamill, the figure skater who was Dino Martin's girlfriend at the time, and later his wife, was there, along with Billy Hinsche, who used to be in Dino, Desi, and Billy. At the time, Billy was playing with the Beach Boys and had just come off the road from an extensive tour with the group. He was sleeping in a downstairs bedroom.

We went over to Hamburger Hamlet, and Desi Jr.'s manager met us there. He told me if I'd get rid of my braces and take some acting classes he could get me into the movies, but I had no interest in acting. Desi Jr. was getting ready to leave town to film a movie called *The Wedding* in Chicago, and any ideas I had of starting a band kind of fizzled out from there.

After Desi Jr. left for Chicago, Tony Martin Jr., the son of Cyd Charrese and Tony Martin, called me one day. Tony, who was one of Desi Jr.'s good friends, told me Desi Jr. liked me and didn't want to hurt me, but Tony said I shouldn't call Desi Jr. anymore to try to pursue my idea of a music group because Desi Jr. was too busy.

I was really upset by Tony's call and thought: *Okay, if that's the way Desi feels, so be it!* I didn't call Desi Jr. again while we were in California.

So far our move to the west coast was not going as I had anticipated.

Kathy and I stayed in our room at my uncle's house for hours at a time. Although she was going to ballet classes and staying in shape, Kathy wasn't really pursuing her ballet career while we were in California.

But God was orchestrating things and events to move us to the place we needed to be in life. Our trip to the west coast had stretched into months, and by this time it was 1977.

During our time in California, I started watching the "700 Club" on television. For the first time, I saw something called "contemporary Christian music."

I watched various musicians singing praises to the Lord and thought: *Wouldn't it be neat to play music for the Lord?*

Contemporary Christian music was in its infancy, and I was fascinated by it. It was like the idea I had in 1974, when I'd urged David to play rock music with godly lyrics!

Watching the "700 Club" also helped to solidify my faith and became an oasis during a very dry time in my spiritual life. Pat Robertson talked about how you can't say you are a Christian and then live in sin, which really related to me!

Away from the club scene, with my Bible and my new wife, I felt optimistic for the first time in a long time, despite the fact that things were not turning out as I had hoped.

One day Kathy and I went to see a band called Starbuck that was playing at Magic Mountain. The group had a big hit with a song called "Moonlight (Feels Right)."

Bo Wagner, a musician I had known from other bands was playing with the group at the time. "Hey, man, how ya' doing?" Bo asked as soon as he saw me.

"Okay," I answered nonchalantly.

"Still playing drums?" he asked.

"Not right now," I answered. "I'm just kicking around."

"You know, our group is looking for a drummer," he said.

"Oh, yeah?" I replied with only vague interest. But I did give Bo my phone number.

Within a few days, the group's manager called and offered me the job. "But you'll have to be in Atlanta as soon as possible so you can start rehearsing with the group," he said.

I went to Starbuck's management office in Beverly Hills for a $200 advance to get Kathy and me to Atlanta. We had been in California about seven months when we finally left my uncle's home and headed east again.

We headed for Atlanta with high hopes, but they were soon dashed. I didn't get along with the keyboard player for some reason, and after only a few weeks the band leader told me, "Things just aren't working out," and dismissed me.

It was the first and only time I had ever been fired from a music job, and my pride was deeply wounded.

I told the band, "You guys will be sorry!" as I left the rehearsal studio.

Kathy cried and was very upset when I came home and told her the news. She was young, a new bride, and had married this guy who was dragging her across the country! She probably wondered what she had gotten herself into by marrying me.

Despite the fact that I'd been fired, I knew God was working on our behalf.

Starbuck was scheduled to play at a big upcoming music festival with Elvin Bishop. After I left, that was their last major performance. Starbuck seemed to fade from the whole music scene after that.

Kathy and I went back to Jackson and moved in with her mother until we could get a place of our own. Kathy's dad suggested that I go back to school, which seemed to be a good idea to me, so I enrolled at Hinds Junior College in Jackson. I did pretty well in junior college, maintaining a 3.0 average in the business classes I was taking.

At the same time, I started playing in little jazz clubs on the weekends and doing studio session work at North American Recording Studio.

As 1978 turned into 1979, Kathy had started dancing with the ballet again, and we soon moved to our own place. We had a bed propped up on bricks for a frame for the mattress to rest on, and all black furniture.

We got a shetland sheep dog and named her Honey and spent some great times just walking Honey in a field near a school in Jackson. She was a really neat dog; whenever we took her for a walk, she'd run around us in circles, trying to "herd" us like sheep!

I was completely off drugs by then, although I still wasn't really growing spiritually.

I hadn't seen David, Rayburn, and Clayborn for awhile, but gradually word reached me that all the Huff brothers had committed their lives to Christ, and bit by bit, I learned what had happened to them.

Shortly before I met Kathy and got married, David and I had to drive back to Laurel one night after a gig we were playing at the

Sheraton Hotel in Jackson for Mississippi State University. On the hour and a half drive to Laurel, I talked to David about Jesus the whole way. Even though I wasn't living a sold-out life myself, David listened to me, and the Word of God started to take effect in his life. I left a Bible in his room, and he started reading it.

We played another gig at the University of Alabama at Auburn, and once again, David and I talked about Jesus in the car all the way there and all the way back.

David continued to have problems in his life, including car wrecks and being busted for marijuana possession, but he also kept reading the Bible after Kathy and I moved to California.

One day he told Rayborn, "There's more to the Bible than what man has told us."

At first Rayborn didn't think much about what David had said, but soon he was reading the Bible, and Clayborn started reading it, too.

Clayborn was living with a girl named Mandy at the time.

One day when Clayborn came into a room where Rayborn was reading his Bible, Rayborn told him, "I've been reading in the Bible that what you're doing is wrong. Did you know you are living in sin with Mandy?"

I had planted a seed in their hearts back in 1974, and through reading the Bible for themselves, the twins both came to the Lord.

The next day, the twins tried to convert Mandy, but it wasn't to be, and she eventually moved out.

Later she wrote the boys a poem, which said, "There was a river which all three of us were crossing, and Rayborn and Clayborn made it across, but the current was too strong for me and it carried me away." She moved to New Orleans, married, had a child, and died at age 27.

The twins were still playing in their band, Magic, but decided to leave, concluding that it would be very hard to serve God while playing in a rock band. They lived in their Volkswagen van for awhile until David invited them to share his apartment, where they started having home Bible studies.

Rayborn and Clayborn spent a lot of time talking to David about Jesus.

Through the twins, David was introduced to a Christian man

named Brother Windham, who point-blank asked him, "David, do you want to be saved or not?"

That one question stopped David in his tracks, and he accepted the Lord. David later wrote a song about this experience called "In My Father's House."

No longer interested in playing secular music, David quit his rock band and planned to teach guitar lessons to earn a living.

Without a steady income, all three brothers found themselves really living by faith! They didn't play music for a time, but the pastor of the church they had been attending encouraged them to use their musical gifts for the glory of God. Skeptical at first, David didn't think churches would accept the kind of contemporary Christian music he wanted to play.

In fact, he once told a reporter, "I thought if we sang like Willie Nelson and put Jesus in the words we'd be accepted, but I could not conceive that God could use rock music!"

Eventually the Huff brothers started singing and playing music in churches, and in 1977, they recorded their first contemporary Christian album, *Song of Songs,* a custom album that they self-produced and put out on their own Song of Songs label. A second custom album, *This One's for You,* was released in 1978, and a third, *Step in My Shoes,* came out in 1979.

I was happy to hear about what had happened to the Huff brothers since I had witnessed to all of them.

David called me in Jackson one day to tell me about what was happening with this new, Christian version of David and the Giants, the band that had kept their old name but was now filled with recreated people.

"Keith, God is really blessing us! We're playing at churches and seeing people come to the Lord, but we believe God wants to bring us into some big places," David told me. "We'd like you to be part of it."

At first I put them off. I had dropped out of college because I had the opportunity to work six nights a week, playing in a disco band at a local club. Kathy was pregnant with our first child, and I needed to work full-time. She was still dancing in the ballet; in fact, she only missed 10 days of dancing because of her pregnancy, which was an easy one. She gained very little weight and never looked very pregnant. In fact, she never even had to wear maternity clothes.

Despite my joy at upcoming fatherhood, doing secular music was wearing me down fast. In spite of the fact that it was a secure job, I was starting to hate every minute of it. The words to the songs the band played were so sexually suggestive.

I would be playing, supplying the rhythm for the group, and think: *What am I doing? This isn't godly!*

During breaks, I would read the Bible in my dressing room and witness about Jesus to the other guys in the band.

In late 1978, I had finally been baptized in the name of the Lord. As I came up out of the water I felt that I was truly a new man. The world even looked new to me.

Yet here I was, still playing with a disco band! What was I doing?

David was giving me the opportunity I had dreamed of for so long: the chance to play Christian music with a Christian band!

"Is your offer to join the Christian band still open?" I asked David.

"Brother, we were praying you would call this week because if you didn't call this week, we were going to go ahead and get another drummer," David said.

The band didn't have a drummer until I joined them. They started with Rayborn on two keyboards, Clayborn on bass guitar, and David on lead guitar and lead vocals.

As we talked, I became more and more excited about finally being able to play music for God. No longer would I have to feel guilty about the environment where I worked or the songs I had to play.

Contemporary Christian music in 1979 was still a fledgling enterprise, and David and the Giants were pioneers in the genre, especially in the south. The church was still resistant to rock music, and David spent a lot of time defending their musical ministry and explaining why it could be effective to people who were skeptical.

In an effort to be more acceptable to church audiences, the twins had to cut their hair that had once reached halfway down their back! When I joined the group, my hair was still on the long side.

One day on the way to the first church date I played with them, the guys told me, "You gotta get a haircut."

"Maybe tomorrow," I said.

"No, now," David said and got out his scissors.

None of us will ever forget that haircut, especially me, because David also cut my ear!

It didn't take long for me to realize playing and traveling with a contemporary Christian music group was much different from drumming with a rock and roll band in nightclubs! For one thing, all of us had totally changed. Rayborn, Clayborn, and David were totally different people.

Rayborn and Clayborn had been real womanizers in our rock days, and they had totally forsaken that sort of life. Their hearts had been totally transformed, and we all tried to live in a way that was pleasing to the Lord.

Some of the early days as a Christian rock band were incredible, to say the least! The mega-success of some of today's top Christian artists would not have been possible without musicians who were really pioneers in contemporary Christian music.

Most churches would not let the band use our lights in the early days. They thought a lot of lights was somehow "worldly."

There were no big bucks in the world of Christian music in those days. At first we usually played for "love offerings," a free-will donation offering given to us by churches. Later we did suggest fees to our sponsors in order to cover travel expenses and support the band members and our families. Most of the early Christian bands were motivated by a desire to minister in a musical medium that young people understood; no one thought about Christian music in terms of a "career" in those days.

My only desire was to play music for God. In fact, most of the first Christian musicians, like Larry Norman, DeGarmo and Key, or Petra, had the same motivation.

David and the Giants played mostly in southern states, and some people still had a resistance to gospel music with a pop beat.

Once a minister came with a group of people he had brought to our concert. In the middle of our concert, he stood up, looked around so everyone could see him, and promptly ushered his people out in what appeared to be a public protest of our music!

Our music back then was a real light, pop/rock style, not a heavy sort of music at all, but to some church people it was obviously offensive! We understood that this minister was just trying to protect his flock, so we took his departure with a grain of salt. Despite such early barriers, most people seemed to accept our brand of Christian music.

In the beginning, I didn't want to make a big deal out of my Little Ricky fame because I felt my drumming and our musical ministry should stand on its own. I didn't want to use it to try to promote myself or the band.

That August I learned that Vivian Vance, who played Ethel Mertz on "I Love Lucy," had died from cancer, and I was deeply saddened. But the world of "I Love Lucy" now seemed far removed from my life.

From the earliest days of my life, music and drumming had been my life, but now my motivation was different. In the rock world, all of us had dreams of stardom; now we just wanted to glorify God and share His love with people through our music.

The ministry aspect of doing Christian music was gratifying. For me, it was refreshing to be able to play music with the ability to help change peoples' lives and lead them to Jesus! We played mostly church dates in the beginning and started to see hundreds of people come to the Lord.

For me, the hardest part was being on the road and away from Kathy, especially when her delivery date drew near.

The morning of April 8, 1979, Kathy awakened me with the news that she thought it "was time." I rushed her to the hospital at eight in the morning, only to wait all day for the baby's birth. Kathy had an easy pregnancy but a hard labor.

The baby's head was not in the right position.

The doctor told us, "If things don't change, I will have to deliver the baby by cesarean section."

It was almost ten o'clock at night, and Kathy had been in labor all day. I left Kathy and went to a nearby bathroom, praying for God's intervention. When the doctor returned and checked Kathy again, the baby had turned!

Kathy was able to have a normal delivery, and I was able to be in the delivery room when our beautiful daughter Tara made her appearance, all six pounds of her. As I saw the miracle of a life coming into the world, a new life on the planet that God had given us the care and responsibility of, I suddenly realized that Tara wasn't really ours. We were just taking care of her for the Lord, and I realized what an awesome responsibility that was!

The name Tara came from Kathy's love of *Gone with the Wind,* but the name also means "high tower." I wanted her middle name to be Kristen because it means "follower of Christ," and more than anything, I wanted my child to follow Christ!

Now I had another person to think about in my family, and it made me look at life more seriously. I resolved to be the best parent I could be and made up my mind not to push anything on Tara, as acting and the entertainment business had been pushed on me as a child.

Becoming a good parent was a learning process for me. I always felt I had to be a strict disciplinarian like Dad, because he was my only role model of what a father should be. But slowly I was able to learn how to be the right kind of parent.

Kathy had grown up in a family much different than mine, and parenting came instinctively to her. Kathy had most of the responsibility for Tara during our daughter's early days because a month after her birth, I was back on the road with David and the Giants.

Ten days after Tara's birth, Kathy was dancing again. Kathy's grandmother kept the baby while Kathy rehearsed, dancing from ten in the morning until two or three in the afternoon. Her ballet performances were held in Jackson, so she was busy with her career while I was out on the road with the band. Her parents, Mary and Bo, and Kathy's grandmother, Honey, helped a lot, which gave me a sense of relief about having to leave my little family.

God had been working in both of our lives to draw us closer to Him. We had been visiting various churches but still did not have a church home for our family. It was even harder to find a church now that I was out with the band. It wasn't unusual for me to be gone 40 days in a row before I was able to come home again.

Kathy had been drawn to God for a long time, but she did not commit her life to the Lord until July of 1979 — at a David and the Giants concert.

The band was playing that night at a little Pentecostal church, and Kathy saw people there who really loved the Lord and thought: *That's what I want.*

Throughout the concert that evening, Kathy found herself being touched by the message of Jesus that was in our music. When the time came for an invitation to be given for people who wanted to give their lives to Jesus to come forward, Kathy was at the front of the church!

She told me later, "All I knew that night was that I wanted the Lord in my life!"

The counselor who prayed with her at the altar that evening told her, "Just start praising God and thanking Him."

Kathy actually fell down under the power of the Holy Spirit — the same way my brother and I had at the Catholic Charismatic meeting. Christians refer to this spiritual state as "being slain in the Spirit."

Kathy and I had been baptized within weeks of each other, but that night we became truly one in the Lord.

Everything I had ever dreamed of was finally coming together in my life. Our times of separation were hard, but Kathy understood the importance of the band's ministry, having been a recipient of it herself! God showed both of us that being in the band was what God wanted for my life, and slowly God brought us even closer as husband and wife. We became best friends as well as lovers, and now we had true spiritual unity.

The band was like a church on the road for me, and I started growing spiritually. My problems with alcohol, drugs, and all the things that had plagued me for so long were over. Surrounded by a group of guys whose lives had been changed by the power of God, we encouraged and lifted each other up, developing a love for each other that far surpassed any sort of camaraderie we had in our past life.

That's just what it was like: a past life. None of us recognized ourselves from that time in our lives because all of us were so different.

I don't know why it took me so long from that first experience with the Lord to settle down in my faith and totally give up the various sins that hounded me after my initial 1974 acceptance of Jesus Christ. The emotional and psychological problems I had were great, and they were compounded by drugs, alcohol, and the whole lifestyle that I was enmeshed in for so long.

David, Rayburn, and Clayborn wisely quit rock music shortly after their experiences with the Lord, and they had each other and a local church to strengthen them in their new walk with God.

I now believe that my main problem was lack of Christian fellowship. Had I been able to totally stay away from the rock world and its temptations, found a good church home, and a body of believers who could have supported and encouraged me as I struggled, I believe the odyssey I endured would have been much, much shorter.

There were big changes in Kathy's life, too, not just in our marriage, but in Kathy as a person.

As I said, Kathy was "born to dance," but this became even more evident after she gave her heart to Jesus.

Kathy once told a reporter, "I love to dance because it is the best way for me to share my faith. I'm not good at talking to people, but when I'm dancing, I can use my whole body and soul in worship."

After giving her life to Christ, Kathy began to see dance as a way to express worship and praise to God, even though she was still dancing with Ballet Mississippi. God gave her a greater joy in her dancing, and her motivation for dancing began to manifest itself in performances. An actual radiance seemed to come from Kathy's face as she danced.

She was not very vocal about what had happened to her, but other people noticed the change and started asking her about it. Kathy always found it difficult to express herself, preferring to let her dancing do that for her. Now her Christianity began to emerge in her dancing, and it was very noticeable.

People often could not put their finger on what was "different" about Kathy Thibodeaux, but to Kathy it was very simple: The reality of Jesus had changed her life.

My lovely wife, Kathy, with our daughter Tara at age 3.

14

Changing Course

Being in the band allowed me to solidify not just my own personal Christian faith, but my purpose and goals in life.

The past held me in chains for a long time. Finally I came to the point where I could either make those chains last forever or have them broken by obeying God and doing what was right.

Although I put my sinful ways behind me, one area of my life remained unsettled: my relationship with my dad.

I hated him for many, many years, blaming him for our family breakup, for what Mom and us kids had to go through, and for abandoning me.

Not long after I accepted Christ into my life, I tried to talk to Dad about Jesus.

At first Dad thought I was just going through another phase in my turbulent life.

"You'll wear outta' that!" he told me.

When I tried to explain to him what the Bible says about salvation, we would always end up in an argument. Dad, who to this day has remained in the Catholic church, refused to budge.

Still, the bitterness that I felt at times was overwhelming. Each time I thought about Dad, the old pain would well up inside of me, dredging up the same old anger and bitterness that I had carried for so long.

One night I was at home, thinking about Dad and all that had happened, when the love God had for me just seemed to overwhelm my heart. Suddenly, I realized that I no longer had bad feelings toward my father. I was surprised to find myself feeling compassion for him.

I thought, *Surely if God can forgive me for all I have done, I can forgive Dad!*

I had not seen Dad for several years. At the time he was living in Baton Rouge with Connie; they had one son, and she was pregnant with another child. I called Mom in Lafayette and asked for Dad's phone number.

Then I called Dad and asked if I could come to see him.

The next day I drove to Baton Rouge alone. I had not seen Connie since my days in California and wondered how I would react to seeing her and my half-brother. They were living in an apartment at the time, and as I walked up to their place and knocked on the door, for just a moment I felt some hesitancy.

Dad came to the door, breaking into a wide grin when he saw me.

He grabbed me and hugged me, calling out to his wife, "Connie! Keith's here!"

Even though I knew I was supposed to be there, it continued to surprise me that I no longer felt anger toward Dad.

Connie came out to the foyer, and I sensed she was approaching me a little tentatively, probably wondering how I would treat her. But she hugged me and accepted me as Dad's son.

My half-brother, little Tate, was about six years old at the time, and he ran out and greeted me, treating me like I was his big brother. The whole situation disarmed me, and I suddenly realized I had wasted so much time by not forgiving Dad!

All of us went into the living room, and I began to share with Dad how I had come to know Christ as my Saviour.

"God has forgiven me of all kinds of things. I've been holding things against you, because of Mom, the divorce, and all that," I told him slowly, choosing my words carefully. "I just wanted to tell you in person that I love you and I forgive you, and God can forgive you, too."

"I know that God can forgive me, Keith," Dad said. "I'm happy for you. I'm happy that you've found God. This is the best thing that's ever happened to you, Keith."

I don't think Dad really understood until several years later what had actually happened in my life. As for me, I felt relieved after our visit, knowing I had obeyed the Lord. It was as if a burden had been lifted from my shoulders.

Only by God's grace was I able to let go of the anger and bitterness that had tortured me for so long; for years the memories were just too painful.

The ability to forgive Dad was supernatural. I could not have done it through my own strength alone, but, with the help of the Holy Spirit, I found there is great freedom in forgiveness.

In the years to come, Dad and I were able to actually talk together and enjoy each other's company. I also got to know Connie and my half-brothers, Tate and Todd.

Although my relationship with Mom and my siblings was strengthened as well, the healing of my relationship with Dad was probably the biggest miracle resulting from my life being changed by God.

Dad wasn't the only member of my family to learn about my new faith in Christ. In fact, I was constantly telling my younger brothers, Dwight and Brian, about what God could do in their lives.

Baptized as an infant in the Catholic church, I felt I had missed the experience of being buried in baptism with Christ and raised to walk in newness of life. That is why I had been baptized again by immersion in water after my commitment to Christ.

"The Bible says we are to be baptized in the name of the Lord Jesus Christ for the remission of sins," I explained to my brothers. "The church in the Book of Acts was very different from the organized monstrosity that is often called the church today!"

When they said they'd like to be baptized, I said excitedly, "Well, come on! I'll baptize you right now!"

"Don't we need a priest?" Dwight asked.

"No. In the Bible, Christians can baptize other people who accept Christ. We don't have to have a priest to do it," I explained.

That answer seemed to satisfy them, and they agreed. Upon their profession of faith in Jesus Christ, I baptized Dwight and Brian at Mom's house in Lafayette in the bathtub!

As a member of David and the Giants, I felt as if a new world had opened up for me. Music is a powerful force that has the ability to carry a message and move people to action, I watched in amazement at how God used the band to change lives. The importance of the band's ministry became more and more evident.

In 1979, our group was invited to England.

The sponsors who arranged our England tour set up a big tent in a park in Oxford with the idea of using our music to attract people who wouldn't set foot in a church.

As we began to play, a crowd of sneering punk rockers, drawn by the music, gathered by the tent. Punk rock music was big then in England, and punk rockers were a pretty rowdy bunch!

From the stage I could see these young people, dressed in black leather, with their noses pierced through with tiny rings, swaying to the music. Many of them had dyed their hair pink and orange, with part of their head shaved.

As they began listening to the lyrics, they realized we were playing godly music.

Suddenly, they began cursing and shouting, "Hey what is this? We don't want that Jesus stuff!"

Picking up rocks, they started throwing them into the tent, knocking down microphones and screaming loudly, "We're going to burn this place down!"

Chaos erupted!

Finally, some of the local Christians in the crowd chased them off. As the punks ran away, they continued to scream threats of burning the place down.

The next day, as we were riding in a van on the way to the meetings, I thought, *This is real spiritual warfare. We're getting a taste of what the Tribulation period will be like.*

That night, the punkers didn't show up, which was a relief.

The following night, they were back again, standing outside the tent.

We played in the tent meetings for 12 days, and each day when we'd go on stage, I'd think, *Oh, boy, here we go again!*

Each day the punk rockers would appear, yelling, chanting, harassing, and threatening us. The spirit of the Lord was drawing them there, and some of them were listening to the lyrics of our songs. As my eyes scanned the crowd, I noticed that a few of them actually had a humble look on their faces!

Surely ,God has done a miracle! I thought.

One night, when we gave an invitation to accept Jesus Christ at the end of our concert, one of the punk rockers walked down to the front of the tent.

"I want to know this Jesus you keep talking about," he said.

We learned the punker's name was Steve. As we prayed with him, suddenly he began lifting his hands in praise to God.

The whole attitude of the other punk rockers began to change after that. By the end of the series of meetings, most had tears in their eyes.

After the last meeting, we led a motorcycle caravan down to the Thames River for a mass nighttime baptism! The punk rockers parked their motorcycles on the river bank and shone their headlights on the water so the baptisms could be done at night.

As I watched the crowd of punk rockers gather to give their lives to Jesus and be baptized, again I was awestruck by how God was using our music!

Sometime during the week, Steve, our first punk rock convert, went home and told his parents what had happened to him.

"Are these people in the Catholic church, or the Church of England?" his parents asked.

"No . . . they're just Christians, believers in Jesus," Steve replied.

"Well, those are the only churches we recognize," his parents said. "We forbid you to go to any more of those meetings!"

As he told me this I shook my head in wonder. These kids were incorrigibles, and I could not understand how his parents could be against something so good happening to their son just because our group was not part of the "official" church.

A friend of Steve's came and told us about what had happened and through him we learned Steve had become so despondent he was actually threatening to drown himself.

Immediately, Rayborn went looking for Steve and was able to talk him out of committing suicide.

After we returned from England and continued our concerts in the states, the work we were doing did not go unnoticed back home.

In December 1979, the then-governor of Mississippi, Gov. Cliff Finch, sent a letter proclaiming the band and me "Goodwill

Ambassadors for Cliff Finch and the State of Mississippi." Along with the letter came a certificate from the State of Mississippi Executive Department, signed by the governor, and officially naming me as a "Goodwill Ambassador."

What a change God had made in my life!

At the end of the year, we received an invitation to attend Desi Jr.'s wedding to actress Linda Purl. The ceremony was to be held on January 13, 1980, at the Stephen S. Wise Temple in Bel Air, with a reception afterwards at the Bistro Hotel in Beverly Hills.

Not long after we received the invitation, Desi Jr. called me. "Keith, I'd love for you to come to my wedding because you've been such a big part of my life," he said.

"I'd love to come," I said.

At the time, I had a break from playing with David and the Giants. Besides, I hadn't seen Desi Jr. since Kathy and I had left California, so we decided to attend.

The wedding was held at a synagogue because Desi Jr. and Linda had a singing teacher who was a cantor at the temple. A minister officiated at the non-denominational ceremony, with vows composed by Desi Jr. and Linda. It was truly a memorable day, with about 250 people in attendance.

Of course, Desi and Lucy were at the wedding with their spouses, and I talked with them briefly. I had not seen Desi since my disastrous appearance on the "Mike Douglas Show" four years earlier, but he was as warm and friendly as ever. I had no way of knowing it would be the last time I would ever see Desi.

At the reception, Kathy and I sat at a table with my old friend Danny Sauer and his wife, Marion, and Lucie's ex-husband, Phil Vandervort.

Although Phil and Lucie were divorced and he had remarried, they remained friends. Phil always called Lucie "Desiree," which is her middle name. The June after Desi's wedding, Lucie married Laurence Luckinbill, an actor 17 years her senior.

The wedding was a special time of renewing old friendships and celebrating Desi Jr.'s marriage. Who would have thought that within two years of that happy day in Desi Jr.'s life, he would check himself into a hospital rehab center to battle drug and alcohol dependency. His marriage later ended in divorce.

I continued to pray for him and for the entire Arnaz family.

Another wedding took place in 1980 when David Huff married a wonderful Christian girl named Twyla. David had been divorced from his first wife for many years when he met Twyla.

After David accepted Christ, he originally planned not to remarry at all. He had been divorced for many years, and his first wife had married again some time ago. Some people had told David that, because he had been divorced before he found Christ, marriage was now not an option for him.

Slowly over the years, as he sought God in prayer and read the Bible, David came to believe that just as God had forgiven him of all his other sins, God could forgive for the sin of divorce.

One evening at a David and the Giants concert, a mutual friend introduced Twyla to David. She was very shy and would never have approached David on her own!

As in every other area of life, David prayed about whether he should marry Twyla. Finally, during an intense prayer session one night, where David was seeking guidance about both his music and his life, he sensed God speaking to him: "David, keep on singing My songs."

When he asked God about Twyla, the answer he sensed was simply: "Marry her."

Twyla brought much happiness to David's life, and together they went on to have two children. To me, it was yet another example of Christ as a redeemer of broken lives!

As a group, David and the Giants did not pursue our ministry as a career but just tried to seek God's leading and direction for our music. We didn't seek a recording contract; we sought the kingdom of God. The band's albums through 1981 were self-produced, custom albums on the Song of Songs label.

We did *Almost Midnight* in 1980 and *Heaven or Hell* in 1981 before being approached by a major label, Priority Records.

A new Christian label developed by CBS Records, Priority was designed to penetrate the growing Christian music market. When Priority approached us, we prayed about going with them for several months before agreeing.

David said, "If God wants to bless us, He can bless us on 'Flop Records' as much as He can on some big-name label with some big record company!"

David's contracts with United Artists, Capitol Records, and MGM Records in his "pre-Christ" days had shown him that self-promotion always fails. The Bible says that God is the One who promotes!

With my background as a Hollywood child star, I had seen firsthand the grief and heartache that fame and fortune can bring. The last thing I wanted at this point in my life was to get off-track with God and His plan.

All of us wanted to make sure that signing with Priority was God's will for the group. As far as we were concerned, the band's main goal was simply to serve God, focus on Jesus, and trust God for our futures.

We did our first album on Priority, called *David and the Giants*, in 1982, followed by *Riders in the Sky* in 1983.

Brown Bannister, a well-known producer in the Christian music industry who has produced records for such notables as Amy Grant, took us out to lunch and was also interested in producing David and the Giants. The Benson Company courted us and was ready to do almost anything to have us sign with them, but we turned them down, too.

Mike Blanton of Blanton-Harrell Management, the company responsible for managing Amy Grant's career, saw us play in Nashville and asked us to call, but we never did.

We had all come from the secular music world, where people were always trying to make a buck by taking advantage of you. David, in particular, seemed to have reservations about going with these widely-recognized, popular labels. I wanted the Lord's will to be done, but often wondered later if we had made the right decision.

Buddy Huey, who was president of Nashville-based Priority at that time, believed in the ministry of David and the Giants. He had heard about us and had purchased all of our custom, self-produced albums before contacting us! He called David to inquire about signing the group and mentioned he had also signed two other singers, Cynthia Clawson, and a new singer he believed would be an up-and-coming Christian artist, a guy with one name: Carman.

The money that Priority gave us provided some of the equipment for the studio David would eventually build. With CBS Records backing us, the albums gave our group national exposure, putting us in every Christian record store in the nation. The exposure, however, proved to be greater than the money from album sales.

Our albums received critical acclaim but were not top sellers. We were known as a great live, in-concert group, and it somehow seemed hard to capture our sound on record the way we performed it in concert. The national exposure definitely boosted our careers, and God continued to provide for us through live concert dates, touring, and record sales.

The 1980s were a busy, fruitful time for our family.

Tara was growing — literally by "leaps and bounds" — and started taking ballet lessons at age three and a half. It was never something Kathy and I forced; Tara just wanted to dance. Since Kathy danced even while pregnant, maybe Tara's attraction to ballet was inevitable!

As principal dancer for Ballet Mississippi, Kathy's career was really taking off, and she often made headlines in our hometown newspaper. Although still dancing in the secular ballet world, Kathy was a committed Christian.

As her ballet expertise grew, Kathy found herself in the running to participate in the annual International Ballet Competition. Often called "the Olympics of the ballet world," its winners are regarded as the world's best dancers. The competition rotates in location from year to year and, in the summer of 1982, was held in Jackson.

Kathy had traveled to Tokyo the year before to participate in a ballet competition there, coming home with no awards at all. Feeling that the outcome of the event had been politically motivated, she vowed not to do any more competitions. But she was being urged to compete in the International Ballet Competition, and she finally changed her mind, on one condition.

Kathy told me, "They want me to compete and I agreed. But

I told them if I make the third and final round of competition, I'll dance to 'We Shall Behold Him.' "

This song, written by Dottie Rambo and popularized by singer Sandi Patti, glorifies Christ in no uncertain terms.

The judges for the 1982 competition included Robert Joffrey, director of the famed Joffrey Ballet in New York, as well as seven judges from Communist countries.

Several Jackson ballet officials opposed her music selection, fearing that the song's explicitly Christian theme would offend some of the judges, especially those from Communist countries. They strongly tried to discourage her from dancing to "We Shall Behold Him."

The local media got wind of the story, generating more controversy, but Kathy remained determined to dance to a song that glorified God.

The more people opposed her position, the more Kathy knew it was of God. When they tried to dissuade her, Kathy became more excited!

As the competition progressed, Kathy made it through the first and second rounds. God gave Kathy favor and she remained determined to dance to "We Shall Behold Him" in the last round.

Excitement and controversy filled the air the last night of the International. A sellout crowd, many of whom were local Christians, had come to see Kathy's performance.

As Sandi Patti's voice echoed throughout the auditorium, and the words "We Shall Behold Him," resounded in the air, Kathy danced gracefully, obviously inspired by the rapturous music.

At the end of her performance — which was really an expression of worship — many in the audience stood to applaud her. Wanting God to get the glory, Kathy cut short her curtain call.

That night Kathy won the silver medal in the senior women's division, missing the gold medal by something like one one-hundredth of a point.

An article featured in the magazine *Christianity Today,* reported, "The solo was a moving moment. One Bostonian who regularly attends ballet competitions said it was the first time he had ever cried at such an event."

Kathy was quoted as saying, "Prayer was my warm-up. While

performing, I could feel His presence, a calming presence."

I had to leave right after the final performance to go on the road with David and the Giants, but I called later to find out what happened.

"I won the silver!" Kathy told me excitedly. "I know God was with me, and it's because of Him that I received the medal!"

I could only say three words in reply: "Praise the Lord!"

Her performance, complete with "We Shall Behold Him" had also been filmed that night by a PBS crew and was later included in a PBS special, *To Dance for Gold,* which aired on 180 PBS stations nationwide.

Governor William Winter proclaimed December 3, 1983, as "Kathy Thibodeaux Day" in Mississippi in recognition of her achievements.

Through it all, Kathy remained resolute about giving God the glory for all the accolades that came her way — even if they were rather unusual.

With the growth of aerobic exercise records and tapes, Priority Records, in 1993, decided to enter the expanding "Christian aerobics" marketplace with the release of *Message in Motion, Volume I.* Such albums were meeting a need among Christians who liked exercising to music but did not like exercising to secular, sometimes ungodly, songs.

Ironically, Kathy, who did not take aerobic exercise classes, was flattered to be asked to pose for the album cover. Apparently, five hours of daily ballet rehearsals certainly made her qualified in the area of physical fitness.

Buddy Huey, president of Priority Records, knew Kathy was well-known in the ballet world. To him, she seemed the a logical choice to be the album cover model.

"Keith," she told me the day she was to fly to Nashville for the photo session, "I'm concerned about what type of outfit they will want me to wear."

She need not have worried. The photo portrayed her beautifully in modest exercise attire with a sweatband around her forehead and her long hair flowing.

In August 1983 our family traveled to California for a visit.

One day my sister Katie, who lives near Los Angeles, went sightseeing with Kathy, Tara, and I.

Kathy and Katie suggested, "Let's go see Lucy!"

"Yeah," I said, "maybe Desi Jr. will be there, and I can see him, too." It had been three years earlier, at the wedding, since I'd seen anyone from the Arnaz family.

As we drove over to Beverly Hills, Tara kept saying, "I want to meet Lucy."

Nearing North Roxbury Drive, we noticed a cluster of people outside Lucy's house.

"Who are all those people?" Kathy asked.

"They're fans and sightseers waiting for just a glimpse of Lucy," I explained.

I pulled into the long driveway, parked out front, and went around to the back door, where a maid greeted me.

"Hello," I said, "I used to play Little Ricky on the "I Love Lucy" show, and I wondered if I could see Lucy."

The maid, who could barely speak English, seemed to have trouble understanding who I was.

"Lucy not here. Lucy not here," she kept saying in broken English.

I went back out to the car, and Kathy suggested that I leave a note for Lucy.

After scribbling out a note, I ran back to the house and gave it to the maid. Just as I was backing the car out of the driveway, both the maid and Lucy appeared at the front door shouting, "Wait, wait!"

For a moment, I thought maybe I was back in an "I Love Lucy" episode as I watched Lucy waving and calling to us.

I drove back toward the house, and we got out and went to the front door where Lucy was waiting and welcoming us with outstretched arms. She started crying and hugging me, as if she didn't want to let go.

"Keith, you've gotten better-looking. You sure didn't get it from your dad!" Lucy joked as she ushered us into the den.

Her hair was darker and not as dyed.

"You look great!" I said, noticing that she certainly didn't look her age. Appearing youthful in slacks and the little flat shoes she always wore, Lucy hadn't changed much from the old days. I didn't realize until later that it was August 6, her seventy-second birthday.

Straw baskets filled with loose cigarettes, not cigarettes in cartons, sat on nearby tables, and the room was filled with plants.

We sat on the couch, talking and catching up on what had been happening in all our lives.

Lucy told us about her grandchildren, Lucie's kids, and said, "I've been hearing some good things about you."

I'm not sure what she meant; maybe she had read some articles about me or the band. Although I didn't get to talk to Lucy specifically about Jesus, I did tell her about playing with David and the Giants and what was going on in my life.

Kathy was her usual quiet, cordial self. Later, she told me she kept thinking, *I'm actually in Lucy's house, sitting on Lucy's couch!*

Lucy seemed enthralled by Tara, who was three years old and chattered away nonstop.

"I can't get over how much she talks for such a little girl," Lucy kept saying. "She must have a vocabulary of 2,000 words!"

Tara, who had seen reruns of "I Love Lucy" shows, piped up to Lucy, "You don't look like you did on TV!" Fortunately, Lucy didn't hear her!

While our visit wasn't very long, it was good to see Lucy again. Even though our lives had changed so much, I was now an adult and felt comfortable around her.

I no longer felt the pressure I had experienced in my younger days when Lucy was my boss.

As we left Lucy's house that day, all the tourists out front stopped us and asked who we were. When they found out I was Little Ricky, they all wanted to take our pictures!

While Kathy and I felt a little silly about all the attention, Tara enjoyed every minute of it!

Two years later, in 1985, Lucy returned to television in her first dramatic role since her movie days in the 1930s and 1940s. In a television movie called *Stone Pillow,* she played a homeless old bag lady, and the dramatic role was a real departure for her. The critics thought she was great in it and so did I.

Early in 1986, she began another weekly television show

called *Life With Lucy,* amid great media hoopla — the comedy queen of television was returning! Seventy-five years old in real life, Lucy played a grandmother who lived with her daughter, son-in-law, and two grandchildren. Unlike Lucy's previous success, "Life With Lucy" was canceled due to low ratings after only 13 episodes.

Desi Jr. later told me he could not understand why, with all her success, his mother chose to do that show at her age.

Back in Mississippi, we resumed our lives. Kathy continued as principal dancer for Ballet Mississippi, and I went back on the road with the band.

Priority Records dissolved, and we were left without a record label. Even though Priority went under, a lot of good came out of our experience with them. They did a lot of promotion for us, and we met some wonderful people.

The guys in the band knew God had His hand on our lives, so we simply prayed about the next step to take.

In 1984 Word/Myrrh Records, the largest Christian record company in the nation at the time, signed David and the Giants to a recording contract, and we went on to record three albums: *Inhabitants of the Rock* in 1984, *Under Control* in 1985, and *Magnificat* in 1987, a theme-based work built around the gospel. The band's popularity steadily increased with each new album, and our following grew.

In addition to drumming and singing background vocals, I began trying my hand at songwriting. "He's Got It Under Control," a song that David and I co-wrote, appeared on *Under Control.* A song that I wrote alone, "Why," appeared on the *Magnificat* album and made it to Number 4 on the Adult Contemporary Christian music charts.

During the mid to late 1980s, I became more comfortable with people knowing I had been Little Ricky. In stories about the band, my past as Little Ricky was usually mentioned, but fortunately record reviewers and reporters didn't focus on that! I still felt our music had to stand alone, but I no longer had as much difficulty discussing my "I Love Lucy" past because I was now secure in Christ.

One writer called us "critically acclaimed but perennially underrated," which was, in a sense, true. Reviews of our albums were pretty good, and we were getting some good radio air play and hit singles. Our records sold well, yet we were not "Christian superstars." Bands like ours, however, did help pave the way for other Christian acts. Our live concerts often brought the house down, yet some people in the Christian music audience remained unaware of us.

As acceptance of Christian rock music grew, we used the lights, fog machines, and other effects that were not accepted by audiences in the early days of contemporary Christian music. Although we strove for excellence in our albums and on-stage live in concert, our most important goal remained reaching people for Jesus Christ.

Jesus said in Matthew 9:12, "It is not the healthy who need a doctor but the sick," and that verse was a sort of motto for us. We were particularly conscious of people who once had been as we were — those involved in the bar and club scene, people who were seeking truth through alcohol or drugs.

At the conclusion of each concert, we issued an invitation to receive Christ as Saviour and stayed long after the performance, talking to people who crowded around us. These usually weren't autograph seekers; they were searching for truth. We would spend hours talking with them about the Lord, or about some problem they were experiencing in their lives.

It wasn't unusual for parents to approach us after a concert with tear-stained faces, explaining, "We didn't want to come tonight because we don't like rock music, but my child just responded to your invitation to accept Jesus!"

During each concert performance, I would leave my drum kit to join Clayborn down front onstage. There I "played" his bass guitar with my drumsticks! This drum solo segment of our concert allowed me to share the gift of drumming that God had given me, and the audiences loved it.

The idea for one of the more popular songs, "Highway to Heaven," came about while the band was in a Pizza Hut in Mississippi one night, sitting around talking about the Lord. A guy in the next booth overheard us and evidently didn't like what we had to say because he very pointedly went to the jukebox and played the AC-DC song, "Highway to Hell."

"That poor guy is on the wrong highway," one of us said.

"Yeah, what we need is a song about what Jesus has to offer people on the highway to heaven," someone else suggested.

That's how we came up with the idea for a protest song against the "see you in hell" mentality.

Another popular song, "Noah," describes how the crowds taunted Noah for building a boat in the middle of a desert. The song featured sound effects of lighting, thunder, rushing wind, and the cries of the people left outside the ark when the flood came.

Jesus predicted in Matthew 24:37-39, "As it was in the days of Noah, so it will be at the coming of the Son of Man. For in the days before the flood, people were eating, drinking, marrying, and giving in marriage, up to the day Noah entered the ark; and they knew nothing about what would happen until the flood came and took them all away. That is how it will be at the coming of the Son of Man" (NIV).

We often closed our concerts with the simple message of the "Noah" song — Jesus is coming back and we need to be ready. It always had a sobering effect on our audiences and helped bring many people into the kingdom of God.

Over the years, David and the Giants played in churches, auditoriums, and at Christian music festivals. Although our music attracted a predominantly youthful crowd, people of all ages seemed to enjoy our concerts.

It was always thrilling for us to go back to a town where we had played before and have someone approach us and say, "I found the Lord at your last David and the Giants concert."

With the number of road miles that the band traveled each year, we were all aware of God's protection for us, but one particular incident stands out in my mind.

At the time, we all took turns driving the band's van, which also pulled an equipment trailer, containing all our instruments, sound equipment, lights, and stage gear. If the back of the trailer was particularly loaded down, it would sometimes sway from side to side and could be difficult to control.

Late one night on our way to Florida for another performance, I was driving on the interstate while the guys slept in the back of the van. As I sped up to pass a big tractor-trailer truck, the equipment trailer behind our van started to sway particularly hard.

The movement woke up the other guys.

"What's going on?" someone shouted.

Just then, a gust of air from the passing truck started the trailer moving in a fish-tail pattern.

"We're gonna turn over!" another of the guys screamed.

Suddenly one of our trailer's tires blew out as I struggled to control the van.

"God, help us!" someone else prayed in terror.

Finally, I was able to pull off the road and stop.

"I thought we'd be killed for sure!" a voice, still horrified by the traumatic experience, called from the back of the van.

I was scared, too, but I never felt we were near death.

"Thank God He protected us," I said.

We were all aware that night of God's protection, and everyone was very thankful.

The experience was a little too much for our sound man. Not long after that, he quit the band!

In 1985, a prophetic word was given to Kathy and me.

We did not understand everything that was said at the time, but we did take the words seriously and prayed about it, trusting God to direct us and to unfold His perfect plan for our lives.

The prophecy said that our lives would be changing course, and that we would begin to see greater days and greater ways to use our testimonies for Him. The prophecy noted that God had set us apart for a special purpose, not only individually but as a team, and predicted that God would use Kathy as a pioneer in the arts to bring glory to Jesus.

Another part of the prophecy that was directed specifically at me said, "You will have your past come to the forefront. Use that door of influence to have further opportunities for ministry."

The beginning of the prophecy began to take shape in 1986.

For a long time, Kathy had struggled with continuing to dance for Ballet Mississippi. She loved dancing with the ballet but felt

God had something more for her to do. While she enjoyed dancing in traditional ballet pieces like "The Nutcracker," she longed to use her entire body in worship to God.

Kathy had a vision for something totally unheard of — a touring Christian ballet troupe that would dance to the glory of God. She envisioned Christian dancers coming together for the purpose of glorifying God in dance. In addition to bringing people into worship, Kathy wanted the group to be an outreach ministry in which dancers would share the love of Jesus with their audiences.

After much prayer, Kathy and I felt certain that God did not want her to renew her contract with Ballet Mississippi.

She went before the ballet's board of directors and tried to explain what she felt God wanted her to do. At 29, Kathy was the principal dancer and the highest paid performer in Ballet Mississippi's 12-person company.

"Why would you want to quit?" they asked, unable to understand her vision for a Christian ballet company.

"All I know is that God does not want me to stay with the ballet any longer," she replied boldly.

"If you'll agree to sign a new contract," one of the board of directors pleaded, "we'll offer you more money."

"Stay with the ballet," another board member pleaded, trying to talk her out of leaving.

"Kathy, please don't give up your career!" the others urged her.

"I appreciate your offer and understand your concern, but I cannot stay. My time here is over," Kathy said.

When she told me what had happened at the meeting, she said, "God has given me a vision for a Christian dance company, but I have no idea how to do it!"

"Well, neither do I!" I replied.

Some people thought Kathy was being completely irrational. She had no studio, no name, no financial support, and no dancers. But she had God!

Word soon leaked to the press that Ballet Mississippi's star ballerina, Kathy Thibodeaux, was leaving to start a Christian dance troupe.

The next day, Kathy received a phone call from Newton Wilson, the new president of Belhaven College, a Presbyterian college based in Jackson.

"It's his first day in office, and he told me, 'Whatever we can do to help you get started, just let me know!' " Kathy told me excitedly. "God is already confirming this, Keith!"

Money and donations began to pour in for the still-unnamed dance company.

By July, Gregory Smith, the choreographer who had choreographed Kathy's 1982 silver medal winning performance of "We Shall Behold Him" joined Kathy as company director. One other member, Lesa Roman, had been recruited, and the new company was practicing, without pay, on a scarred tile floor above the Belhaven College gym.

In return for performances at special college functions, like fundraisers and awards banquets, the college also agreed to provide office space and computer access. By the time they moved into the office, Kathy had a name for the company, which I had suggested: Ballet Magnificat.

The local newspaper reported that several people in the ballet community who knew Kathy seemed surprised at Kathy's "new firmness" about Ballet Magnificat.

Ballet Mississippi artistic director Alan Woodard was quoted as saying, "I told her she's taking the grand jete into an area where there's no guarantee. I like to think I'm pretty persuasive, but she was absolutely resolute. She's being very brave in this. It's a new facet of her personality."

Kathy and I knew this was much more than a new personality trait! Above all, we knew this new venture was an answer to the prayer of Kathy's heart, and the beginning of the prophecy given to us the year before.

Soon churches began to call to request bookings, and Ballet Magnificat was on its way.

I wondered about the words of the prophecy as they pertained to me, and I wondered what this Christian life, this great adventure of following Jesus, would bring next for me!

Dad, my sister Leslie, and Mom, at Leslie's wedding.

The Thibodeaux family — Tara, Keith, Kathy.

15

Stepping Stones

The phone rang very early one morning, jolting me out of a sound sleep.

"Mr. Thibodeaux?" an unfamiliar voice asked.

"Yes," I replied sleepily, looking at the clock on the night stand. It was 6:30 in the morning.

"We have just learned that Desi Arnaz has died," he said matter-of-factly. "Can you give me your reaction to his death?"

Tears filled my eyes, and I groped for the right words to say. All that came to mind was, "He was a kind and compassionate man, and I will miss him very much."

I had heard that Desi was very ill and knew that, barring a miracle, he did not have long to live. When I first learned about his illness, he was in Mexico at his home there. I never really thought about going to see him because he had his family near him, and I felt that was enough.

After his death, Desi's physician was quoted in a newspaper article: "He died of lung cancer. It was from smoking those Cuban cigars, and that's the truth."

I later found out more details about his death. Desi had been in ill health with other problems for several years before he was diagnosed with lung cancer. His wife Edie had died the year before, following her own three-year battle with cancer. Desi was hospitalized frequently during the final months of his life and went through debilitating chemotherapy and radiation treatments.

When the doctors said he had little time left, Lucie took her son Joe, who was four at the time, and moved into Desi's house to help take care of him. Lucie went prepared to stay months if necessary; instead, she was with her father for only three and a half weeks.

On December 2, 1986, Desi died at his Del Mar home in Lucie's arms. He was 69 years old.

It must have been very difficult for Lucie. She later told me, "He was scared to death and angry and morphined. He was not in a frame of mind to discuss that he might die."

Lucy stayed in touch with Desi and visited him a few times during his final illness. Shortly before his death, Lucy phoned on November 30 and told Desi she loved him, according to Lucie. It was only later that the family realized that November 30 was Lucy and Desi's wedding anniversary.

When Desi died, Lucy was quoted as saying, "He was the father of my children, and we were always friends. He suffered a lot. We have prayed for his being free of pain."

Dad called when he heard about Desi and said he wanted to go to the funeral in California with me. We flew out to the west coast together, where I was interviewed by Joan Lunden on "Good Morning America" via satellite hookup on the morning of Desi's memorial service.

As I talked about Desi on "Good Morning America," suddenly the reality of his passing hit me. When they showed a clip of him, I struggled to hold back my tears. Desi was still close to my heart, despite all the years that had passed.

On the "I Love Lucy" set, Desi's raging outbursts would frighten me, but when things went wrong, Desi was the one who could always comfort me. He seemed to sense how I was feeling, and he knew how to settle me down. He was a warm, generous man.

When I recall all my times with Desi on the show, I especially remember doing the "Babalu" number with him on "I Love Lucy." I had so much fun performing with him!

I loved Desi and was very sad that he was gone.

Ironically, I didn't learn until later that Horace Heidt, the man who put me on the road with his big band tour when I was just a toddler, passed away in Los Angeles on the exact same day as Desi Arnaz! Heidt died from pneumonia at the age of 85.

My old friend Danny Sauer picked Dad and me up at our hotel and drove us to Desi's memorial service. Danny is very active in the Catholic Charismatic community, and during our drive from Los Angeles to the church, he shared his own Christian testimony with Dad.

Dad seemed to listen intently to what Danny had to say.

Desi's body was cremated, and the memorial service, held at St. James Catholic Church in Salona Beach, just north of Del Mar, was small, with just family and close friends present. A picture of Desi stood at the front of the sanctuary, and Danny Thomas gave the eulogy.

The wake was held afterwards at Desi's house in Del Mar. As soon as I walked through the door, I saw Lucy, who was with her husband Gary.

She came over and hugged me and wouldn't let me go for a long time.

"I watched you this morning on 'Good Morning America,' " Lucy said. "I was really proud of you today on the show. You did a great job, Keith."

Such words were high praise coming from Lucy. I knew she didn't pass out compliments unless she really meant them.

Dad had not seen Lucy in years, not since he was fired from Desilu. I don't know what they said to each other at the wake, but I know Dad felt as if he had made up with Lucy over the past.

The Del Mar house was as I had remembered it. Everything was the same, yet it was so different because Desi wasn't there.

Pictures and photographs were placed all around the house. The family said it was okay to take one if we wanted. Danny found a photograph of himself with Desi, and put it in his pocket to take home.

People seemed to be relaxed and talkative. Marge Durante and her daughter came over to talk with me; I hadn't seen them in years. She and Jimmy, who had died six years earlier at the age of 87, had lived just a few doors down from Desi's place in Del Mar, so I often saw them during the time I spent there.

Desi Jr.'s stepbrother Greg, or "Butchie" as we called him, was there, too.

Desi Jr. seemed to be taking his father's death pretty stoically.

I didn't see any tears; he just seemed to reason everything out in his mind. I am sure he had his own private grief, but at the funeral he seemed calm.

"My father is not suffering anymore. He fought a good fight," Desi Jr. told me. "It's just a shame that after he did finally get off alcohol, those cigars he smoked for years killed him."

There was probably a sense of relief in the family because Desi had suffered so much during his illness. Since Lucie spent the final weeks of her dad's life with him, I'm sure she was hit hardest by his death. She was very close to her father.

We all loved Desi. I don't think Lucy ever stopped loving him, even though both of them married other people. I think the love they experienced with their new mates in their second marriages was a different kind of love, but I don't think either one of them ever stopped loving the other.

Billy Hinsche, who used to be with Dino, Desi, and Billy but was now playing with the Beach Boys, was there and we spoke briefly.

"Hi, Keith. I've been hearing some good things about you, man!" Billy said with a smile.

Dino — Dean Martin Jr. — also made a point to talk with me. It was the first time we had seen each other in years, and he seemed genuinely glad to see me. I was somewhat stunned since, when we were younger, Dino had always seemed somewhat egotistical — trying to act cool all the time. Maybe I had just felt that way because of my own insecurities.

"What are you doing these days, man?" I asked.

"I'm doing a little acting. In fact, I'm trying out for a role on 'Miami Vice.' "

"Miami Vice" was a popular TV series starring Don Johnson. It was rumored that Johnson might be leaving the show, but I don't know if Dino was trying out for Johnson's part or another role.

As we talked, it was as if all that outer veneer had crumbled, and he seemed more like a regular guy. Our conversation changed my whole perception of him.

I didn't know I would never see him again. Dino was killed only a few months after we'd talked in California. Hollywood was stunned by his death.

A captain in the California Air National Guard, Dino was killed when the F-4C Phantom jet he was flying on a routine exercise crashed into the top of a ravine at 400 miles per hour. He died on March 21, 1987, leaving a 14-year-old son, Alex, from his first marriage to actress Olivia Hussey.

It was hard to believe Dino was gone. He was only one year younger than I was at the time — 36.

Kathy was busy running Ballet Magnificat, which was now performing across the country.

David and the Giants' record contract with Word/Myrrh had expired, and several other major record companies had approached the band about recording our next album. As we prayed about what to do, we decided to release our next album on our own label.

David had formed Giant Records several years earlier to record new artists who wanted to be "spiritual giants" in the Christian music industry. To accomplish this David built Huff Recording Studio, a state-of-the-art recording studio near his home.

In 1988, we released our eleventh Christian album, *Strangers to the Night,* on Giant Records and distributed by the Benson Company, a large Nashville-based Christian music company. The album received excellent reviews and resulted in several radio hit singles. It was a blend of pop/praise tunes, soulful ballads, Cajun and soul-flavored songs, and just plain rock.

David's 15-year-old daughter Kellye, from his first marriage, sang a duet with her dad on the ballad, "Perfect Love." Later Kellye went on to pursue a solo singing career in Christian music.

I was continuing to write songs, and one tune, "Lively Stones," was included on our new album. We followed *Strangers* with *R U Gonna Stand Up* in 1989. Things were going well with the band, but I still wondered about the prophecy that had been given about me — although parts of it were already coming to pass.

I started getting calls from various shows, asking me to appear in "whatever-happened-to" segments. People seemed very interested in what Little Ricky was doing now.

When I did Gary Collins' "Hour Magazine" show, I was asked a lot of questions about the "I Love Lucy" days, which I had expected. Then, when he asked me some direct questions about my life, I seized the opportunity to express my faith in Christ.

"What kinds of drugs have you used, Keith?" Gary asked.

"Everything from amphetamines to heroin," I replied candidly.

"What helped you come off the drugs? How did you get away from that lifestyle you lived?" he persisted.

I began telling him my story, and just basically shared the gospel. I don't recall my exact words.

Jane Fonda, a guest on the same segment, was seated quietly beside me as I gave my testimony of how Jesus had changed my life. For some reason, Jane struck me as being nervous that day. During one of the commercial breaks, she turned to me and asked, "Do you still play the drums?"

"Yes, I play in a Christian rock group right now," I explained.

She was very nice and unlike the strident feminist I had pictured her to be.

After the show, one of the technicians ran up to me, shook my hand, and said, "I'm a Christian, too! That was great — what you said about the Lord. I'm proud of you."

I felt seeds were sown that day, and for the first time, I began to see how my past — the past that I was reluctant to discuss for so long — could actually be used by God. Perhaps hearing the story of Little Ricky would help someone else who was struggling with the problems I had battled for so long.

I went on to appear on a number of national shows, and whenever possible, I tried to tell the audience what God had done in my life.

I also continued to pray and waited in anticipation about what God had in store for my future!

When the news came that Lucy had been hospitalized for emergency heart surgery, I was not particularly upset. Even though Lucy was 77 years old, she had so much energy and always seemed robust to me, even in her old age. The month before her hospitalization, she had appeared on the Academy Awards telecast with Bob Hope, and she looked great.

I was concerned, of course, and followed the news reports updating her condition, but I wasn't really worried.

Lucy will pull through, I thought. *She is one tough lady!*

On April 18, 1989, Lucy had complained of chest pains and breathing difficulties and was rushed to Cedars-Sinai Hospital. After nearly seven hours of surgery to repair a tear in her aorta near her heart, news reports said she was doing well. She had been able to get out of bed and was joking with the hospital staff.

The hospital was swamped with flowers, get-well cards, and telegrams once word of her surgery reached the public. Thousands of calls came into the hospital from worried fans around the world, and the media gave daily bulletins on her progress. From all accounts she seemed to be doing well, and I believed she would recover.

Lucy had been in the hospital for eight days when I was awakened from a sound sleep by a reporter from the Associated Press. "Lucille Ball just died. How do you feel, Mr. Thibodeaux?" the reporter asked.

I was barely awake and tried to digest what the man was asking me. *Lucy? Dead? It couldn't be!* I thought.

I mumbled some sort of answer about how Lucy was a great lady and said, "I'm sure all this is going to hit me a little later on" before I hung up.

Lucy's death was unexpected even by her doctors. I learned she had awakened early on the morning of April 26, with pain in her back and was gone within minutes. A tear had developed in the abdominal portion of her aorta, causing cardiac arrest, and doctors were unable to revive her.

The phone rang all that day, as reporters from across the country called to ask my reaction to Lucy's passing. Even "shock jock" Howard Stern called!

Unlike Desi's quiet, nearly unheralded passing, Lucy's death unleashed a flood of media attention. People seemed to take her death very hard, almost as if she had been a personal friend or a member of the family. Until that time, I had not realized the enormous, continuing popularity of "I Love Lucy." There was something about Lucy and the show that made her seem like an old friend to millions of people. The media coverage continued for days following her death.

By this time, Desi Jr. had married again, to dancer Amy Bargiel, and had become a stepfather to her daughter. I tried to get in touch with him to find out about the funeral, but I kept getting his answering machine.

Then it was announced that there would be no funeral, just a private, family-only memorial service. I was not invited; the only people there were Gary and Lucy's children. That's what Lucy would have wanted because her kids and grandkids were the most important people in her life.

Like Desi, Lucy's body was also cremated. Lucie knew that her mother hated funerals and didn't want one.

After Lucy's death, Lucie found notes from her mother's planned but unfinished autobiography recalling a happy childhood picnic. Reading the notes gave Lucie the idea for a somewhat unorthodox memorial service following the family-only services: a picnic, which was held on May 7 — Mother's Day. I did not attend the memorial picnic.

I was saddened by Lucy's death, and it seemed very unreal at first. My initial reaction had been shock and surprise because it seemed that Lucy would live forever — even though I knew that wasn't true!

Both Desi and Lucy had appeared larger than life to me from the time I first met them as a child. Now both of them were gone, and it seemed as if an era had died with them.

I think I grieved more for Desi than for Lucy simply because I had always felt closer to him. I loved Lucy, but most of my life I was in awe of the lady. I'd always felt more at home around Desi.

With Lucy gone, the world had lost a great person; the kids had lost their mother; and I had lost part of my past.

I had been praying for a long time about what God had for me in the future, and the more I prayed, the more I felt that it was time to leave David and the Giants. I still was not completely certain what I should do, but the desire to leave would not go away.

For 20 years, I had been with David and the Giants, playing secular and later Christian music. We were good friends and brothers in the Lord, but I could not shake the impression that God had something else for me to do.

I decided it was time to tell David, Rayborn, and Clayborn.

"I don't know how to say this, but I feel it's time for me to leave the band," I said, hoping they would understand my reason.

They were surprised but supportive.

David said, "It's okay, man. We know you believe it's what God wants you to do, and we would never stand in the way of God's will."

David asked Lance, his grown son from his previous marriage, to replace me as the group's drummer, and the group continued their traveling musical ministry.

I had started playing the piano and was devoting more time to song writing. When I made my last appearance as drummer for David and the Giants in the early part of 1990, it was with a sense of anticipation about the next chapter in my life.

I formed my own band, Lively Stones, from talented musicians I had met while playing with David and the Giants. These included Jim Cooper, Jody Davis, and Terry Ostovich, with Todd White as our road manager. Our debut single was a song I had written called "Get Down on My Knees."

The song was later featured as part of *Ultimate Rock 2,* a collection of Christian rock songs released by StarSong Records, a well-known Nashville-based Christian record company. Our band was the only unsigned act (unsigned to a record label) on *Ultimate Rock 2,* which included such popular Christian artists as Petra, White Heart, DeGarmo and Key, the Newsboys, and Mylon and Broken Heart.

Lively Stones was signed by a Nashville management company, and soon we were out on the road. Things went well at first, but by the end of 1990, problems among the members began to trouble me more and more.

At the same time, I felt I was neglecting Kathy.

During my years with David and the Giants, I was on the road probably half of each year. When Kathy started Ballet Magnificat, she went on the road, too, so we were not able to have much of a family life. It seemed ridiculous to be married and not spend time with my own family. Now here I was, back on the road again with another band — and the same grueling schedule!

After I became a Christian, I continued to play with David and the Giants for 10 years because I knew God was specifically calling me to do it. But I was having doubts about Lively

Stones; something was wrong.

In addition to my inner struggles, I developed an unusual sore throat that I couldn't shake, in spite of several rounds of antibiotics. I could not eat, and it seemed like Satan was hounding me in every area of my life. My faith in the goodness of God was also being tested and shaken to the core. At times, I felt as if Satan had his hand on my throat and that my very life was at stake.

At the same time, I couldn't quit touring because I felt responsible to the guys who had quit their jobs to get the band going. The financial pressure constantly hounded me, and I had taken out my frustrations on Kathy, pushing her away with my harsh words.

One day as the band was traveling to San Antonio, Texas, I sat in the back nursing my sore throat and clutching a blanket of Tara's that I had brought with me. Feeling sorry for myself, I thought, *Tara is the only person I have left to love and care about.*

With no one to turn to, I had never felt so lonely. That amazed me since I had thought the worst period of my life had been before I had come to the Lord. Now the loneliness and depression I felt enveloped me like a dark cloud that wouldn't go away. I couldn't seem to shake it.

One night, while traveling with the band on a bus somewhere in South Carolina, I wanted answers from God so badly, I prayed, "Lord, I'll do anything that You want me to do!"

Immediately, I sensed God speaking directly to me, not in an audible voice, but in my heart: "I want you to join Kathy and work with Ballet Magnificat."

That answer was very humbling because the last thing I wanted to do was quit music in spite of the fact I no longer felt comfortable with my new band. I feared that if I stopped playing the drums, I'd lose my identity, even though I knew my true identity was in Jesus Christ.

I remember talking with Steve Garrett, a talented guitar player who auditioned for the band and traveled with us for a time, and had become a close friend. I told him, "I'm thinking about leaving the band. I'm really struggling with feeling so responsible for the band, and yet thinking about abandoning the ship."

The struggle continued until I got back home and went to

our church, New Covenant, in Jackson. During the singing and worship that day, the tears flowed from my eyes as I wept and cried. Afterward, I went forward for prayer and told my pastor, Jim Singleton, all the burdens I had been carrying with the band, my health, and the finances.

He listened and then prayed, "I rebuke the angel of death in the name of Jesus!"

Suddenly, the burdens lifted, and hope took their place in my heart. I knew God wanted to get me to the point where I could trust only Him, instead of depending on my wife or the band or my own talent. That day I let go and gave God everything, and He transformed my life.

I told Kathy what the Lord had spoken to my heart.

"You're kidding," she said. "Surely, you're not thinking of quitting your music. It's your life!"

"Yes," I replied, "I really feel the Lord wants me to work with you and the ballet."

When she realized I was serious, she said, "That's wonderful, honey. Actually, nothing would please me more than for us to be together all the time."

The band dissolved at the end of 1990, and everyone went their separate ways. The guys really gave it their all and were with me 100 percent. They sacrificed and labored together with me through it all. Jim Cooper, our keyboard player, now performs and ministers with Petra. Our lead singer, Jody Davis joined another group called the Newsboys, and Terry Ostovich today works in management, as does Todd White.

The Lord showed me that Lively Stones was not a mistake but a stepping stone because "We know that all things work together for good to them that love God, to them who are called according to his purpose," (Rom. 8:28).

I joined the Ballet Magnificat staff in 1991.

Kathy's Christian ballet company, with the favor and blessing of God, had continued to grow and prosper. The ministry is funded completely by donations and revenues from the touring ministry and school.

In 1989, the ballet had moved into a building that once housed a health spa on North State Street in Jackson. There was space for dance rehearsals, dressing areas, showers, and offices for support staff.

As the ministry of Ballet Magnificat had grown, God had made it clear to Kathy that — in addition to the touring performance company — it was time to establish a permanent ballet school as part of Ballet Magnificat. Although the State Street building needed renovations, it was an ideal site for both a ballet school and a home base for the touring company. It is a 10,000 square foot facility.

Putting music on the shelf was hard for me, but it was necessary. I needed to learn to be a servant. I discovered the hard part doesn't last too long when you are in the will of God.

When I joined the ballet, I was an all-purpose worker, doing whatever was necessary to help. I drove the tour bus, operated light and sound equipment for performances, and assisted with some of the administrative work. I found that I enjoyed working with the ballet, and I loved being able to travel with my wife!

Our daughter Tara was now 12 years old and joined us on the road as much as possible, often performing a special solo number.

As I continued to work with the ballet, my responsibilities grew, and in 1993 I was named executive director. Overseeing a company of professional ballet dancers and office staff is a challenge and very different from what I have done in the past.

What does God have for me to do next? Who knows? I still am writing songs, and I may record a solo album. I don't think God is finished with me yet in terms of a music career, but I am content to wait for God's timing and leading. Whatever the future holds, as the song says, "I know Who holds the future," so I'm confident and expectant.

When I think back to the prophecy that was given about Kathy and me back in 1985, I am reminded of God's Word that He would use my past to bring glory to Him.

I believe this book may be part of the fulfillment of that prophecy, as I share with you what God has done in my life.

When Tara was little and our family would relax at home watching "I Love Lucy" reruns, Tara would look at the television and then back at me and say, "Daddy, I can't believe that was really you!"

Sometimes I can hardly believe it myself. I realize now what an honor it was to have been part of a classic like "I Love Lucy." Over 40 years have passed since the first "I Love Lucy" show aired in October 1951, yet its amazing popularity continues.

In 1991, a Lucy museum, officially called "Lucy: A Tribute," opened as a new exhibit at Hollywood's Universal Studios, attracting thousands of visitors eager to view Lucy's life as shown through costumes, photos, clips from her TV shows, and recreations of "I Love Lucy" stage sets.

That same year, the magazine *Special Reports* picked the character of Lucy Ricardo, as played by Lucille Ball, as the most influential television character of all time. A second Lucy tribute museum has also opened at Universal Studios in Florida, near Disney World.

Thanks to Desi Arnaz — who invented the rerun — people around the world can turn on their TVs and watch as Lucy, Ricky, Fred, Ethel — and yes, Little Ricky! — get involved in one zany situation after another.

In 1994, the popular national cable television network, Nickelodeon, began airing original uncut, unedited "I Love Lucy" episodes on weeknights in prime time, marking the first time "I Love Lucy" has appeared in prime time in its original form in over 30 years.

CBS' Home Video collection featuring "I Love Lucy" episodes has thousands of subscribers eager to own their own "I Love Lucy" shows. Lucie and her husband Laurence Luckinbill's video production company, Arluck Entertainment, has also produced several Lucy and Desi-related videos for sale.

One video, *Lucy & Desi: A Home Movie,* won an Emmy Award for outstanding informational special, something that was very gratifying for Lucie! The film, which includes never-before-seen home movie footage along with clips from Lucy and Desi's early movies and candid interviews with close friends, was co-produced by Lucie and her husband and hosted by Lucie. The film, a moving tribute to Lucie's parents, first aired on television on Valentine's Day 1993, and the for-sale version includes 18 additional minutes not seen in the televised version.

It would be useless to analyze why, after all these years, a television show still generates such interest. The greatness of Lucille Ball and Desi Arnaz has been scrutinized by numerous television critics, writers, social scientists, and journalists over the years.

When I think about "I Love Lucy" and my part in it, I am still amazed.

Proverbs 18:16 says, "A man's gift maketh room for him, and bringeth him before great men." My gift — playing the drums — brought me before a great man and a great woman, Desi Arnaz and Lucille Ball. The results of that meeting are still being played out around the world today: Someone, somewhere is watching "I Love Lucy" even as you read this. The gift of laughter is the legacy of Lucy and Desi, and I am grateful to have played a small part in that legacy.

I am also grateful that I have a new, bigger boss, One who is greater than Lucy. His name is Jesus.

One of our more interesting ballet dates: In 1993 Ballet Magnificat stopped in Phoenix for a scheduled performance at a local church. The pastor drove us to a church member's home for the night. Lo and behold, the church member was Alice Cooper (real name: Vince Cooper)! The former rock crazy man is now a dedicated Christian and a great testimony for the Lord. He was a gracious host to our family. In this photo Tara, Kathy, and I flank Alice and his son.

Epilogue

In a sense, I have been born three times: first in Lafayette, Louisiana, as the first child of Mary Ann and Lionel Thibodeaux; second, when Little Ricky was "born" on television, leading to another life as Little Ricky on "I Love Lucy;" and finally in 1974, when I first experienced the reality and truth of Jesus Christ as the Son of God.

I thought you might want to know more about what has happened to some of the people discussed in this book; hence, this epilogue.

I still talk to both Lucie and Desi Jr. from time to time, and I'm always happy to hear about good things going on in their lives.

I last saw Desi Jr. when both of us appeared on the "Maury Povich Show" in 1991, when Desi was promoting a movie, *The Mambo Kings*. Desi Jr. played his father in that movie, gathering a lot of publicity for the film in the process.

Lucie lives with her family in upper Westchester County, New York, and Desi Jr. lives with Amy and their daughter in Boulder City, Nevada. Lucie will always be "Little Lucie" to me, and I love and pray for both her and Desi Jr.

I appreciate very much the time they spent, talking and reminiscing with my co-author, Audrey Hingley, in preparation for this book about my life.

Desi was my best friend as a child, and our lives have taken many similar twists and turns. We continue to discover new ironies about our lives.

One night as Amy and Desi were at home watching a television show about ballet, Amy noticed that one of the dancers looked very familiar. The dancer was Kathy Denton Thibodeaux.

"I know that girl!" Amy told Desi.

"I know that guy!" Desi replied.

It turns out that Desi's wife Amy, who is also a ballet dancer, roomed together with Kathy one summer when both were teenagers and studying ballet at the famed Joffrey School in New York.

Desi and I found the story amazing. We were best friends for years; we both married ballet dancers; and now it turns out our wives knew each other long before Desi or I met either one of them!

Truth is definitely stranger than fiction.

My old buddy Danny Sauer also married a ballet dancer — maybe Desi, Danny, and I all just like girls with great legs! Danny lives in Tempe, Arizona, where he operates a travel agency and is vice-president of a firm that distributes school textbooks. He and Marion, a ballet teacher, have a large family, keeping up the Catholic tradition and are active in a Charismatic Catholic community.

My Louisiana high school buddy, Gary Lamson, still lives in Lafayette and runs his family's oil business. Gary, who is a Christian, also pastors a church in Lafayette. When I played with David and the Giants, Gary would often come to our Christian concerts.

When I last saw my old friend, Tony, he was living in sort of a residential halfway house under constant supervision. Before he did drugs, Tony had a great sense of humor. During our visit, however, I noticed his humor was more far out, and much of what he said did not make sense. In his mind, he seemed to be living back in the same days when we hung out together. Tony was looking for the ultimate trip and, unfortunately, he got it. Tony was my best friend, and I'm saddened that I have lost him to drugs. But as long as there is life there is hope, and I continue to pray for Tony.

Hal Leach, the guy who used to live in our house in Laurel, Mississippi — the guy mentioned in the "rattling love beads" incident—eventually went to work for Casablanca Records in Los Angeles.

One day, while I was still playing in the Christian David and the Giants, Kathy and I got a call to come and visit Hal who had melanoma cancer and was hospitalized.

When we walked into his room, we saw Scripture verses taped to the walls. "I didn't know you were a Christian, Hal," I exclaimed as Kathy and I hugged him.

Although very thin and weak, Hal smiled and said, "It's the best thing that ever happened to me."

We talked a lot about the Lord that day, and Hal told us, "I am not afraid to die. In fact, I'm looking forward to going to be with Jesus."

Sometime later, Hal did die, but I know I will see him in heaven!

Some of the people I was connected with in my Hollywood days have also died in recent years.

Frances Bavier, who played Aunt Bee on "The Andy Griffith Show," died at age 86 in December of 1989.

The trials and tribulations of many child stars have been highly publicized in recent years, including the suicide of actor Rusty Hamer in 1990. Rusty played Rusty Williams, the television son of Danny Thomas in another Desilu production, "Make Room for Daddy." News reports said he was despondent about his life when he shot himself in the head with a .357 Magnum; he was just 43 years old.

George Murphy, who worked with Dad at Desilu and later became a U.S. Senator, died at age 89 of leukemia in 1992. I'll never forget his kindness in securing a grant for me to attend the University of Southwestern Louisiana.

Claude Akins, who played an Indian in the "I Love Lucy" episode "Desert Island," died in 1994.

I am still close friends with David, Lance, Rayborn, and Clayborn Huff who live about an hour's drive away from Kathy and me in Forest, Mississippi. Over the years, they have shared some of the most exciting — and most desperate — times of my life, and they are my brothers in the Lord.

Clayborn recently married a girl he met at church, Mandy, and they have an infant son. David and his wife, Twyla, have two children, Tate and Tamara. Rayborn has never married.

The Huff brothers continue to record and tour as David and the Giants, and their 1990 album *Distant Journey* was nominated for a Dove Award — Christian music's version of the Grammy. Between their concert touring schedule and my work with the ballet, it's difficult for us to get together, but our friendship endures.

I see my parents when we can arrange to get together. Dad and Connie live in St. Petersburg, Florida, where Dad does public relations work for a cruise ship line. Mom still lives and works in Lafayette and usually comes to see the ballet's annual Christmas performance in Jackson.

My siblings, Katie, Leslie, Debbie, Dwight, and Brian, and their families, are scattered in different areas of the country, but we keep in touch and remain close. My two half-brothers, Tate and Todd, are grown now and live in Hawaii.

My daughter Tara is a teenager, and as I write this she is training for the junior division of the International Ballet Competition. She seems to be following in her mother's footsteps — a great role model! Tara has received Jesus as her Saviour and loves God, and I am very proud of her.

With over 100 live performances each year, Ballet Magnificat continues to live up to its motto of praising God with dance. We currently have nine professional dancers in our touring company, supported by 10 additional office staff and ballet school teachers.

In addition, we operate a full-time ballet school in Jackson, and each summer Ballet Magnificat sponsors a three-week summer ballet workshop for dancers ages 12 to 30 at nearby Belhaven College. The workshop attracts 150 dancers from around the world who enjoy daily ballet classes and weekly classes in creative, modern, and jazz dance and choreography. In addition, daily chapel services and a Bible study centering around scriptural foundations for dance, minister to their spirits. Belhaven College has also added a dance minor, which we are responsible for operating, as part of their program.

Being in the body of Christ has given me a whole new family in addition to my natural family. Kathy, Tara, and I attend a thriving church in Jackson, and I continue to meet brothers and sisters in the Lord as we travel around the country. I am continually awestruck by God's love and mercy in my life and His patience and long-suffering in freeing me from the sin that plagued me for so long.

Years ago, a reporter asked me, "What do you want to be most in life?"

I told her, "I want to be somebody."

I'm sure people who read that article thought I meant I wanted to be somebody big, somebody famous. But I simply wanted to know who I was.

Today, because of Jesus, I know who I am: a child of the King and a servant of the Most High God! I have peace, contentment, and an expectancy for the future, whatever it may bring—because God is in control.

I have more than life after Lucy. I have eternal life, and in my life after Lucy, despite some dark times, I have found true life in Jesus Christ.

I am truly a blessed man.

If you would like to contact Keith or would like information about Ballet Magnificat, write:

Ballet Magnificat
4455 N. State Street
Jackson, MS 39206

We would also like to recommend Lucie's award-winning video, *Lucy & Desi: A Home Movie.* Write to:

Arluck Entertainment
P.O. Box 636
Cross River, NY 10518

The address for the "We Love Lucy Fan Club" is:

We Love Lucy Fan Club
P.O. Box 56234
Sherman Oaks, CA 91413

About the writer

Audrey T. Hingley is an award-winning freelance writer, reporter, and public relations consultant whose work has appeared in numerous national magazines. Her credits include articles in the *Saturday Evening Post, Woman's World, Home Mechanix, the Christian Reader, Christian Parenting,* and many more.

She holds a B.S. degree in journalism from Virginia Commonwealth University, and is a member of the National Federation of Press Women. She lives near Richmond, Virginia, with her husband, Brian, and son Robert.